CGP

Face the (GCSE) Spanish Inquisition with CGP!

No doubt about it, you'll be asked some difficult questions in AQA GCSE Spanish. Luckily, this CGP Revision Guide is bursting with brilliant notes for every topic, plus crystal-clear explanations of all the vocab and grammar you'll need.

But that's not all. We've also packed in plenty of exam-style reading, writing, translation, speaking and listening questions — with **free audio files** available from this page:

www.cgpbooks.co.uk/GCSESpanishAudio

How to access your free Online Edition

You can read this entire book on your PC, Mac or tablet, with handy links to all the online audio files. Just go to **cgpbooks.co.uk/extras** and enter this code:

1907 0028 7550 8573

By the way, this code only works for one person. If somebody else has used this book before you, they might have already claimed the Online Edition.

CGP — still the best! ☺

Our sole aim here at CGP is to produce the highest quality books — carefully written, immaculately presented and dangerously close to being funny.

Then we work our socks off to get them out to you — at the cheapest possible prices.

CONTENTS

CONTENTS

Published by CGP

Editors:
Chloe Anderson
Rachel Grocott
Rose Jones
Jennifer Underwood

Contributors:
Matthew Parkinson
Jacqui Richards
Clare Swayne

With thanks to Encarna Aparicio-Dominguez, Karen Gascoigne, Pippa Mayfield,
Sabrina Robinson and Glenda Simpson for the proofreading.

With thanks to Ana Pungartnik for the copyright research.

Acknowledgements:
Audio produced by Naomi Laredo of Small Print.
Recorded, edited and mastered by Graham Williams of the Speech Recording Studio,
with the assistance of Andy le Vien at RMS Studios.

Voice Artists:
Jessica Gonzalez Campos
David Martel Santana
Ángela Lobato del Castillo

AQA material is reproduced by permission of AQA.
With thanks to iStock.com for permission to use the images on pages 29, 46 and 55
Abridged and adapted extract on page 16 from 'Las inquietudes de Shanti Andía' by Pío Baroja.
Abridged and adapted extract on page 32 from 'Pepita Jiménez' by Juan Valera.
Abridged and adapted extract on page 48 from 'Viajes por Europa y América' by Gorgonio Petano y Mazariegos.

ISBN: 978 1 78294 546 8
Printed by Elanders Ltd, Newcastle upon Tyne.
Clipart from Corel®

Based on the classic CGP style created by Richard Parsons.

Numbers

There are some tricky customers among Spanish numbers so make sure you're first in line for top marks.

Uno, dos, tres — *One, two, three*

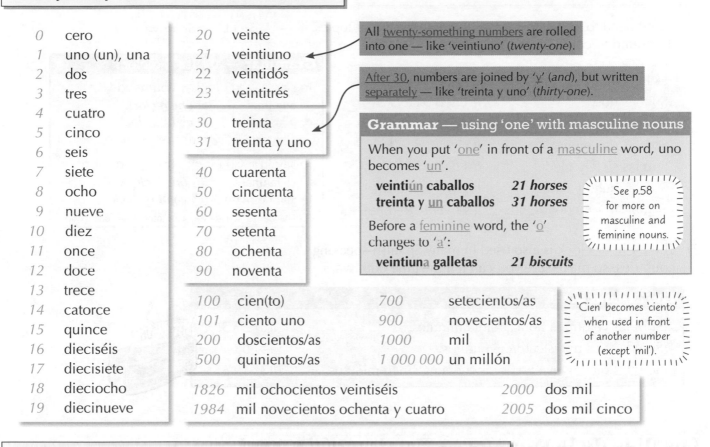

0	cero		20	veinte
1	uno (un), una		21	veintiuno
2	dos		22	veintidós
3	tres		23	veintitrés
4	cuatro			
5	cinco		30	treinta
6	seis		31	treinta y uno
7	siete		40	cuarenta
8	ocho		50	cincuenta
9	nueve		60	sesenta
10	diez		70	setenta
11	once		80	ochenta
12	doce		90	noventa
13	trece			
14	catorce			
15	quince			
16	dieciséis			
17	diecisiete			
18	dieciocho			
19	diecinueve			

All twenty-something numbers are rolled into one — like 'veintiuno' (*twenty-one*).

After 30, numbers are joined by 'y' (*and*), but written separately — like 'treinta y uno' (*thirty-one*).

Grammar — using 'one' with masculine nouns

When you put 'one' in front of a masculine word, uno becomes 'un'.

veintiún caballos	*21 horses*
treinta y un caballos	*31 horses*

Before a feminine word, the 'o' changes to 'a':

veintiuna galletas	*21 biscuits*

See p.58 for more on masculine and feminine nouns.

100	cien(to)		700	setecientos/as
101	ciento uno		900	novecientos/as
200	doscientos/as		1000	mil
500	quinientos/as		1 000 000	un millón

'Cien' becomes 'ciento' when used in front of another number (except 'mil').

1826	mil ochocientos veintiséis	2000	dos mil
1984	mil novecientos ochenta y cuatro	2005	dos mil cinco

Primero, segundo, tercero — *First, second, third*

These words always end in 'o' for masculine things and 'a' for feminine things.

1st	primero/primera (1°/1ª)	6th	sexto/a
2nd	segundo/a (2°/2ª)	7th	séptimo/a
3rd	tercero/a (3°/3ª)	8th	octavo/a
4th	cuarto/a	9th	noveno/a
5th	quinto/a	10th	décimo/a

Grammar — 'primero', 'tercero' + masculine nouns

When 'primero' or 'tercero' appear in front of a masculine word, they drop the 'o'.

el primer baile	*the first dance*
el tercer cantante	*the third singer*

Other useful number phrases

el número = number

una docena	*a dozen*	un par	*a couple / pair*	unos/as	*some / a few / about*

unas diez peras
about ten pears

1st the worst, 2nd the best, 3rd the one with the Spanish test...

Lee el texto y contesta a las preguntas en **español**.

'Tener' is a radical-changing verb. See p.76.

Marta tiene veintidós años. Su hermana solo tiene diecisiete años, pero su abuelo tiene ochenta y ocho años. Marta vive muy cerca de aquí — en la segunda calle a la derecha.

e.g. ¿Cuántos años tiene Marta? **Tiene veintidós años.**

1. ¿Cuántos años tiene su hermana? [1]
2. ¿Cuántos años tiene su abuelo? [1]
3. ¿Dónde vive Marta? [1]

Times and Dates

Time to learn some really useful phrases which are sure to get you good marks in your Spanish GCSE.

¿Qué hora es? — *What time is it?*

1) You'll need to know how to <u>tell the time</u> for lots of topics. It's bound to come up in your exams...

See p.1 for more numbers.

Es la una.	*It's one o'clock.*
Son las dos.	*It's two o'clock.*
Son las cinco y cuarto.	*It's quarter past five.*
Son las dos menos cuarto.	*It's quarter to two.*
Son las siete y media.	*It's half past seven.*
Son las ocho y cinco.	*It's five past eight.*
Son las tres menos veinte.	*It's twenty to three.*

Grammar — at / it's X o'clock

To say '<u>at X o'clock</u>', you need '<u>a</u>':
a <u>la</u> una	at *one o'clock*
a <u>las</u> ocho	at *eight o'clock*

('La' changes to 'las' for anything other than 'one o'clock'.)

To say '<u>it's X o'clock</u>', use '<u>es</u>' or '<u>son</u>':
<u>es</u> la una	*it's* one o'clock
<u>son</u> las ocho	*it's* eight o'clock

('Es changes to 'son' for anything other than 'one o'clock'.)

2) The <u>24-hour clock</u> is also used in many Spanish-speaking countries, so make sure you can tell the time <u>both</u> ways.

The 24-hour clock

(Son) las veintiuna horas treinta minutos.	*(It's)* 21.30.
(Son) las tres horas catorce minutos.	*(It's)* 03.14.
(Son) las diecinueve horas cincuenta y cinco minutos.	*(It's)* 19.55.

Los días de la semana — *The days of the week*

la semana	*the week*	hoy	*today*	
el fin de semana	*(at) the weekend*	mañana	*tomorrow*	
lunes	*Monday*	ayer	*yesterday*	
martes	*Tuesday*	anoche	*last night*	
miércoles	*Wednesday*	pasado mañana	*the day after tomorrow*	
jueves	*Thursday*	anteayer	*the day before yesterday*	
viernes	*Friday*	el lunes	*on Monday*	
sábado	*Saturday*	los lunes	*on Mondays*	
domingo	*Sunday*	todos los días	*every day*	
		quince días	*a fortnight*	
		cada quince días	*every fortnight*	
		cada tres días	*every three days*	

Days of the week are always masculine and lower case.

In English, a fortnight is fourteen days, but if you're talking about a fortnight in <u>Spanish</u>, you actually say <u>fifteen days</u>.

Fui de compras ayer.	*I went shopping yesterday.*
Tengo un examen pasado mañana.	*I have an exam the day after tomorrow.*
Voy al cine los sábados.	*I go to the cinema on Saturdays.*

the day before yesterday — anteayer

tomorrow — mañana

every six days — cada seis días

Times and Dates

Knowing about dates is important — they do tend to crop up every now and then. What's even better is that they can help you sort out your Spanish social life. What's not to love?

More useful time phrases

esta mañana	*this morning*
esta tarde	*this afternoon/evening*
esta noche	*tonight*
mañana por la mañana	*tomorrow morning*
la semana que viene	*next week*
la semana pasada	*last week*

See p.2 for more time phrases.

To say 'in the evening', you add 'por':

Juego al tenis por la mañana.
I play tennis in the morning.

You don't translate 'at' here — you literally say 'I play tennis the weekend'.

in the afternoon — por la tarde
at the weekend — el fin de semana

Los meses del año — *The months of the year*

Just like the days of the week, the months of the year are all <u>masculine</u> and <u>shouldn't have capital letters</u>.

enero	*January*	julio	*July*	la estación	*season*
febrero	*February*	agosto	*August*	la primavera	*spring*
marzo	*March*	septiembre	*September*	el verano	*summer*
abril	*April*	octubre	*October*	el otoño	*autumn*
mayo	*May*	noviembre	*November*	el invierno	*winter*
junio	*June*	diciembre	*December*		

Voy a la playa todos los años en agosto. *I go to the beach every year in August.*

En invierno, iremos a esquiar. *In winter, we will go skiing.*

Bern hoped to impress his date with his alternative choice of transport.

¿Qué fecha es? — *What's the date?*

In English, you say 'the third of May' or 'the twentieth of December'. In Spanish, you can say either 'el primero de' or 'el uno de' for the <u>first</u> of the month, but for all the other dates, you say 'the three of May' or 'the twenty of December'...

el tres de mayo	*(on) the third of May*
el veinte de diciembre	*(on) the twentieth of December*
Es el uno de / el primero de febrero.	*It's the first of February.*
Es el dos de marzo de dos mil dieciocho.	*It's the second of March 2018.*

You <u>don't</u> translate '<u>on</u>' at the start of dates in Spanish, so <u>both</u> 'the third of May' and 'on the third of May' are written '<u>el tres de mayo</u>'.

Sultanas, raisins, dates — *tasty treats for exam revision...*

*Listen to what Carlos, Anabel and Julia have to say, and then answer the questions in **English**.*

e.g. How often does Carlos go to the gym? **Every day.**

1. When was Anabel's birthday meal? [1]
2. Where did Anabel go yesterday? [1]
3. When is Julia going to the theatre? [1]

Questions

Knowing about questions will come in handy in your speaking test — you'll have to understand what you're being asked, and in the role-play you'll have to ask your teacher a question too. Best to be prepared.

Question marks and tone of voice

1) To turn a statement into a question, put an <u>upside down question mark</u> at the <u>beginning</u> and a <u>normal one</u> at the <u>end</u>.

2) When speaking, <u>raise your voice</u> at the <u>end</u> of the sentence to show you're asking a question.

¿Tu sombrero es azul?   *Is your hat blue?*

Literally: 'Your hat is blue?'

¿Tienes un coche?   *Do you have a car?*

Literally: 'You have a car?'

"Of course I have a car — why wouldn't a dog have a car?"

¿Qué... — *What...?*

If your question starts with '<u>What...</u>', you normally need to start it with '<u>¿Qué...</u>' in Spanish.

¿Qué comes por la mañana?   *What do you eat in the morning?*

¿Qué quieres hacer el fin de semana?   *What do you want to do at the weekend?*

Go back to p.2-3 for more time phrases.

¿Cuál... — *Which one..? What...?*

1) '<u>¿Cuál...</u>' normally means '<u>Which...</u>' or '<u>Which one...</u>':

¿Cuál quieres?   *Which (one) do you want?*

2) However, sometimes you might need to use '<u>¿Cuál...</u>' even if you'd use '<u>What...</u>' in English. This is usually when you use the verb '<u>ser</u>' and you're asking for a <u>piece of information</u>, rather than a definition.

¿Cuál es tu problema?   *What is your problem?*

¿Cuál es tu dirección?   *What is your address?*

¿Cuándo? ¿Por qué? ¿Dónde? — *When? Why? Where?*

There are <u>loads of other words</u> you can use to <u>begin a question</u> — get them <u>all</u> learnt.

Question words like this are known as interrogatives. See p.70.

¿Cuándo?	*When?*
¿Por qué?	*Why?*
¿Dónde?	*Where?*
¿Cómo?	*How?*
¿Cuánto/a?	*How much?*
¿Cuántos/as?	*How many?*
¿Quién(es)?	*Who?*
¿Cuál?	*Which?*
¿Es...?	*Is it...?*

Remember that question words need accents.

¿Cuántos/as tienes?	*How many do you have?*
¿Por qué haces eso?	*Why are you doing that?*
¿De dónde eres?	*Where are you from?*
¿Cuál prefieres?	*Which do you prefer?*
¿Es muy difícil?	*Is it very difficult?*

Questions

Now you know how to form questions, you need to get practising them in conversations. If you're asking loads of questions, you might need to be able to say 'please', too — there's more about being polite on p.6.

Tengo una pregunta — *I have a question*

Here are some of the most common ways you can use the question words from p.4.

¿Qué fecha?	*What date?*
¿Qué día?	*What day?*
¿Cuándo es tu cumpleaños?	*When is your birthday?*
¿Cuántos años tienes?	*How old are you?*
¿A qué hora...?	*At what time...?*
¿Qué hora es?	*What time is it?*
¿Por cuánto tiempo?	*For how long?*
¿Cuánto cuesta(n)?	*How much does it / do they cost?*
¿Cuánto vale(n)?	*How much does it / do they cost?*
¿Cuánto es?	*How much is it?*
¿De qué color (es)?	*What colour (is it)?*

Question	**Simple Answer**	**Extended Answer**
¿Cuánto cuesta ir al cine? *How much does it cost to go to the cinema?*	Cuesta siete euros. *It costs seven euros.*	Cuesta siete euros, cincuenta céntimos. Es muy caro. *It costs seven euros, fifty cents. It's very expensive.*

SPEAKING — To learn Spanish or not to learn Spanish, that is the question...

Have a look at the role-play that Carla did with her teacher.

Teacher: ¿A qué hora vas al gimnasio, Carla?

Carla: Voy al gimnasio a las cuatro de la tarde.

Teacher: ¿Cuánto cuesta ir al gimnasio?

Carla: Cuesta tres euros cada vez.

Teacher: ¿Vas al gimnasio todos los días?

Carla: No, solo los fines de semana, pero los jueves, juego al **baloncesto**[1] porque me gusta mucho.

Teacher: Ah, **vale**[2], muy bien.

Carla: Y tú, ¿cuándo practicas **deporte**[3]?

Teacher: Juego al fútbol los sábados.

Grade 8-9

[1]basketball
[2]OK
[3]sport

Tick list:
✓ tenses: present
✓ opinion phrase
✓ correct time phrases e.g. los jueves
✓ correctly formed question

To improve:
+ add a few more complex structures, e.g. cada tres días

Estás hablando con tu amiga española sobre el deporte.
- *la hora cuando juegas al tenis*
- *la frecuencia con que juegas al tenis*
- *!*
- *el precio de jugar al tenis*
- *? deporte preferido*

Use the instructions on the role-play card to prepare your own role-play. Address your friend as 'tú' and speak for about two minutes. [15 marks]

'!' means you'll need to answer a question you haven't prepared. You can have a good guess at what you might be asked though — here, the question is likely to still be on the topic of tennis as the questions before and after the '!' are about tennis too.

When you see '?', you need to ask your teacher a question.

Section 1 — General Stuff

Being Polite

Being polite is an important part of the speaking test — so mind your manners with these tips.

Los saludos — *Greetings*

If you're writing these greetings as exclamations, you need an upside down exclamation mark at the start and a normal one at the end, for example: ¡Hola!

hola	*hello*
buenos días	*good day / good morning*
buenas tardes	*good afternoon / good evening*
buenas noches	*good night*
hasta luego	*see you later*
hasta el lunes	*see you on Monday*
hasta mañana	*see you tomorrow*
hasta pronto	*see you soon*
adiós	*goodbye*

¿Qué tal?	*How are you? (informal)*
¿Cómo estás?	*How are you? (informal)*
¿Cómo está?	*How are you? (formal)*

muy bien	*very well*	great — fenomenal
bien	*well*	so-so — así así
no muy bien	*not very well*	terrible — fatal

Question	**Simple Answer**	**Extended Answer**
¿Qué tal?	Bien, gracias.	Estoy fatal. Me duele la cabeza.
How are you?	*Well, thanks.*	*I feel terrible. I've got a headache.*

See p.41 for more illnesses.

Por favor y gracias — *Please and thank you*

You don't want to sound <u>rude</u> in the exam, so learn these <u>charming</u> little words and phrases.

por favor	*please*	Eres muy amable.	*That's very kind of you. (informal)*
gracias	*thank you*	Es muy amable.	*That's very kind of you. (formal)*
muchas gracias	*thank you very much*	De nada.	*You're welcome.*
Lo siento.	*I'm sorry.*	vale	*ok*
Lo siento mucho.	*I'm really sorry.*	¡Claro!	*Of course!*

¡Por favor! / ¡Perdone!	*Excuse me!*	(E.g. for asking someone the way)
¡Con permiso!	*Excuse me!*	(E.g. for wanting to get past someone)

Le presento a ... — *May I introduce ... ?*

If you're <u>male</u>, you say 'encantad<u>o</u>', and if you're <u>female</u>, it's 'encantad<u>a</u>'.

Use 'Esta es...' for introducing someone <u>female</u>.

Le presento a ...	*May I introduce ... ?*	Encantado/a.	*Pleased to meet you.*
Este es ...	*This is ...*	Mucho gusto.	*Pleased to meet you.*

Here's how a conversation might go if you wanted to <u>introduce someone</u>:

Señora Valls:	Hola Ana, ¿qué tal?	*Hello Ana, how are you?*
Ana:	Muy bien. ¿Cómo está?	*Very well. How are you?*
Señora Valls:	Así así.	*So-so.*
Ana:	Le presento a Arturo.	*May I introduce Arturo?*
Señora Valls:	Encantada.	*Pleased to meet you.*

Ana uses the <u>formal</u> way to ask how Señora Valls is because Señora Valls is <u>older</u> than her. See p.7 for more information.

If you're talking to someone you call 'tú', you say 'Te presento a...' — it's <u>informal</u>.

Being Polite

And the politeness doesn't end there — here are some more ways to charm the examiner...

Quisiera — *I would like*

1) Don't just say 'I want' — make sure you <u>ask politely</u> for what you would like:

> Quisiera un café. *I would like a coffee.*

2) And this is how to say that you <u>would like to do</u> something:

> Quisiera hablar. *I would like to talk.*
> ¿Puedo sentarme? *May I sit down?*

> go to the toilet — ir al baño
> have a drink — beber algo

'Poder' is a radical-changing verb. See p.76.'

Tú y usted — *Informal and Formal 'you'*

Grammar — 'tú' and 'usted'

In Spanish, there are <u>four</u> different ways of saying '<u>you</u>'.

Informal 'you':

① '<u>Tú</u>' — for <u>one person</u> who's your <u>friend</u>, a <u>family member</u> or of a <u>similar age</u>.

② '<u>Vosotros/as</u>' — for a group of <u>two or more people</u> that you <u>know</u>.
Only use '<u>vosotras</u>' if all the people in the group are <u>female</u>.

Formal 'you':

③ '<u>Usted</u>' — for <u>one person</u> that is <u>older than you</u> or someone you <u>don't know</u>.

④ '<u>Ustedes</u>' — for a group of <u>two or more people</u> that you <u>don't know</u>.

'Usted' and 'ustedes' <u>don't use the same 'you' part of the verb</u> as 'tú' and 'vosotros'.

* For '<u>usted</u>', use the '<u>he/she/it</u>' part of the verb (see p.75-85).
* For '<u>ustedes</u>', use the '<u>they</u>' part of the verb.

One does not appreciate being called 'tú'.

'Tú', 'vosotros/as', 'usted' and 'ustedes' are all pronouns — see p.68.

So, here are the <u>four</u> different ways of asking where someone is from:

Tú	Vosotros/as	Usted	Ustedes
¿De dónde eres?	¿De dónde sois?	¿De dónde es?	¿De dónde son?

Argh, so many 'you's — I'm seeing quadruple...

Here, Andrés is introducing his two friends Mateo and Lucía to each other.

Andrés:	¡Buenos días, Mateo! ¿Qué tal?
Mateo:	Muy bien, gracias, ¿y tú?
Andrés:	Sí, bien. Esta es mi amiga, Lucía.
Mateo:	¡Hola Lucía! Encantado.
Lucía:	Mucho gusto.
Mateo:	¿Cómo estás, Lucía?
Lucía:	No muy bien, estoy enferma.
Mateo:	Ay, ¡qué lástima!¹
Lucía:	Sí, es una pena².
Andrés:	Pues³, hasta luego, Mateo.
Mateo:	¡Adiós!

Grade 4-5

¹Oh, what a shame!
²a pity
³Well

Tick list:
✓ variety of phrases
✓ correct Spanish punctuation
✓ gender agreement

To improve:
+ develop each idea a bit further
+ different tenses (add a past or future)
+ use more varied adjectives, e.g. 'fatal' instead of 'no muy bien'

Now have a go yourself:

*Escribe tu propio diálogo en el que te presentas. Escribe aproximadamente **40** palabras en **español**.*

[8 marks]

Opinions

Having opinions stops you sounding dull — but more importantly, it gets you marks, and lots of them.

¿Qué piensas de...? — *What do you think of...?*

¿Qué piensas?	*What do you think?*
¿Qué piensas de...?	*What do you think of...?*
¿Qué te parece...?	*What do you think of...?*
¿Cuál es tu opinión de...?	*What's your opinion of...?*
¿Le encuentras simpático/a?	*Do you find him/her nice?*
Pienso que / Creo que	*I think that...*
...me parece...	*I think ... is ...* ← If you're talking about more than one thing, you need 'me parecen'.
Estoy de acuerdo.	*I agree.*
No estoy de acuerdo.	*I disagree.*
(No) es verdad.	*That's (not) true.*

Urgh. So many questions, so little time.

¿Qué piensas de **mi novio**?   What do you think of **my boyfriend**?

Pienso que **es amable.**   I think **he's kind.**

What's your opinion of...? — ¿Cuál es tu opinión de...?

I think — creo que

See p.14 for more useful describing words.

Las opiniones — *opinions*

Me gusta... (sing.)	*I like... (singular)*
Me gustan... (pl.)	*I like... (plural)*
Me gusta(n) mucho...	*I really like...*
Me encanta... (sing.)	*I love... (singular)*
Me encantan... (pl.)	*I love...*
Me interesa(n)...	*I'm interested in...*
Encuentro ... fantástico.	*I find ... fantastic.*

No me gusta(n)...	*I don't like...*
No me gusta(n)... para nada.	*I don't like ... at all.*
... no me interesa(n).	*... doesn't / don't interest me.*
Encuentro ... horrible.	*I find ... awful.*
Odio...	*I hate...*

Grammar — 'gustar' and 'encantar'

Use '<u>me gusta</u>' and '<u>me encanta</u>' when you want to say you like or love a <u>singular</u> thing.

If you want to say you like or love a <u>plural</u> thing, <u>add</u> an '<u>n</u>' to the end.

   Me gusta<u>n</u> las uvas.   *I like grapes.*
   Me encanta<u>n</u> las películas.   *I love films.*

To say you <u>like doing an activity</u>, use an <u>infinitive</u> (see p.75) after the correct form of 'gustar' or 'encantar'.

   e.g. **Me gusta <u>bailar</u>.**   *I like <u>dancing</u>.*
   infinitive ↗

If you <u>don't like</u> something, always try to say what you <u>prefer</u>:   Prefiero...   *I prefer...*

Grammar — 'preferir' is a radical-changing verb

'<u>Preferir</u>' (*to prefer*) is a <u>radical-changing verb</u> (see p.76 for more). With 'preferir', the second '<u>e</u>' changes to '<u>ie</u>':

prefiero	*I prefer*
prefieres	*you prefer*
prefiere	*he/she/it prefers*
prefieren	*they prefer*

The stem of the 'we' and 'you inf., pl.' forms doesn't change:
'preferimos' = 'we prefer'
'preferís' = 'you (inf., pl.) prefer'

Me gusta el té, pero prefiero el café.
I like tea, but I prefer coffee.

No me gusta cantar — prefiero bailar.
I don't like singing — I prefer dancing.

Opinions

Being able to express your opinion is great — but it's even better if you can justify it. Why? Because it makes you sound great, cool, fabulous, marvellous and definitely not boring...

Porque — *because*

To start justifying your opinion, you need '<u>porque</u>' (*because*). Look out, though — '<u>porque</u>' and '<u>¿por qué?</u>' <u>sound very similar</u>, but they're <u>written differently</u> and <u>mean different things</u>.

¿Por qué te gusta ir al cine?	*Why do you like going to the cinema?*
Me gusta ir al cine porque...	*I like going to the cinema because...*

(No) me gusta porque es... — *I (don't) like it because it's...*

Here's a nice long list of <u>adjectives</u> you can use to <u>justify</u> your opinions and <u>collect some good marks</u> too.

bueno/a	*good*	agradable	*nice, kind*	interesante	*interesting*
estupendo/a	*fantastic*	amable	*friendly*	divertido/a	*amusing, entertaining, fun*
fenomenal	*great*	fabuloso/a	*fabulous*	malo/a	*bad*
genial	*brilliant*	increíble	*incredible*	desagradable	*unpleasant*
guay	*cool*	maravilloso/a	*marvellous*	aburrido/a	*boring*
emocionante	*exciting*	precioso/a	*beautiful*	ridículo/a	*ridiculous*
perfecto/a	*perfect*	bonito/a	*pretty*	decepcionante	*disappointing*
impresionante	*impressive*	entretenido/a	*entertaining*	raro/a	*strange*

These <u>useful little phrases</u> could also help you out:

Me fastidia.	*It annoys me.*
Me aburre.	*It bores me.*
Me hace llorar.	*It makes me cry.*
Me hace reír.	*It makes me laugh.*

Adjectives change to agree with plural nouns too — see p.60 for more on agreement.

Grammar — nouns and adjectives agree

The <u>ending</u> of the <u>adjective</u> must <u>agree</u> with the <u>noun (p.60)</u>.

'el cine' is masculine so 'bueno' must end in 'o'.

El cine es bueno.	*The cinema is good.*
La película es buena.	*The film is good.*

'la película' is feminine so the adjective ends in 'a'.

Adjectives that end with other letters like '<u>interesante</u>' stay the <u>same</u> for both masculine and feminine nouns.

READING I think, therefore I get good marks in Spanish...

Luis and Elena are discussing the cinema. Read what they say and answer the questions in **English**.

Luis:	¿Te gusta ir al cine, Elena?
Elena:	Sí, me encanta ir al cine porque es divertido. Me gustan las películas de acción. Y tú, ¿qué piensas del cine?
Luis:	No me gusta ir al cine. Prefiero ver las películas en casa. Me encantan las comedias pero odio las películas románticas porque me parecen aburridas. ¿Qué piensas, Elena?
Elena:	Sí, estoy de acuerdo. A veces son ridículas.

e.g. Why does Elena like going to the cinema? **Because it's fun.**

1. Does Luis prefer going to the cinema or watching films at home? [1]
2. Does Luis like romantic films? Why / Why not? [2]
3. What does Elena think of romantic films? [1]

Putting it All Together

Now you know all the ingredients that go into giving and justifying opinions, you need to be able to put them all together. This is really useful — you'll have something to say about any of the GCSE topics.

Putting your opinions together

este equipo	this team
esta revista	this magazine
esta música	this music
este grupo	this band
esta novela	this novel
este actor	this actor
esta actriz	this actress
esta película	this film
este periódico	this newspaper
esta canción	this song
esta tienda	this shop

Grammar — 'este' and 'esta'

'Este' means 'this', but it has to agree with the noun it comes before — see p.62 for more information.

	masculine	feminine
singular	este	esta
plural	estos	estas

¿Qué te parece este grupo? — *What do you think of this band?*

Esta música es fenomenal. — *This music is great.*

¿Qué piensas de estos actores? — *What do you think of these actors?*

Question	Simple Answer	Extended Answer
¿Cuál es tu opinión de esta revista? *What's your opinion of this magazine?*	Me gusta mucho esta revista. *I really like this magazine.*	Me gusta mucho esta revista porque es muy interesante. *I really like this magazine because it's very interesting.*

Remember to always back up your opinions

¿Qué piensas de este grupo? — *What do you think of this band?*   [this team — este equipo]

Me encanta este grupo porque me gusta la música rock. — *I love this band because I like rock music.*   [their music is brilliant — su música es genial]

¿Estás de acuerdo? — *Do you agree?*   [And you, what do you think? — Y tú, ¿qué piensas?]

No, odio la música rock — prefiero la música pop. — *No, I hate rock music — I prefer pop music.*   [I find rock music awful — encuentro la música rock horrible]

🎧 LISTENING TRACK 02 — *Don't keep your opinions to yourself — share 'em.*

Listen to Antonio and Carolina talking about what they like doing. Decide whether the statements are true (T) or false (F), and write T or F next to them. The first one has been done for you.

e.g. Carolina likes going to the swimming pool. **T**

1. Antonio likes listening to music. [1]
2. Antonio thinks the shops in his city are fantastic. [1]
3. Antonio doesn't like reading newspapers. [1]
4. Carolina likes both reading and listening to music. [1]
5. Carolina thinks pop bands are awful. [1]

About Yourself

Being able to talk about yourself is really important — you just can't get by without it.

Preséntate — *Introduce yourself*

el nombre	*name*	el cumpleaños	*birthday*	
el apellido	*surname*	cumplir años	*to have a birthday*	
llamarse	*to be called*	la edad	*age*	
nacer	*to be born*	tener ... años	*to be ... years old*	
el nacimiento	*birth*	la nacionalidad	*nationality*	

Grammar — saying your age

In Spanish, you 'have' an age, so you need the verb 'tener' to say how old you are. 'Tener' is a radical-changing verb — see p.76.

Tengo 16 años. *I'm 16 years old.*

¡Hola! Me llamo Juan.　　　　*Hello! I'm called Juan.*

My name is Juan. — Mi nombre es Juan.
I'm Juan. — Soy Juan.

Tengo quince años.　　　　*I'm 15 years old.*

Mi cumpleaños es el dos de abril.　　　　*My birthday is the 2ⁿᵈ of April.*

Check p.3 for a reminder of how to say dates.

Nací en (el año) dos mil dos.　　　　*I was born in (the year) 2002.*

Soy británico/a. Nací en Surrey.　　　　*I'm British. I was born in Surrey.*

English — inglés / inglesa
Scottish — escocés / escocesa
Welsh — galés / galesa
Irish — irlandés / irlandesa

Vivo en Málaga, en el sur de España.　　　　*I live in Málaga, in the south of Spain.*

See p.47 for more countries and nationalities.

the north — el norte
the east — el este
the west — el oeste

¿Cómo se escribe? — *How do you spell it?*

You might have to spell something out, so learn how to pronounce the letters of the Spanish alphabet.

A — ah	F — effay	K — ka	O — oh	U — ooh
B — bay	G — hay	L — elay	P — pay	V — oohbay
C — thay	H — atchay	M — emay	Q — coo	W — oohbay doblay
D — day	I — ee	N — enay	R — eray	X — ekis
E — ay	J — hota	Ñ — enyay	S — essay	Y — yay
			T — tay	Z — thayta

'h' like 'lo**ch**'　　　Double 'l' makes a '**y**' sound.

Some Spanish words like 'adiós' have an accent to show which vowel you need to emphasise. Remember to write the accent too.

SPEAKING ***It's all about me, me, me...***

Read the question and then look at how Estefanía has answered it.
Háblame un poco de ti.

¡Hola! Me llamo Estefanía y soy de Venezuela.
Vivo en el norte del país, cerca de la ciudad de Caracas.
Mi cumpleaños es el veinticuatro de diciembre. Es un día muy
especial, porque celebramos mi cumpleaños y la Navidad al
mismo tiempo. Nací en el año dos mil.

Grade 6-7

Tick list:
✓ tenses: present, preterite
✓ correctly formed dates and years
✓ justifying opinions with 'porque'

To improve:
+ include an opinion about where you live

Now try to answer the same question. Mention your name, where you're from and your birthday.
Try to speak for about two minutes. [10 marks]

My Family

Learning to talk about who's in your family is an absolute must — examiners seem to love asking about it.

Mi familia — *My family*

los parientes	*relatives*	los hijos	*children*	el abuelo	*grandfather*
el padre	*father*	el marido	*husband*	la abuela	*grandmother*
la madre	*mother*	la mujer	*wife*	los nietos	*grandchildren*
los padres	*parents*	el hermanastro	*stepbrother*	el/la tío/a	*uncle/aunt*
el padrastro	*stepfather*	la hermanastra	*stepsister*	el/la primo/a	*cousin*
la madrastra	*stepmother*	el/la gemelo/a	*twin*	el/la sobrino/a	*nephew/niece*

Háblame de tu familia — *Tell me about your family*

Grammar — saying 'my' and 'your'

Possessive adjectives like 'my' and 'your' etc. have to agree with the noun they come before (see p.62). Remember — 'su(s)' could also mean 'your' if you're being formal — see p.62.

mi padre	*my father*	**tu** hermana	*your sister*	**su** tía	*his / her / their aunt*
mis padres	*my parents*	**tus** hermanas	*your sisters*	**sus** tías	*his / her / their aunts*

And don't go asking your father either... The answer is no!

Tengo una hermana mayor. Ella se llama Ramona.

I have an older sister. She is called Ramona.

an older brother — un hermano mayor
a younger sister — una hermana menor
a younger brother — un hermano menor

Hay cinco personas en mi familia — mi madre, mi padrastro, mis dos hermanastros menores y yo. Mis hermanastros se llaman David y Gabriel.

There are five people in my family — my mother, my stepfather, my two younger stepbrothers and me. My stepbrothers are called David and Gabriel.

only child (female) — hija única

Soy hijo único, pero me gustaría tener hermanos.

I'm an only child (male), but I would like to have brothers and sisters.

I like not having brothers and sisters — me gusta no tener hermanos

Question	Simple Answer	Extended Answer
¿Cómo es tu familia? *What's your family like?*	Soy hijo único, pero tengo muchos primos. *I'm an only child, but I have a lot of cousins.*	Soy hijo único, pero mi padre tiene cinco hermanos, así que en realidad, tengo muchos parientes. Mis primos viven cerca de aquí y siempre lo pasamos bien juntos. *I'm an only child, but my father has five brothers and sisters, so really, I have lots of relatives. My cousins live near here and we always have a good time together.*

Examiners are fans of families — don't forget to revise them...

Translate this text into **English**. *[9 marks]*

Vivo con mi madre, mi hermana mayor y mis dos hermanas menores. Son gemelas. Para mí, es importante tener hermanos porque siempre tienes alguien con quien puedes salir. Los fines de semana, visito a mi padre, su mujer y mi hermanastro. Nació el año pasado y solo tiene seis meses. Me gustaría pasar más tiempo allí con ellos porque es muy divertido.

Describing People

You'll probably have to describe what people look like at some point in your exam — so carry on reading.

¿Cómo eres? — *What are you like?*

> You'll need the verbs 'tener' (*to have*) and 'ser' (*to be*) for this page. They're irregular, so check p.76-77 to see how they work.

alto/a	*tall*	joven	*young*	negro	*black*
bajo/a	*short*	viejo/a	*old*	castaño	*chestnut-brown*
de altura mediana	*medium height*	marrón	*brown*	largo	*long*
gordo/a	*fat*	azul	*blue*	corto	*short (hair)*
delgado/a	*slim*	verde	*green*	liso	*straight*
guapo/a	*good-looking*	rubio/a	*blonde*	rizado	*curly*

> 'Marrón' loses its accent in the plural form.

El aspecto físico — *Physical appearance*

Question	Simple Answer	Extended Answer
¿Cómo eres? *What are you like?*	Soy alta. Tengo los ojos azules y tengo el pelo castaño. *I'm tall. I have blue eyes and I have brown hair.*	Soy bastante alta. No soy ni gorda ni delgada. Tengo los ojos azules y llevo gafas. Tengo el pelo corto y rizado, y no tengo pecas. *I'm quite tall. I'm neither fat nor slim. I have blue eyes and I wear glasses. I have short, curly hair, and I don't have freckles.*

Grammar — adjectives agree

Adjectives must agree with the noun they describe.

'Los ojos' are masculine plural, so adjectives like 'blue' must be in the masculine plural form — azules.

'El pelo' is masculine singular, so adjectives like 'curly' need to be in the masculine singular form — rizado — even if you're a girl.

Soy muy bajo como mis padres. Sin embargo, mi hermano es mucho más alto que yo. Tengo el pelo rubio y tengo los ojos verdes.
I'm very short like my parents. However, my brother is much taller than me. I have blonde hair and I have green eyes.

Soy bajo y delgado. Tengo el pelo negro y tengo los ojos marrones. Tengo una barba también.

I'm short and slim. I have black hair and I have brown eyes. I also have a beard.

dark — moreno

a moustache — un bigote

Es altísima. Lleva gafas y tiene los ojos azules. Tiene el pelo castaño y liso.

She's really tall. She wears glasses and she has blue eyes. She has straight, chestnut-brown hair.

make-up — maquillaje

curly — rizado

Es de altura mediana y bastante gordo. Es pelirrojo y tiene los ojos verdes.

He's medium height and quite fat. He's red-haired and he has green eyes.

He's bald — Es calvo

Describe people well and you'll look like a first-rate student...

(TRACK LISTENING 03)

María y Jaime describen estas cuatro personas. Empareja cada foto con la descripción de la persona.

 a)  b)  c)  d)

Descripción 1 = foto .....
Descripción 2 = foto .....
Descripción 3 = foto .....
Descripción 4 = foto .....

[4 marks]

Personalities

Just saying everyone's nice gets pretty dull pretty quickly, so use these adjectives to spice up your writing.

Mi personalidad — *My personality*

animado/a	*lively*	hablador/a	*chatty / talkative*	egoísta	*selfish*
alegre	*happy*	atrevido/a	*daring / cheeky*	maleducado/a	*rude*
cariñoso/a	*affectionate*	serio/a	*serious*	perezoso/a	*lazy*
comprensivo/a	*understanding*	sensible	*sensitive*	travieso/a	*naughty*
cortés	*polite*	callado/a	*quiet*	torpe	*clumsy*
gracioso/a	*funny*	valiente	*brave*	celoso/a	*jealous*

¿Cómo es ...? — *What's ... like?*

Mi mejor amigo es gracioso y siempre alegre. Es sensible también. Sin embargo, a veces es un poco maleducado porque dice cosas sin pensar.

My best friend is funny and always happy. He's sensitive too. However, sometimes he's a bit rude because he says things without thinking.

My best friend (girl) — Mi mejor amiga

he always arrives late when we go to the cinema — siempre llega tarde cuando vamos al cine

Mis padres son comprensivos y amables. Mi madre es habladora pero mi padre es más callado.

My parents are understanding and kind. My mother is chatty but my father is quieter.

serious — serios

Mis profesoras son amables pero estrictas al mismo tiempo.

My teachers are friendly but strict at the same time.

kind — simpáticas

Grammar — making adjectives agree

<u>Adjectives</u> have to <u>agree</u> with the <u>nouns</u> they describe.
See the <u>normal</u> rules for adjective agreement on p.60.
But some adjectives work <u>differently</u>, like those ending in '<u>-or</u>' or '<u>-ísta</u>/-<u>ista</u>'.

1) '<u>Hablador</u>' — <u>add</u> an '<u>a</u>' on the end for the <u>feminine</u> form and then '<u>es</u>' and '<u>as</u>' for the masculine and feminine <u>plurals</u>.

2) '<u>Egoísta</u>' stays the same in the <u>singular</u> and becomes '<u>egoístas</u>' for both the masculine and feminine <u>plurals</u>.

Mis amigos son habladores.
My friends are chatty.

Mi primo es un poco egoísta.
My cousin is a bit selfish.

Me? I'm intelligent, good-looking, wonderful, humble...

Benjamín has written you an email telling you about himself, and his family and friends.

A decir verdad[1], mis padres son muy cariñosos, **aunque**[2] pueden ser estrictos, sobre todo **si no arreglo mi dormitorio**[3]. En mi opinión, mis amigos son alegres y atrevidos, pero **según**[4] mis padres, son maleducados. **Cuando era pequeño**[5], era bastante travieso, pero ahora creo que soy comprensivo y gracioso. Me gustaría ser más valiente. Y tú, ¿cómo eres?

Grade 6-7

[1]To tell the truth
[2]although
[3]if I don't tidy my bedroom
[4]according to
[5]When I was little

Tick list:
✓ tenses: present, imperfect, conditional
✓ varied adjectives that agree correctly
✓ conjunctions e.g. aunque, pero

To improve:
+ complex structures, e.g. subjunctive
+ use a wider range of tenses, e.g. future

Contesta a Benjamín y describe a tu familia. Escribe aproximadamente **90** *palabras en* **español**. *[16 marks]*

Relationships

Saying whether you get on with people is a good way of showing you can use some more complex verbs.

Las relaciones — *Relationships*

conocer	*to know (a person or place)*
aguantar	*to put up with*
confiar	*to trust*
fastidiar	*to annoy*
pelearse	*to fight*
llevarse bien / mal (con)	*to get on well / badly (with)*
relacionarse (con)	*to be in contact (with)*

You need the personal 'a' with 'conocer' and 'aguantar'. Have a look at p.73 for more information.

el amor	*love*
el novio	*boyfriend*
la novia	*girlfriend*
la pareja	*couple, partner*
la disputa	*argument*
besar	*to kiss*
enamorarse	*to fall in love*

Grammar — 'confiar'

'Confiar' is an irregular verb. In the present tense, the 'i' has an accent on it in every form except the 'we' and 'you inf., plural' forms.

Confío en él.   *I trust him.*

To say you trust someone, you need to use 'en'.

Grammar — reflexive verbs

'Llevarse', 'relacionarse' and 'pelearse' are reflexive verbs. Take off the 'se' and add the correct ending to the stem like a normal verb (see p.75). Then choose the right pronoun (see p.84) and put it in front of the verb.

Me llevo bien con mi hermana.   ***I get on well** with my sister.*
¿Te relacionas con ella?   ***Are you in contact** with her?*
Nos peleamos mucho.   ***We fight** a lot.*

Mis padres tienen una buena relación pero yo no me llevo bien con ellos debido a la barrera generacional entre nosotros.

My parents get on very well, but I don't get on with them due to the generation gap between us.

I get on badly with them — me llevo mal con ellos

Me llevo mejor con mi hermano porque me ayuda mucho. Tiene un buen sentido del humor.

I get on better with my brother because he helps me a lot. He has a good sense of humour.

Mi hermana y yo nos peleamos mucho porque me fastidia.

My sister and I fight a lot because she annoys me.

I can't stand my sister — No aguanto a mi hermana

Conozco muy bien a mi novio y confío en él. Nos enamoramos hace dos años y tenemos muy pocas disputas.

I know my boyfriend really well and I trust him. We fell in love two years ago and we have very few arguments.

'Conozco' (*I know*) is the only irregular bit of the verb 'conocer'. See p.76.

'Enamorarse' (*to fall in love*) is a reflexive verb too.

SPEAKING

Luckily, I get on really well with Spanish revision...

Read the questions and Víctor's responses below.

¿Qué hay en la foto? ¿Te llevas bien con tu familia?

En esta foto, hay dos chicos — **quizás**[1] son hermanos, pero se llevan bien porque no se pelean.

Grade 6-7

Tick list:
✓ range of adjectives which agree
✓ complex verbs e.g. 'confiar en'
✓ extended reasons given

Generalmente, sí. Confío en mi madre, así que hablo con ella cuando tengo **dificultades**[2] con **amistades**[3], por ejemplo. Mi padre es muy simpático y me conoce bien. No aguanto a mi hermana porque es muy maleducada y estúpida a veces.

[1]perhaps
[2]difficulties
[3]friendships

To improve:
+ a few more complex structures
+ try to use another tense

*Now answer these questions in **Spanish**. ¿Te llevas bien con tus padres? ¿Tienes una buena relación con tus hermanos? ¿Confías en tus amigos?*
[10 marks]

Partnership

Thinking about getting married is just round the corner — it might come up in your Spanish GCSE, in fact.

En el futuro... — *In the future...*

estar enamorado/a de	*to be in love with*
comprometerse	*to get engaged*
el casamiento / la boda	*wedding*
el matrimonio	*marriage, married couple*
el anillo	*ring*
el esposo / el marido	*husband*
la esposa / la mujer	*wife*
ser soltero/a	*to be single*
el estado civil	*marital status*

en mi opinión	*in my opinion*
a mi modo de ver	*the way I see it*
desde mi punto de vista	*from my point of view*
debo admitir que...	*I must admit that...*

Grammar — When I'm X years old...

To say '<u>when I'm 30</u>' (or to say 'when' with a future event), use the <u>subjunctive</u>. See p.88.

Cuando <u>tenga</u> 60 años... *When <u>I'm</u> 60 years old...*

Question	Simple Answer	Extended Answer
¿Te gustaría casarte y tener hijos en el futuro?	No sé si quiero casarme, pero me gustaría tener hijos.	No sé si me casaré porque no me importa mucho. Me gustaría tener hijos cuando tenga treinta años, pero no sé cuántos hijos quiero tener.
Would you like to get married and have children in the future?	*I don't know if I want to get married, but I'd like to have children.*	*I don't know if I'll get married because it's not very important to me. I'd like to have children when I'm 30, but I don't know how many I want to have.*

¿El matrimonio es importante? — *Is marriage important?*

Quiero casarme porque estoy enamorado de mi novia, y desde mi punto de vista, las bodas son muy románticas.

I want to get married because I'm in love with my girlfriend, and from my point of view, weddings are very romantic.

I want to celebrate with my family — quiero celebrar con mi familia

Debo admitir que preferiría no casarme, porque una boda es bastante cara.

I must admit that I would prefer not to get married, because a wedding is quite expensive.

I never want to get married — no quiero casarme nunca

I'd prefer to buy myself a house — preferiría comprarme una casa

A mi modo de ver, no es necesario casarse antes de tener hijos, pero me gustaría hacerlo de todos modos.

The way I see it, it's not necessary to get married before having children, but I'd like to do it anyway.

marriage is important because it gives you stability — el matrimonio es importante porque te da estabilidad

---

Turkey and stuffing — a marriage made in heaven...

Read this extract from 'Las inquietudes de Shanti Andía' by Pío Baroja, and answer the questions.

Dolorcitas parecía **decidirse por**[1] mí; pero, al mismo tiempo, todo el mundo decía que iba a casarse con el hijo del **marqués**[2] de Vernay, un señor de Jerez, no muy rico, pero de familia aristocrática. Le escribí a Dolorcitas y le hablé varias veces **por la reja**[3].

[1] decide on
[2] marquis
[3] through the window bars

1. *Decide whether these statements are true or false.*
   a) Nobody thought Dolorcitas was going to get married.
   b) The Marquis of Vernay's son didn't have much money.
   c) The narrator never spoke to Dolorcitas.

2. *Use the information in the text to fill in the gap.*
   The Marquis of Vernay's son came from ....

   [4 marks]

Music

Music often comes up in GCSE exams, so learn your stuff and dazzle the examiners.

La música — *Music*

la batería	*drums*
la canción	*song*
el / la cantante	*singer*
cantar	*to sing*
la letra	*song lyrics*
el grupo	*band*
el / la músico/a	*musician*
tocar	*to play (an instrument)*
la grabación	*recording*
en directo	*live*

Grammar — 'tocar' + instrument

Use the verb '<u>tocar</u>' to say you <u>play an instrument</u>.

When you're using the 'yo' form of 'tocar' in the <u>preterite</u> tense (see p.78), the '<u>c</u>' changes to '<u>qu</u>'.

<u>**Toco**</u> el violín.	***I play** the violin.*
<u>**Toqué**</u> el violín ayer.	***I played** the violin yesterday.*
<u>**Tocaba**</u> el violín.	***I used to play** the violin.*

Use the <u>imperfect</u> tense (p.79) to say what you <u>used to do</u>.

Question

¿Tocas algún instrumento?

Do you play an instrument?

Simple Answer

Sí, toco la guitarra y el clarinete.

Yes, I play the guitar and the clarinet.

Extended Answer

Sí, toco la guitarra en un grupo. Cuando era pequeño, tocaba el piano. Me gustaría aprender a tocar la batería, pero mis padres no me dejarán hacerlo.

Yes, I play the guitar in a band. When I was little, I used to play the piano. I would like to learn to play the drums, but my parents won't let me do it.

¿Te gusta escuchar música? — *Do you like listening to music?*

Me encanta escuchar música porque me hace sentir relajado/a. No me gusta la música pop. Diría que mi género de música preferido es el hip-hop.

I love listening to music because it makes me feel relaxed. I don't like pop music. I'd say that my favourite genre of music is hip-hop.

For a reminder of how to express your opinion, see p.8.

rap music — la música rap
rock music — la música rock
classical music — la música clásica

Puedo descargar muchos tipos de música instantáneamente, lo que me parece fenomenal.

I can download many types of music instantly, which seems great to me.

take my music with me and listen to it while I'm jogging or on the train — llevar la música conmigo y escucharla cuando salgo a correr o cuando estoy en el tren

Adoro a DiskoBeetz e intento ir a todos sus conciertos. Sus videos musicales son siempre entretenidos y originales.

I adore DiskoBeetz and I try to go to all their concerts. Their music videos are always entertaining and original.

Their song lyrics are interesting. — La letra de sus canciones es interesante.
I love live music. — Me encanta la música en directo.

TRACK LISTENING 04

It's time to face the music and try this exam style question...

*Marisol is a Spanish singer. Listen to the interview and then answer the questions in **English**.*

e.g. What kind of music is most important to Marisol's sister? **pop music**

1. Which instrument would Marisol like to learn to play? [1]

2. What two advantages of listening to music on the Internet does Marisol mention? [2]

3. Why does Marisol like going to concerts? [1]

Cinema

Make sure you can talk about a film you saw recently — and remember to always back up your opinions.

En el cine — *At the cinema*

la película	*film*	el papel	*role*	la estrella	*star, celebrity*
el actor	*actor*	la trama	*plot*	la banda sonora	*soundtrack*
la actriz	*actress*	el reparto	*cast*	la entrada	*ticket*

Me encantan las películas policíacas porque son muy emocionantes.
I love detective films because they're very exciting.

science fiction — de ciencia ficción

Prefiero las películas de aventura porque me dan menos miedo que las películas de terror.
I prefer adventure films because they scare me less than horror films.

often the special effects are great — muchas veces los efectos especiales son fenomenales

Romantic films annoy me — Las películas románticas me fastidian

No me gustan las películas de ciencia ficción porque es difícil seguir la trama.
I don't like science fiction films because it's difficult to follow the plot.

you always know what's going to happen — siempre sabes lo que va a pasar

Grammar — I saw...

To say '<u>I saw...</u>' you need the <u>preterite</u> tense.
Check how to form it on p.78.

El viernes, <u>vi</u> una comedia.
On Friday, <u>I saw</u> a comedy.

<u>Unlike</u> most verbs when they're in the '<u>yo</u>' form of the <u>preterite</u> tense, '<u>vi</u>' <u>doesn't</u> have an <u>accent</u>.

La última película que vi... — *The last film I saw...*

Question

Describe la última película que viste.
Describe the last film you saw.

Simple Answer

El sábado, vi una película de acción. Me gustó mucho.
On Saturday, I saw an action film. I really liked it.

Extended Answer

El fin de semana pasado, vi una película de acción. Se trataba de dos familias que luchaban durante cientos de años. Tengo ganas de ver la nueva película de Geoff Frank porque me gusta el reparto.
Last weekend, I saw an action film. It was about two families who were fighting for hundreds of years. I'm looking forward to seeing the new film by Geoff Frank because I like the cast.

Grammar — 'se trata de'

Use '<u>se trata de</u>' to say what a film is about:
<u>Se trata de</u> unos jóvenes muy ricos.
<u>It's about</u> some very rich young people.

And you can use it in the <u>imperfect</u> to say what a film <u>was</u> about:

<u>Se trataba del</u> amor.   **<u>It was about</u> love.**
Remember — 'de' + 'el' = 'del' (p.72).

Don't let your Spanish GCSE become a horror film...

Translate this text into **Spanish**. *[12 marks]*

I love films. In my opinion, detective films are the best. They are the most entertaining films because you have to think about the plot. Last week, I saw a really funny film. I like seeing films with my friends at the weekend. In the future, I would love to be an actress.

Make sure you're always using the right tense.

TV

Here's the page where you get to chat about all the TV programmes you watch — hurrah.

¿Qué hay en la tele? — *What's on TV?*

el programa	*programme*	las noticias	*the news*	los dibujos animados	*cartoons*
la cadena	*channel*	el documental	*documentary*	la telenovela	*soap opera*
el anuncio	*advert*	el concurso	*game show, contest*	el reality show	*reality show*

Question	**Simple Answer**	**Extended Answer**
¿Te gusta ver la tele? *Do you like watching TV?*	Sí, me gusta ver la tele los fines de semana. *Yes, I like watching TV at the weekend.*	Sí, me gusta ver la tele los fines de semana. Mi cadena preferida es BBC1 porque no hay anuncios. *Yes, I like watching TV at the weekend. My favourite channel is BBC1 because there aren't any adverts.*

¿Qué te gusta ver? — *What do you like watching?*

The race for the remote control was always a hard-fought contest...

Grammar — 'la gente' is singular

In English, 'people' is a plural noun. In Spanish, 'la gente' is singular, so you need the 'he/she/it' bit of the verb and the feminine singular form of 'many'.

Mucha gente cree que...   *Many people believe that...*

A mí me gusta ver las telenovelas. Mucha gente dice que son aburridas y ridículas pero me ayudan a relajarme. No me gusta ver las noticias, especialmente cuando hablan sobre política.

I like watching soap operas. Many people say that they're boring and ridiculous but they help me relax. I don't like watching the news, especially when they're talking about politics.

Suelo ver varios tipos de programas. Hoy en día hay tanta diversidad. Sin embargo, quisiera ver más documentales y menos dibujos animados.

I usually watch several types of programmes. These days there is so much diversity. However, I would like to see more documentaries and fewer cartoons.

Mi abuelo pasa todos los días viendo la tele porque no puede salir. A él le encantan los concursos porque puede participar desde el sofá.

My grandad spends every day watching TV because he can't go out. He loves game shows because he can join in from the sofa.

Some people think that — Alguna gente piensa que

I don't understand why people complain — no entiendo por qué la gente se queja

See p.23 for how to use the verb 'soler'.

there's so much rubbish — hay tanta basura

Now there's something for everyone. — Ahora hay algo para todo el mundo.

TV is very important for him. — La televisión es muy importante para él.

Don't let revising TV give you square eyes...

Read Eli's email about TV, then decide whether the statements are true or false.

¡Hola Melissa! ¡Lo pasé fenomenal durante el intercambio contigo! Lo que me sorprendió fue la cantidad de telenovelas en la televisión británica. Sin embargo, no había tantos anuncios como en España. En España preferimos los dramas, sobre todo los que se tratan de figuras históricas. Creo que son muy emocionantes y han tenido mucho éxito recientemente.

e.g. Eli enjoyed the exchange. **True.**

1. The number of soap operas didn't surprise Eli. [1]

2. British TV had more adverts than Spanish TV. [1]

3. Historical dramas are popular in Spain. [1]

4. Eli thinks historical dramas are exciting. [1]

Food

This page is guaranteed to get your taste buds tingling — and it'll come in handy for your exam, too.

Los alimentos — *Foods*

la manzana	*apple*	las legumbres	*vegetables, pulses*	la zanahoria	*carrot*
el melocotón	*peach*	las verduras	*vegetables*	la col	*cabbage*
la fresa	*strawberry*	las judías verdes	*string beans*	la patata	*potato*
la naranja	*orange*	los champiñones	*mushrooms*	la cebolla	*onion*
el plátano	*banana*	los guisantes	*peas*	la lechuga	*lettuce*
la pera	*pear*				
las uvas	*grapes*	el aceite	*oil*	el arroz	*rice*
la piña	*pineapple*	el ajo	*garlic*	una barra de pan	*a loaf of bread*
		el huevo	*egg*	la tostada	*toast*
la carne	*meat*	la pimienta	*ground pepper*		
la carne de vaca	*beef*	la sal	*salt*	el café	*coffee*
la carne de cordero	*lamb*	el azúcar	*sugar*	el té	*tea*
la carne de cerdo	*pork*	la nata	*cream*	el zumo	*juice*
la carne de ternera	*veal*	el queso	*cheese*	la leche	*milk*
el filete	*steak*	la mantequilla	*butter*	el vino	*wine*
el jamón	*ham*			la cerveza	*beer*
el pollo	*chicken*	los calamares	*squid*		
la salchicha	*sausage*	el chorizo	*Spanish sausage*	el caramelo	*boiled sweet*
el pescado	*fish*	el gazpacho	*cold soup*	la mermelada	*jam*
el atún	*tuna*	la tortilla	*omelette*	la galleta	*biscuit*
las gambas	*prawns*	las tapas	*nibbles, bar snacks*	el pastel	*cake, pie*
los mariscos	*seafood*	los churros	*long doughnuts*	el helado	*ice cream*

¿Qué te gusta comer? — *What do you like to eat?*

Grammar — meal times

These are the <u>nouns</u> for Spanish meals:

el desayuno	*breakfast*
el almuerzo	*lunch* ← You can also say 'la comida'.
la merienda	*afternoon snack*
la cena	*dinner*

These nouns can be made into <u>verbs</u>:

desayunar	*to have breakfast*
almorzar	*to have lunch* ← You can say 'comer' too.
merendar	*to have an afternoon snack*
cenar	*to have dinner*

Almuerzo a la una. Suelo comer un bocadillo.

I have lunch at one o'clock. I usually eat a sandwich.

'Almorzar' (*to have lunch*) is a <u>radical-changing verb</u> ('o' to 'ue'). See p.76.

Mis padres trabajan mucho, así que comemos mucha comida basura. Mi plato preferido es pollo al curry.

My parents work a lot, so we eat a lot of junk food. My favourite meal is chicken curry.

I love Chinese / Mediterranean food. — Me encanta la comida china / mediterránea.

Whenever I seafood, I eat it...

TRACK LISTENING 05

Listen to three people's opinions about food. Tick the statements that are true. [3 marks]

e.g. When he was younger, Joaquín ate lots of sweets. ✓

1. Joaquín likes eating junk food.
2. Alejandra doesn't think she eats enough fruit.
3. Raquel thinks it's difficult to find things she can eat in restaurants.

Eating Out

Restaurants often come up in the role-play section of the exam — so get learning your stuff.

¡Vamos al restaurante! — *Let's go to the restaurant!*

pedir	*to order, ask for*	el plato (combinado)	*(set) dish*
traer	*to bring*	el primer plato	*starter*
el camarero	*waiter*	el segundo plato	*main course*
la camarera	*waitress*	el postre	*dessert*
la carta	*the menu*	la bebida	*drink*
el tenedor	*fork*	la cuenta	*bill*
el cuchillo	*knife*	la propina	*tip*
la cuchara	*spoon*	a la plancha	*grilled*
el vaso	*glass*	tener hambre	*to be hungry*
incluido	*included*	tener sed	*to be thirsty*

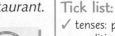

Grammar — ordering politely

Use 'quisiera' to order what you'd like politely. 'Quisiera' comes from the imperfect subjunctive of 'querer' (*to want*). See p.83 and 89.

> **Quisiera** un filete.
> *I'd like a steak.*

You can also say 'me apetece', which means 'I fancy'.

> **Me apetece** un café.
> *I fancy a coffee.*

Question	Simple Answer	Extended Answer
¿Qué le gustaría tomar?	Quiero la sopa, por favor.	Para el primer plato, quisiera la sopa, y para el segundo plato, el atún.
What would you like?	*I want the soup, please.*	*For the starter, I'd like the soup, and for main course, the tuna.*

Me encanta ir a restaurantes pero normalmente no puedo comer mucho. Sin embargo, siempre pido un postre porque me gustan las cosas dulces.

I love going to restaurants but normally I can't eat much. However, I always order a dessert because I like sweet things.

> but sometimes it's hard to choose what you want to eat — pero a veces es difícil elegir lo que quieres comer

Comemos en restaurantes a menudo, especialmente cuando tenemos hambre y no tenemos tiempo para cocinar.

We often eat in restaurants, especially when we're hungry and we don't have time to cook.

> To say you're hungry or thirsty, you need to use the verb 'tener' (*to have*). I'm thirsty — tengo sed

Una vez probé unas gambas a la plancha — estaban muy saladas.

Once I tried some grilled prawns — they were very salty.

> fried — fritas
> spicy — picantes

SPEAKING — Hopefully this page has given you some food for thought...

Here's an example of a role-play — Pedro is eating in a restaurant.

Pedro está hablando con un camarero en un restaurante.   **Grade 8-9**

Camarero: Buenas tardes. **¿En qué puedo servirle?**[1]

Pedro: Quisiera gambas a la plancha con verduras y arroz.

Camarero: De acuerdo.

Pedro: ¿Usted tiene algo para mi amigo? No le gustan los mariscos.

Camarero: Sí, le recomendaría una pizza margarita con ensalada.

Pedro: ¡Muy bien! Y, para el postre, me apetece un helado grande con dos cucharas.

Camarero: Sí, muy bien.

[1]How can I help you?

Tick list:
✓ tenses: present, imperfect subjunctive, conditional
✓ correct use of 'usted'

To improve:
+ justify opinions more

Estás hablando con un camarero.
- lo que quieres comer
- lo que no te gusta comer
- !
- ? comida vegetariana
- lo que comiste durante tu última visita al restaurante

*Prepare the role-play on the right. Address the waiter as 'usted', and try to speak in **Spanish** for about **two** minutes.* [15 marks]

Sport

...t matter if you're not the sportiest person on earth — you still need to learn the vocab on this
pag... so you can recognise the names of sports and say which ones you like or don't like doing.

¿Practicas algún deporte? — *Do you play any sports?*

el fútbol	*football*	el baloncesto	*basketball*	la pesca	*fishing*
el rugby	*rugby*	la equitación	*horse riding*	el atletismo	*athletics*
el tenis	*tennis*	la natación	*swimming*	el alpinismo	*mountain climbing*
el hockey	*hockey*	la vela	*sailing*	el patinaje	*skating*
el bádminton	*badminton*	el piragüismo	*canoeing*	los deportes de riesgo	*adventure sports*

jugar al fútbol / tenis	*to play football / tennis*	correr	*to run*	el polideportivo	*sports centre*
montar a caballo	*to ride a horse*	bailar	*to dance*	la piscina	*swimming pool*
montar en bici	*to ride a bike*	nadar	*to swim*	el estadio	*stadium*
ir en monopatín	*to go by skateboard*	patinar	*to skate*	la pista	*track, court, slope*
ser aficionado/a a...	*to be fond / a fan of...*	pescar	*to fish*	la pista de hielo	*ice rink*

Question

¿Te gusta practicar deporte?
Do you like doing sport?

Simple Answer

Me gusta montar en bici porque es divertido.
I like riding my bike because it's fun.

Extended Answer

Me gusta montar en bici después del colegio porque
es divertido estar con mis amigos al aire libre.
*I like riding my bike after school because it's fun to
be with my friends in the fresh air.*

Grammar — 'jugar' + 'a' + sport

Use 'jugar a' to say what sports you play. In Spanish,
you can't say 'Juego a el fútbol'. So if the sport is
a masculine noun (like 'el fútbol'), the 'a' and the
article 'el' combine to form 'al' (see p.72).

Juego al hockey. *I play hockey.*
Juegas al tenis. *You play tennis.*

'Jugar' is a radical-changing verb — its stem changes
from 'u' to 'ue' in the present tense. See p.76.

Mi deporte preferido es... — *My favourite sport is...*

Me encanta montar a caballo
varias veces por semana. Para
mí, es crucial hacer deporte.

*I love going horse riding a few
times per week. For me, it's
crucial to do sport.*

*I like going to the ice rink —
Me gusta ir a la pista de hielo*

Juego al rugby los lunes. Me
gusta porque puedo divertirme
con mis amigos y hacer deporte
al mismo tiempo.

*I play rugby on Mondays. I like it
because I can have a good time
with my friends and do sport at
the same time.*

*the sports centre where we
practise is near my house —
el polideportivo donde
practicamos está cerca de mi casa*

See how to make the adjective 'deportista' agree on p.14.

No soy exactamente deportista,
pero el deporte es bastante
importante para mí — voy al
colegio en monopatín y los fines
de semana, pesco con mi padre.

*I'm not exactly sporty, but sport
is quite important to me — I go
to school on my skateboard and
at the weekend, I fish with my
father.*

*and sport isn't very important
to me — y el deporte no es
muy importante para mí*

*but in my spare time, I prefer to
cook or read — pero en mi tiempo
libre, prefiero cocinar o leer*

Sport

A double sport session — aren't you lucky? It's really important that you can talk about sports in an interesting way, showing off your Spanish as you go, so — on your marks, get set, go!

El deporte en la tele — *Sport on TV*

el partido	*match*	marcar un gol	*to score a goal*
la carrera	*race*	el campeón	*champion*
ganar	*to win*	el campeonato	*championship*
perder	*to lose*	el torneo	*tournament*
el equipo	*team*	la copa	*trophy, cup*
el jugador	*player*	los Juegos Olímpicos	*the Olympic Games*

Grammar — 'usually' + infinitive

Use the verb '<u>soler</u>' plus the <u>infinitive</u> to say what you <u>usually do</u>. It's a <u>radical-changing verb</u> — its <u>stem</u> changes from '<u>o</u>' to '<u>ue</u>'. See p.76.

<u>Suelo</u> ver el tenis los viernes.
***I usually** watch tennis on Fridays.*

Prefiero jugar al hockey que verlo en la tele. En vez de pasar mucho tiempo viendo la tele, los jóvenes deberían practicar deporte.

I prefer playing hockey to watching it on TV. Instead of spending a lot of time watching TV, young people should do sport.

Suelo ver el fútbol en la tele los fines de semana. Me encantaría visitar un estadio. Me imagino que sería muy emocionante estar allí si tu equipo marca muchos goles y gana el partido.

I usually watch football on TV at the weekend. I would love to visit a stadium. I imagine that it would be very exciting to be there if your team scores a lot of goals and wins the match.

Me encanta ver los Juegos Olímpicos porque es interesante ver los deportes menos populares como el piragüismo. Sueles aprender algo sobre ellos y son emocionantes también.

I love watching the Olympic Games because it's interesting to watch the less popular sports like canoeing. You usually learn something about them and they're exciting too.

I'm a fan of basketball. — Soy aficionado/a al baloncesto.

At primary school, I usually played football during break time. — En la escuela primaria, solía jugar al fútbol en el recreo. ('Solía' is the imperfect tense of 'soler'.)

The verb '<u>imaginarse</u>' means 'to imagine / suppose'.

the championship — el campeonato
the tournament — el torneo

it's exciting when someone from your country wins a medal — es emocionante cuando alguien de tu país gana una medalla

---

WRITING *Be a good sport and try out this practice writing question...*

Julia has written a blog about the sporting opportunities her school provides.

Mi colegio se llama Westwater College. Quisiera compartir unos **datos**[1] con vosotros **para que sepáis**[2] por qué es un colegio excepcional. **En cuanto a**[3] la educación física, se puede elegir entre varios deportes, entre ellos el tenis, el baloncesto y el hockey. **Tenemos mucha suerte**[4] porque nuestro profesor de hockey participó en los Juegos Olímpicos. Además, tenemos una piscina enorme. Después del colegio, se puede practicar deportes de riesgo, **incluso**[5] el piragüismo.

Grade 8-9

[1]information, facts
[2]so that you know
[3]With regard to
[4]We're very lucky
[5]even

To improve:
+ use another tense e.g. future

Escribe tu propio blog sobre el deporte en tu colegio. Menciona:

* *por qué las oportunidades deportivas en tu colegio son excelentes*
* *una actividad deportiva reciente en el colegio*

*Escribe aproximadamente **150** palabras en **español**.*
Responde a los dos aspectos de la pregunta. [32 marks]

Tick list:
✓ tenses: present, preterite, present and imperfect subjunctives
✓ connectives e.g. 'además'
✓ idiomatic phrases e.g. 'tenemos mucha suerte'
✓ complex sentences including opinions

Technology

Technology changes really quickly — make sure you keep up to speed by looking carefully at these pages.

La tecnología en la vida diaria — *Technology in everyday life*

el ordenador	*computer*
el portátil	*laptop*
el móvil	*mobile phone*
el mensaje (de texto)	*(text) message*
mandar / enviar	*to send*
recibir	*to receive*
usar / utilizar	*to use*

Grammar — I could / couldn't ...

To imagine what you 'could do' or 'couldn't do', use the conditional tense of 'poder' (see p.83) followed by the infinitive.

Sin mi móvil, no podría hablar con mis amigos.
Without my mobile phone, I couldn't talk to my friends.

No podría hacer mis deberes sin un portátil.
I couldn't do my homework without a laptop.

Question

¿Para qué usas tu móvil?
What do you use your mobile phone for?

Simple Answer

Uso mi móvil para mandar mensajes.
I use my mobile phone to send messages.

Extended Answer

Tener un móvil es muy importante para mí. Sin mi móvil, no podría ni mandar ni recibir mensajes.
Having a mobile phone is very important for me. Without my mobile phone, I couldn't send or receive messages.

Navegando por la red — *Surfing the Internet*

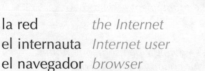

la red	*the Internet*	el usuario	*user*	el videojuego	*video game*
el internauta	*Internet user*	el correo electrónico	*email*	el buscador	*search engine*
el navegador	*browser*	descargar	*to download*	la herramienta	*tool*

Me encanta descargar canciones.	*I love downloading songs.*
Me gustan los videojuegos porque puedes comunicarte con otros usuarios.	*I like video games because you can communicate with other users.*

La red es una herramienta muy útil porque puedes usar un buscador para encontrar información.

The Internet is a very useful tool because you can use a search engine to find information.

crucial for modern life — crucial para la vida moderna

Mis padres usan la red para sus cuentas bancarias porque es más fácil que ir al banco.

My parents use the web for their bank accounts because it's easier than going to the bank.

Many Internet users — Muchos internautas

Gracias a la red, es más cómodo hacer las compras. Hace unos días, compré unos regalos por Internet y ya están aquí.

Thanks to the Internet, it's more convenient to do your shopping. A few days ago, I bought some presents online and they're already here.

However, it's difficult to know if you like the product or not because you buy it without seeing it in reality. — Sin embargo, es difícil saber si te gusta el producto o no porque lo compras sin verlo en realidad.

Technology

Singing technology's praises isn't enough — you also need to be able to talk about its disadvantages.

Lo malo de la tecnología... — *The bad thing about technology...*

Grammar — the ... thing is that...

In Spanish, you can say 'the good thing' or 'the bad thing' by using '<u>lo</u>' followed by '<u>bueno</u>' or '<u>malo</u>'.

Lo bueno / malo es que... *The good / bad thing is that...*

You can do this with <u>any adjective</u>:

Lo mejor / peor es que... *The best / worst thing is that...*

Lo peligroso es que... *The dangerous thing is that...*

To say '<u>the most... thing</u>', just add '<u>más</u>' before the adjective:

Lo más útil es que... *The most useful thing is that...*

acceder	*to access*
el archivo	*file*
borrar	*to erase / delete*
el buzón	*inbox, mailbox*
adjuntar	*to attach*
el correo basura	*spam*
la contraseña	*password*
el servidor de seguridad	*firewall*
el disco duro	*hard disk/drive*

Lo peor de los móviles es que la gente puede grabar videos sin informarte.

The worst thing about mobiles is that people can record videos without telling you.

share your photos with other people you don't know — compartir tus fotos con otra gente a la que no conoces

Es importante tener una contraseña para proteger tu identidad. Si alguien averigua tu contraseña, puede acceder a tus archivos. Por eso no se debe utilizar nunca la red sin un buen servidor de seguridad.

It's important to have a password to protect your identity. If someone finds out your password, they can access your files. Therefore you should never use the Internet without a good firewall.

ruin your hard disk — estropear tu disco duro

Me molesta cuando recibo correo basura porque tengo que borrar todos los mensajes de mi buzón para encontrar los que me importan.

It annoys me when I receive spam because I have to delete all the messages from my inbox to find the ones that matter to me.

sometimes it harms your computer and causes you problems — a veces daña tu ordenador y te causa problemas

Question

Dáme una desventaja de la tecnología.
Give me one disadvantage of technology.

Simple Answer

Una desventaja es que no puedes escapar de la tecnología.
One disadvantage is that you can't escape from technology.

Extended Answer

Una desventaja es que siempre tienes que estar conectado. Lo más irritante es cuando mis amigos se enfadan cuando no contesto a sus mensajes enseguida.
One disadvantage is that you always have to be connected. The most irritating thing is when my friends get angry when I don't reply to their messages straightaway.

WRITING

Technically speaking, this page is really, really useful...

*Translate this text into **Spanish**. [12 marks]*

I couldn't live without technology because it is very useful. I like playing video games online with my brother. We speak to Internet users in other countries. Yesterday, I played with a boy in Chile, but in order to protect my identity, I never use my name. The best thing about mobile phones is that you don't have to be at home to use the Internet. In the future, I think children will have mobile phones when they are 2 or 3 years old.

Social Media

...dia — love it or hate it, it's everywhere. And what's more, it might just come up in your exams.

Las redes sociales — *Social networks*

la red social	*social network*
el sitio web	*website*
la sala de chat	*chat room*
el blog	*blog*
la cuenta	*account*
desactivar	*to deactivate / block*
charlar	*to chat*
colgar	*to post (online)*

Grammar — colgar (*to post*)

'Colgar' (*to post*) is a <u>radical-changing verb</u> (see p.76) that changes in the <u>present</u> tense:

Mis amigos <u>cuelgan</u> fotos en mi muro.
My friends <u>post</u> photos on my wall.

Question

¿Usas las redes sociales?
Do you use social networks?

Simple Answer

Sí, me gusta charlar con mis amigos en las redes sociales.
Yes, I like chatting with my friends on social networks.

Extended Answer

Sí, comparto fotos con mis amigos. Mis padres tienen miedo de las redes sociales porque no las entienden.
Yes, I share photos with my friends. My parents are scared of social networks because they don't understand them.

After much posing, Gertrudis was finally happy with her profile picture...

Uso los medios sociales para... — *I use social media to...*

Me encanta usar las redes sociales para hablar con mis amigos que viven lejos de mí.

I love using social networks to talk to my friends who live far away from me.

→ my cousins who live in Canada — mis primos que viven en Canadá

Diría que los jóvenes pasan demasiado tiempo en las redes sociales.

I would say that young people spend too much time on social networks.

→ should spend more time outside — deberían pasar más tiempo al aire libre

Uso las redes sociales todos los días para charlar con la gente que comparte mis intereses. Me gusta cocinar, así que cuelgo recetas y fotos de la comida en unos sitios web.

I use social networks every day to chat to people who share my interests. I like cooking, so I post recipes and photos of food on some websites.

→ I watch videos to learn more about cooking — veo vídeos para aprender más sobre la cocina

Time to make friends with social media...

Lee lo que dice Belén sobre las redes sociales y decide si las frases son verdaderas (V) o falsas (F).

Uso las redes sociales después del colegio. Es relajante charlar sobre cosas estúpidas. Sin embargo, a veces, mis amigos se pelean si alguien ha colgado una foto sin permiso. No podría vivir sin las redes sociales, pero me molesta cuando salgo con mi novio y pasa todo el tiempo viendo cosas ridículas en su móvil en lugar de charlar conmigo.

e.g. Belén sólo usa las redes sociales los sábados. **F**

1. Belén charla sobre cosas no muy serias. [1]

2. Las redes sociales causan problemas entre sus amigos. [1]

3. Según ella, la vida sería mejor sin las redes sociales. [1]

4. El novio de Belén cree que la red es estúpida. [1]

The Problems with Social Media

Being able to talk about the pros and cons of social media is really important for your GCSE.

Las ventajas y desventajas — *Advantages and disadvantages*

la ventaja	*advantage*	por una parte	*on one hand*
la desventaja	*disadvantage*	por otra parte	*on the other hand*

debido a *due to*
gracias a *thanks to*

Me encanta que siempre hay alguien con quien puedo charlar en las redes sociales.

I love it that there's always someone I can chat to on social networks.

Por una parte, es muy fácil mantenerte en contacto con los amigos, pero por otra parte, creo que es muy importante salir con los amigos y estar juntos en la vida real.

On the one hand, it's very easy to keep in contact with your friends, but on the other hand, I believe it's very important to go out with your friends and be together in real life.

Debido a las redes sociales, sé lo que está pasando en el mundo.

Due to social networks, I know what's happening in the world.

Chat rooms are useful but they can be dangerous. — Las salas de chat son útiles, pero pueden ser peligrosas.

often, the friends you have on social media aren't real friends — muchas veces, los amigos que tienes en las redes sociales no son amigos de verdad

Looking at pug videos? Me?

I waste time looking at useless things — pierdo tiempo mirando cosas inútiles. 'Pierdo' comes from 'perder', which is a radical-changing verb. See p.76.

Question
¿Cuál es tu opinión de las redes sociales?
What's your opinion of social networks?

Simple Answer
Es divertido usar las redes sociales pero pueden ser peligrosas también.
It's fun to use social networks but they can be dangerous too.

Extended Answer
Una ventaja es que no te aburres nunca. Sin embargo, no me gustan las salas de chat porque la gente te puede mentir. Pienso que voy a desactivar mi cuenta.
An advantage is that you never get bored. However, I don't like chat rooms because people can lie to you. I think I'm going to deactivate my account.

 ## *Update your status to 'revising' and try these questions...*

Have a look at Manuel's answer to this question.

¿Crees que los jóvenes deberían pasar menos tiempo en las redes sociales?

A mi modo de ver, las redes sociales tienen más ventajas que desventajas. Mucha gente dice que pasamos demasiado tiempo charlando con los amigos en el mundo virtual, pero yo no estoy de acuerdo. No puedo salir con mis amigos después del colegio, así que es conveniente usar las redes sociales para comunicarme con ellos. Además, las redes sociales te pueden **enseñar**[1] mucho sobre el mundo y lo que pasa en tu **barrio**[2]. Puede ser más barato navegar por Internet para aprender estas cosas que comprar un periódico.

Grade 8-9

[1]teach
[2]neighbourhood

Tick list:
✓ tenses: present
✓ comparatives
✓ connectives e.g. además
✓ opinions

To improve:
+ use more tenses, e.g. future, conditional
+ use intensifiers e.g. muy, bastante

*Contesta a estas preguntas en **español** — intenta hablar durante 5 minutos.*

- ¿Te gusta usar las redes sociales?
- ¿Cuáles son las desventajas de las redes sociales?
- ¿Crees que los jóvenes deberían pasar menos tiempo en las redes sociales? *[30 marks]*

Customs and Festivals

Spanish-speaking countries have lots of different festivals that they celebrate throughout the year.
In this section you'll find out about some of the most famous ones — life could be worse...

¡Celebremos! — *Let's celebrate!*

la fiesta	*festival, party*	¡Feliz cumpleaños!	*Happy Birthday!*
festejar	*to celebrate*	¡Felicitaciones!	*Congratulations!*
el día festivo	*public holiday*	¡Feliz año nuevo!	*Happy New Year!*
el santo	*saint's day*	Nochevieja	*New Year's Eve*
la fecha patria	*national independence day*	el Año Nuevo	*New Year*
		tener suerte	*to be lucky*

> **Grammar** — Let's...
>
> To say '<u>let's</u>...', use the '<u>we</u>' form of the <u>present subjunctive</u> (see p.88).
>
> **<u>Hablemos</u>** de las fiestas.
> ***Let's talk*** about festivals.

'La Tomatina' es una fiesta que tiene lugar en agosto en Buñol, Valencia. Los participantes se lanzan tomates los unos a los otros. Atrae a miles de turistas cada año.

En Nochevieja en España, es tradicional comer 12 uvas para traer buena suerte.

'La Tomatina' is a festival that takes place in August in Buñol, Valencia. Participants throw tomatoes at each other. It attracts thousands of tourists each year.

On New Year's Eve in Spain, it's traditional to eat 12 grapes to bring good luck.

San Fermín — *The running of the bulls*

One festival in Spain that causes some controversy is <u>San Fermín</u>, which takes place in <u>Pamplona</u> each July.

el toro	*bull*		la plaza de toros	*bullring*	polémico	*controversial*
la corrida	*bullfight*		el torero	*bullfighter*	la tradición	*tradition*

Muchas personas corren por las calles estrechas con los toros peligrosos hasta la plaza de toros.

Durante la fiesta, los habitantes y los turistas llevan ropa blanca y pañuelos rojos.

La corrida de toros es una tradición común en España, pero es polémica porque alguna gente piensa que es cruel. Sin embargo, otros creen que es un arte.

Many people run through the narrow streets with the dangerous bulls to the bullring.

During the festival, locals and tourists wear white clothes and red scarves.

Bullfighting is a common tradition in Spain, but it's controversial because some people think that it's cruel. However, others believe it's an art.

 ## Fest-iv-al, a reading question...

Read the text on the right, and then decide whether the sentences below are true (T) or false (F).

The festival started because of an argument between a local man and a tourist.	
The argument was settled calmly.	
The streets are full of people.	
'La Tomatina' takes place in Valencia.	
They grow the tomatoes in Extremadura.	

[5 marks]

La fiesta que se llama 'La Tomatina' comenzó en 1945 a causa de una disputa entre los habitantes. La disputa se convirtió en una pelea con verduras. Hoy en día, mucha gente viaja a Buñol para participar en la fiesta. **Toneladas**[1] de tomates vuelan por el aire y las calles están llenas de gente. La fiesta tiene lugar en Valencia, pero los tomates se cultivan en Extremadura.

[1]Tonnes

Customs and Festivals

Next up it's All Souls' Day and a day that's a bit like April Fools' Day. But, spoiler alert — it's not in April in the Spanish-speaking world. And that's not me just trying to fool you...

El Día de los Muertos — *All Souls' Day*

El <u>Día de los Muertos</u> is a Mexican, Central American and Filipino tradition. According to <u>folklore</u>, heaven's gates open at midnight on <u>1st November</u> and the spirits of the dead <u>reunite</u> with their families for <u>24 hours</u>.

la Catrina	*popular female skeleton icon*	morir	*to die*
la calavera de azúcar	*skull made of sugar*	el muerto	*dead (person)*
el maquillaje	*make-up*	el mariachi	*Mexican musician*

'Muerto' is an irregular past participle — see p.81 for more.

En la tradición mexicana, la muerte no es espantosa.

In Mexican tradition, death isn't frightening.

the lives of the dead are celebrated — se celebran las vidas de los muertos

El Día de los Muertos, las familias limpian y arreglan las tumbas de sus parientes y celebran fiestas.

On All Souls' Day, families clean and tidy the graves of their relatives and throw parties.

friends — amigos

share stories — comparten historias

Alguna gente se disfraza de 'la Catrina'. Honran a los muertos y lo demuestran con calaveras de azúcar, flores y música del mariachi.

Some people dress up as 'la Catrina'. They respect the dead and show it with sugar skulls, flowers and Mexican music.

wear make-up like — lleva maquillaje como

An example of how some people dress to celebrate All Souls' Day.

© iStock.com/hbrizard

El Día de los Inocentes — *28th December*

El Día de los Inocentes is like <u>April Fools' Day</u>, but it takes place in December in the Spanish-speaking world.

la broma	*joke, trick*
los medios de comunicación	*the media*

Es tradicional gastar una broma a alguien, por ejemplo sustituir el azúcar con la sal.

It's traditional to play a joke on someone, for example substitute sugar with salt.

Los medios de comunicación presentan noticias falsas como broma.

The media feature false news stories as a joke.

SPEAKING *My tea tastes salty — what's the date today?*

Laura has answered the following questions.

1. **¿Qué hiciste el año pasado para festejar tu cumpleaños?**
2. **¿Cuál es tu opinión de las fiestas en los países donde se habla español?**
3. **¿Cómo celebrarás la Nochevieja?**

Tick list:
✓ tenses: preterite, present, future
✓ good use of reflexive verbs

1. El año pasado fui a patinar sobre hielo para celebrar mi cumpleaños. Me lo pasé bien pero el único problema fue que me hice daño en el hielo.

Grade 6-7

To improve:
+ more detailed answers
+ more adjectives

2. Me fascinan las fiestas del mundo hispanohablante. Por ejemplo, las tradiciones y las costumbres del Día de los Muertos me interesan mucho.

3. No estoy segura, ¡pero quizás comeré uvas como se hace en España!

Now answer the same questions. Speak for about 3 minutes. [15 marks]

Customs and Festivals

Last year, I asked Father Christmas for a third page of festival-based fun — and he didn't disappoint.

Semana Santa — *Easter week*

The Catholic festival <u>Semana Santa</u> is the biggest religious celebration in Spanish-speaking countries.

la Pascua	*Easter*	la iglesia	*church*
el paso	*statue paraded at Easter*	la costumbre	*custom, way*

La Pascua es un evento sombrío. Hay procesiones con música. Se llevan pasos por las calles y los participantes llevan ropa que esconde sus identidades.

Easter is a sombre event. There are processions with music. Statues are carried around the streets and the participants wear clothes that hide their identities.

Grammar — impersonal verbs

To say that something is done <u>without</u> saying <u>who</u> does it, use '<u>se</u>' and the <u>3rd person</u> part of the verb (p.87).

<u>Se ven</u> **las procesiones**.
The processions <u>are watched</u>.

¡Feliz Navidad! — *Merry Christmas!*

Nochebuena	*Christmas Eve*	el Día de Reyes	*Epiphany, 6th January*	Papá Noel	*Father Christmas*
Navidad	*Christmas*	el villancico	*Christmas carol*	el turrón	*Spanish nougat*

Muchas comunidades participan en la lotería el 22 de diciembre.

Many communities participate in the lottery draw on 22nd December.

← *because they want to win 'El Gordo', the big prize — porque quieren ganar 'El Gordo', el gran premio*

Muchos españoles celebran el Día de Reyes. Los Reyes Magos traen regalos a los niños o, si no se han comportado bien, un trozo de carbón.

Many Spaniards celebrate Epiphany. The Three Kings bring the children presents or, if they haven't behaved well, a piece of coal.

I love to sing Christmas carols — me encanta cantar villancicos

we usually eat turkey — solemos comer pavo

En Navidad, me gusta comer turrón.

At Christmas, I like to eat nougat. ←

Otras fiestas religiosas — *Other religious festivals*

El Eid al-Fitr es una fiesta musulmana que marca el fin del mes de Ramadán.

Eid al-Fitr is a Muslim festival that marks the end of the month of Ramadan.

Muchos judíos celebran Hanukkah. Se encienden velas y se comen alimentos fritos.

Many Jews celebrate Hanukkah. Candles are lit and fried food is eaten.

No coal for you, just this lovely present...

TRACK LISTENING 06

Listen to these people talking about Christmas celebrations and complete the sentences below.

1. **The winning lottery number is...**
   A) ...80673.
   B) ...13773.
   C) ...80636.   *[1]*

2. **Ana's going to...**
   A) ...travel the world using her winnings.
   B) ...buy a new car and an island.
   C) ...buy a luxury flat and go on holiday.   *[1]*

3. **Carla's favourite food at Christmas was...**
   A) ...seafood.
   B) ...turkey.
   C) ...chocolate nougat.   *[1]*

4. **For Christmas, Diego's brother got...**
   A) ...some toys.
   B) ...a bike.
   C) ...a mobile.   *[1]*

Talking About Where You Live

For your Spanish GCSE, you'll need to be able to describe where you live, even if it's not remotely exciting...

En mi barrio... — *In my neighbourhood...*

'Correos' doesn't have an article.

el pueblo	*town*	el mercado	*market*	Correos	*Post Office*
el centro	*centre*	el parque	*park*	la comisaría	*police station*
las afueras	*outskirts*	la mezquita	*mosque*	la peluquería	*hairdresser's*
el edificio	*building*	la biblioteca	*library*	la carnicería	*butcher's*
el ayuntamiento	*town hall*	el museo	*museum*	el estanco	*tobacconist's*
el aparcamiento	*parking*	la fábrica	*factory*	el puerto	*port / harbour*

Question

¿Dónde vives?
Where do you live?

Simple Answer

Vivo en un pueblo en Cumbria.
I live in a town in Cumbria.

Grammar — adding 'ito'

In Spanish, you can add bits onto the ends of nouns and adjectives to change their meanings. Adding 'ito/a/os/as' makes the word smaller or cuter. Find out more on p.67.

Extended Answer

Vivo en un pueblo pequeñito en el campo. Preferiría vivir más cerca de Londres porque hay más que hacer. Aquí no hay ni una tienda de ropa, lo que me fastidia mucho.
I live in a really small town in the countryside. I'd prefer to live closer to London because there's more to do. Here there's not a single clothes shop, which annoys me a lot.

Háblame de tu pueblo — *Talk to me about your town*

En mi barrio, hay mucho que hacer. Por ejemplo, el viernes fui al teatro. Sería casi perfecto si tuviera una bolera.

In my neighbourhood, there's a lot to do. For example, on Friday I went to the theatre. It would be almost perfect if it had a bowling alley.

if it had a pedestrian zone — si tuviera una zona peatonal

'tuviera' is the imperfect subjunctive of 'tener' — see p.89.

Mi ciudad tiene varios edificios impresionantes. También hay una carnicería y una librería.

My city has various impressive buildings. There's also a butcher's and a book shop.

pretty — bonitos
modern — modernos

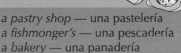

a pastry shop — una pastelería
a fishmonger's — una pescadería
a bakery — una panadería
a stationery shop — una papelería

Creo que es mejor vivir en el campo que en la ciudad. En un mundo ideal, viviría más lejos de las fábricas porque hacen mucho ruido.

I think it's better to live in the countryside than in the city. In an ideal world, I'd live further away from the factories because they make a lot of noise.

from the shopping centre because there are so many people — del centro comercial porque hay tanta gente

WRITING

Go to town on your Spanish revision...

Tu amigo español te ha escrito para describir su pueblo.

¡Hola George! Voy a contarte todo sobre el pueblo que visitarás el mes que viene. **Grade 8-9** En el centro, hay el ayuntamiento y varios edificios oficiales. Además, se puede visitar el museo del pueblo y hay **un montón de**[1] tiendas. Según mi padre, van a construir un polideportivo, lo que sería fenomenal, porque ahora hay poco que hacer por la tarde después del colegio y los jóvenes **acaban**[2] en la calle, molestando a la gente.

[1]loads of
[2]end up

To improve:
+ use a past tense
+ use a comparative

Tick list:
✓ tenses: present, future, conditional
✓ connectives
✓ use of 'se puede'
✓ well-explained opinion

Ahora describe tu barrio, y menciona:
- *cómo es tu pueblo;*
- *cómo cambiarías tu pueblo.*

Escribe aproximadamente **150** *palabras en* **español**.
Responde a los dos aspectos de la pregunta.

[32 marks]

The Home

Home is where the heart is — and where the marks are — so you need to be able to describe it.

Mi casa — *My house*

mudarse (de casa)	*to move house*	el salón	*lounge*
la casa (adosada)	*(semi-detached) house*	la cocina	*kitchen*
el piso	*flat*	el comedor	*dining room*
la planta baja	*ground floor*	la escalera	*stairs*
la segunda planta	*second floor*	el dormitorio	*bedroom*
la habitación	*room*	los muebles	*furniture*
el cuarto de baño	*bathroom*	la estantería	*shelves*
el aseo	*toilet*	la pared	*wall*
la ducha	*shower*	el sótano	*basement*

Grammar — there is / are

To say what there is in your house, use 'hay'. It stays the same regardless of whether the thing you're talking about is singular or plural.

En mi casa, hay un salón.
In my house, there is a lounge.

Hay siete habitaciones.
There are seven rooms.

Vivo en una casa adosada.
En mi dormitorio, hay una cama, un armario, una alfombra en el suelo, una mesita, y un espejo.

I live in a semi-detached house. In my bedroom, there's a bed, a wardrobe, a carpet on the floor, a little table, and a mirror.

In the kitchen, there's a sink, a fridge and an oven. — En la cocina, hay un fregadero, una nevera y un horno.

Vivimos en un piso pequeño.
La habitación que más me gusta es el salón porque es cómodo.

We live in a small flat. The room I like best is the lounge because it's comfortable.

there are armchairs — hay sillones

Me gustaría mudarme a una casa más grande.

I'd like to move to a bigger house.

to have more electrical appliances — tener más electrodomésticos

---

Question

¿Cómo sería tu casa ideal?
What would your ideal house be like?

Simple Answer

Mi casa ideal tendría muchas habitaciones y un jardín grande.
My ideal house would have a lot of rooms and a big garden.

Extended Answer

La casa de mis sueños tendría un jardín enorme y una piscina de lujo. Además, sería mejor si no tuviera que compartir mi habitación.
The house of my dreams would have an enormous garden and a luxury pool. It would also be better if I didn't have to share my room.

READING ## Make yourself at home and try this question for size...

Read this passage from 'Pepita Jiménez' by Juan Valera.

Tiene la casa limpísima y todo en un orden perfecto. Los muebles no son artísticos ni elegantes; pero tampoco **se advierte**[1] en ellos nada pretencioso y de mal gusto. **Para poetizar su estancia**[2], tanto en el patio como en las salas y galerías, hay multitud de flores y plantas. No tiene, en verdad, ninguna planta rara ni ninguna flor exótica; pero sus plantas y sus flores, de lo más común que hay por aquí, están cuidadas con extraordinario **mimo**[3].

[1]is observed
[2]To make her surroundings more poetic
[3]care

Decide whether the following statements are true or false.

e.g. The house is very clean. **True**
1. The furniture is elegant.
2. The flowers are only in the kitchen.
3. There are many flowers and plants.
4. The flowers are mostly exotic.
5. The flowers are well looked after.

[5 marks]

What You Do at Home

Doing chores might be a bit of a drag, but at least talking about them in Spanish is more fun... probably.

Un día típico — *A typical day*

despertarse	*to wake up*
levantarse	*to get up*
ducharse	*to have a shower*
lavarse la cara	*to wash your face*
vestirse	*to get dressed*
acostarse	*to go to bed*
dormirse	*to go to sleep*

Grammar — reflexive verbs

All of these verbs are <u>reflexive</u> — they help you say what you do <u>to yourself</u>. To use them, <u>remove</u> the <u>reflexive pronoun</u>, <u>conjugate the verb</u> as normal, and put the <u>reflexive pronoun</u> back <u>in front of the verb</u> in its <u>correct form</u> (see p.84).

<u>Me despierto</u> a las siete. *<u>I wake up</u> at seven o'clock.*

¿A qué hora <u>te levantas</u>? *What time <u>do you get up</u>?*

<u>Se acuestan</u> temprano. *<u>They go to bed</u> early.*

Some of these verbs are radical-changing too. See p.84.

Question	Simple Answer	Extended Answer
¿Qué haces por la mañana? *What do you do in the morning?*	Me despierto a las siete y luego me ducho. *I wake up at seven o'clock and then I have a shower.*	Me despierto a las siete, pero no me levanto hasta las siete y media. Luego me ducho y me visto rápidamente. *I wake up at seven o'clock, but I don't get up until half past seven. Then I have a shower and get dressed quickly.*

Las tareas domésticas — *Chores*

arreglar	*to tidy*	hacer la cama	*to make the bed*	pasar la aspiradora	*to do the vacuuming*
ayudar	*to help*	pasear al perro	*to walk the dog*	hacer las compras	*to do the shopping*
limpiar	*to clean*	cortar el césped	*to mow the lawn*	sacar la basura	*to take out the rubbish*

Hago mi cama y arreglo mi dormitorio antes de salir de casa. Es importante que todos ayuden en casa.

I make my bed and I tidy my bedroom before leaving the house. It's important that everyone helps at home.

'Es importante que' needs to be followed by the subjunctive form of 'ayudar' — 'ayuden'. See p.88.

Después de la cena, pongo todo en el lavaplatos y paseo al perro.

After dinner, I put everything in the dishwasher and I walk the dog.

I clear the table — quito la mesa
I take out the rubbish — saco la basura

En verano, corto el césped, pero mis padres no me dejan hacer las compras porque siempre compro cosas que no les gustan.

In the summer, I mow the lawn, but my parents don't let me do the shopping because I always buy things they don't like.

lay the table because I break the glasses — poner la mesa porque rompo los vasos

Hopefully your Spanish is now squeaky clean...

Translate this text into **English**. *[9 marks]*

Creo que es importante ayudar en casa, pero no pienso que sea justo si yo hago mucho y mi hermano menor hace muy poco. Me encanta pasear al perro. Mi padre me da dinero si corto el césped, así que lo haré el domingo que viene. La semana pasada tuve que limpiar el cuarto de baño. ¡Qué asco!

Clothes Shopping

Time to indulge in some retail therapy and pick some marks up along the way.

¡Vamos al centro comercial! — *Let's go to the shopping centre!*

las grandes almacenes	*department store*
la tienda de ropa	*clothes shop*
la zapatería	*shoe shop*
la joyería	*jeweller's*

estar de moda	*to be in fashion*
la ropa de marca	*designer clothes*
la camiseta	*T-shirt*
la falda	*skirt*
los vaqueros	*jeans*
el abrigo	*coat*
la rebeca	*cardigan*
los calcetines	*socks*
el bolso	*handbag*
las zapatillas de deporte	*trainers*
la talla	*size*
los probadores	*changing rooms*

Question

¿Qué compraste?
What did you buy?

Simple Answer

Compré una camiseta para mi hermana.
I bought a T-shirt for my sister.

Extended Answer

Tuve que comprar un regalo para mi hermana, así que primero, fui a la zapatería. Ya que no había zapatillas de deporte, fui a otra tienda para comprarle una camiseta.
I had to buy a present for my sister, so I went to the shoe shop first. As there weren't any trainers, I went to another shop to buy her a T-shirt.

Me gustaría... — *I would like...*

Me gustaría esta camisa.	*I would like this shirt.*
Creo que me quedaría bien.	*I think it would suit me.*
Me encanta aquella bufanda.	*I love that scarf over there.*
¿Me la puedo probar?	*Can I try it on?*
Odio esa falda. Es la falda más fea del mundo.	*I hate that skirt. It's the ugliest skirt in the world.*

Grammar — it suits me

To say that something <u>suits you</u>, use the verb '<u>quedar</u>', followed by '<u>bien</u>'. To say something <u>doesn't suit you</u>, use '<u>quedar</u>' followed by '<u>mal</u>'. '<u>Quedar</u>' works like '<u>gustar</u>', so you need to add an <u>indirect object pronoun</u> too (see p.69).

Esta blusa <u>me queda bien</u>.
This blouse <u>suits me</u>.

Estas botas <u>me quedan mal</u>.
These boots <u>don't suit me</u>.

¿Me puede ayudar? — *Can you help me?*

You might have to pretend you're in a shop in the role-play. Make sure you know how to ask a shop assistant for different items.

Me encanta esta rebeca pero me queda grande. ¿Hay otra talla?	*I love this cardigan, but it's too big for me. Is there another size?*
Estoy buscando un bolso de cuero que no sea muy caro.	*I'm looking for a leather bag which is not too expensive.*
Quisiera un collar pero no quiero gastar demasiado.	*I'd like a necklace, but I don't want to spend too much.*

Use '<u>quedar</u>' with '<u>grande</u>' or '<u>pequeño</u>' to say that something is <u>too big</u> or <u>small</u> for you.

When you're <u>imagining something</u> that may or may not exist, you need the <u>present subjunctive</u>. '<u>Sea</u>' is the present subjunctive form of '<u>ser</u>'. See p.88.

some earrings — unos pendientes
a tie — una corbata
a dress — un vestido

Clothes Shopping

Choosing what you want is the nice part — then comes the part where you have to pay...

La caja — *The till*

el/la vendedor/a	*sales assistant*	las rebajas	*the sales*	devolver	*to return*
el/la dependiente/a	*sales assistant*	el recibo	*receipt*	reembolsar	*to refund*
a mitad de precio	*half price*	cambiar	*to change*	en efectivo	*cash*
el descuento	*discount*	pagar	*to pay*	la tarjeta de crédito	*credit card*

Question

¡Buenos días! ¿En qué puedo servirle?
Good morning! How can I help you?

Simple Answer

Quiero devolver esta blusa, por favor.
I want to return this blouse, please.

Extended Answer

Quiero devolver esta blusa. Quisiera que me la cambie, por favor.
I want to return this blouse. I'd like you to change it for me, please.

Grammar — I would like...

To say what you'd like, you can use 'quisiera' as well as 'me gustaría'. 'Quisiera' is the imperfect subjunctive form of the verb 'querer'. See p.89.

Quisiera un descuento, por favor.
***I'd like** a discount, please.*

If you're telling someone what you'd like them to do, you need the present subjunctive form of the verb. See p.88.

Quisiera que me reembolse, por favor.
***I'd like** you (form., sing.) to give me a refund, **please**.*

Quiero quejarme porque la falda tiene un agujero. Quisiera un reembolso, por favor.

I want to complain because the skirt has a hole. I'd like a refund, please.

has a stain — tiene una mancha
is ripped — está rasgada
is broken — está rota

Hoy hay muchas rebajas. Compré este chándal a mitad de precio.

There are a lot of sales today. I bought this tracksuit half price.

I had to queue for ages. — Tuve que hacer cola durante mucho tiempo. 'Tener' is irregular in the preterite tense. See p.78.

The queue for the fancy hats stretched right down the road...

SPEAKING *All shopped out? Time for some more revision, then...*

Have a look at this conversation between Paula and a shop assistant.

Vendedor: Buenas tardes, señorita. ¿En qué puedo servirle? *(Grade 6-7)*

Paula: ¿Dónde están los abrigos, por favor?

Vendedor: Están ahí al fondo, al lado de los probadores.

Paula: ¿Se puede pagar con tarjeta de crédito?

Vendedor: Lo siento. Hoy no se puede porque **la máquina**[1] está rota.

Paula: No pasa nada. ¿Me puede ofrecer **un reembolso**[2] si no me queda bien?

Vendedor: Sí, si tiene el recibo.

Paula: Gracias por su ayuda.

[1] the machine
[2] a refund

Tick list:
✓ tenses: present
✓ correct use of 'usted'
✓ use of 'se puede'

To improve:
+ use another tense e.g., future, conditional
+ some longer, more developed answers

Now prepare your own role-play using the bullet points below. You should address the shop assistant as 'usted' and aim to talk for about **2 minutes**. [15 marks]

• *lo que compraste — cuando*
• *el problema con lo que compraste*
• *? reembolso / cambio*
• *!*
• *tu opinión de la tienda*

More Shopping

You probably thought you'd seen the end of shopping — but there's still one more page to go.

En la tienda de comestibles — *In the grocery shop*

la cantidad	*quantity*	una ración	*portion*	
una caja	*box*	una bolsa	*a bag*	
un cartón	*carton*	lleno/a	*full*	
una lata	*tin*	vacío/a	*empty*	
un pedazo	*piece*	pesar	*to weigh*	
un trozo	*slice, piece*	un kilo	*a kilogram*	
un bote	*jar*	un gramo	*a gram*	

Grammar — agreement with weights

When you're talking in <u>hundreds</u> in Spanish, the <u>number</u> has to <u>agree</u> with the <u>weight</u>.

Doscien<u>tos</u> gramo<u>s</u> de uvas, por favor.
Two hundred grams of grapes, please.

In Spanish, when you say '<u>half a kilo</u>', you <u>don't need</u> the '<u>a</u>' like in English.

Medio kilo de fresas, por favor.
Half <u>a</u> kilo of strawberries, please.

Quisiera un trozo de tarta, por favor. ¿Cuánto cuesta?
I would like a slice of cake, please. How much does it cost?

Deme dos kilos de naranjas, por favor.
Give me two kilos of oranges, please.

¿Puede usted pesar estas peras, por favor?
Could you weigh these pears, please?

Necesitamos unos tomates.
We need some tomatoes.

a portion of Manchego cheese — una ración de queso manchego

Although this sounds a bit rude, it's <u>normal</u> to use the <u>imperative</u> 'give me' in Spanish when you're at a market. See p.90 for more imperatives.

We need — Nos hacen falta
Use '<u>hace</u>' instead of '<u>hacen</u>' to say you need a <u>singular</u> item.

Hacer las compras en la red — *Shopping online*

Question

¿Te gusta hacer las compras en la red?
Do you like shopping online?

Simple Answer

Sí, me gusta hacer las compras en la red porque es fácil.
Yes, I like shopping online because it's easy.

Grammar — before / after doing something

To say '<u>before doing something</u>', use '<u>antes de</u>' and the <u>infinitive</u>. To say '<u>after doing something</u>', use '<u>después de</u>' followed by the <u>infinitive</u>.

<u>Después de hacer</u> las compras, tomo un café.
<u>After doing</u> the shopping, I have a coffee.

Extended Answer

Sí, me gusta hacer las compras en la red porque resulta más barato. Además, no tienes que salir de casa porque hay un servicio de reparto a domicilio.
Yes, I like shopping online because it turns out cheaper. Besides, you don't have to leave the house because there's a home delivery service.

Prefiero ir de compras en un centro comercial porque para mí, es mejor ver las cosas antes de comprarlas.
I prefer to go shopping in a shopping centre because, for me, it's better to see things before buying them.

TRACK LISTENING 07

Don't shop 'til you drop — have a rest and do some practice...

Montse is in a grocery shop. Listen to the dialogue and fill in the blanks.

e.g. Montse is making the tortilla for ___a birthday party___ .

1. She needs .... of onions.   [1]

2. She doesn't need any ....   [1]

3. The shopkeeper doesn't have any olive oil because .... [1]

4. The total price is ....   [1]

Giving and Asking for Directions

If you're feeling a bit lost, this is the page for you — you'll be on the straight and narrow in no time.

¿Dónde está? — *Where is it?*

cruzar	*to cross*
tomar	*to take (a road)*
seguir	*to continue*
a la izquierda	*on the left*
a la derecha	*on the right*
al lado de	*next to*
detrás de	*behind*
delante de	*in front of*
entre	*between*
enfrente de	*opposite*
en la esquina	*on the corner*
al final de	*at the end of*

For more prepositions, see p.72.

Question

¿Dónde está la peluquería?
Where's the hairdresser's?

Simple Answer

La peluquería está al final de la calle.
The hairdresser's is at the end of the street.

Extended Answer

La peluquería está justo al lado de la piscina, enfrente del cine. Es muy fácil encontrarla.
The hairdresser's is right next to the swimming pool, opposite the cinema. It's very easy to find it.

Grammar — 'estar' for locations

In Spanish, there are two verbs for 'to be' — 'ser' and 'estar'. To describe where things are, you need to use 'estar' — see p.77. You can also use 'estar situado' to say where something is situated.

Wilbur was feeling really very lost...

La estación está enfrente de Correos, en el norte de la ciudad.

The station is opposite the post office, in the north of the city.

See p.11 for the other compass points.

El banco está situado detrás de la iglesia.

The bank is situated behind the church.

is on the right of — está a la derecha de

Los servicios están en la esquina.

The toilets are on the corner.

on the left — a la izquierda

¿Cómo se llega a...? — *How do you get to...?*

Siga todo recto y el museo está entre la catedral y la biblioteca.

Continue straight on and the museum is between the cathedral and the library.

behind — detrás de

El parque está detrás del colegio. Tome esa calle y verá un semáforo. Luego gire a la izquierda.

The park is behind the school. Take that road and you'll see some traffic lights. Then turn left.

the police station — la comisaría

Grammar — giving instructions

To give instructions, use the imperative. See how to form it on p.90. You probably won't know the person who's asked for directions, so you should use the 'usted' form.

Siga todo recto y **cruce** la calle.
Continue straight on and cross the street.

Tome la segunda calle a la derecha.
Take the second street on the right.

Stay on the right track with your Spanish revision...

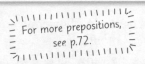

Escucha a Iker describir su barrio y escribe verdadero (V) o falso (F) para cada frase.

e.g. Es un barrio muy viejo. **V**

1. El teatro está al lado del supermercado. [1]
2. Hay tres supermercados. [1]
3. Hay un supermercado enfrente de la comisaría. [1]
4. Para llegar a la iglesia, hay que seguir la calle San Felipe y tomar una calle a la izquierda. [1]

Weather

Come rain or shine, moaning about the weather is a favourite British pastime — enjoy.

Hace buen / mal tiempo — *It's good / bad weather*

Está...	*It's...*	caluroso	*hot*
despejado	*clear*	fresco	*fresh*
nublado	*cloudy*	húmedo	*humid*
lloviendo	*raining*	tormentoso	*stormy*
nevando	*snowing*	seco	*dry*

Hace...	*It's...*
sol	*sunny*
viento	*windy*
calor	*hot*
frío	*cold*

Hay...	*There is / there are...*
niebla	*fog*
hielo	*ice*
tormenta	*a storm*
chubascos	*showers*

el clima   *climate*   el pronóstico   *weather forecast*   el cielo   *sky*

Question

¿Qué tiempo hace?
What's the weather like?

Simple Answer

Hace buen tiempo hoy.
It's good weather today.

The British summer was going swimmingly...

Extended Answer

Hoy hace mucho sol en el sur, pero mañana cambiará: habrá truenos y relámpagos.
Today it's really sunny in the south, but tomorrow it will change: there will be thunder and lightning.

Grammar — weather verbs

To describe the weather in English, you often use 'to be', e.g. 'it's rainy'. You can do this in Spanish with some types of weather:

Está despejado / nublado / nevando / lloviendo.
It's clear / cloudy / snowing / raining.

But sometimes, you have to use the verb 'hacer' instead:

Hace sol / viento / frío.   *It's sunny / windy / cold.*

And sometimes, you need the verb 'haber':

Hay niebla / hielo.   *There's fog / ice.*

It sounds complicated, but just learn which types of weather go with which verb. Remember you can put the verbs into different tenses too.

¿Qué tiempo habrá? — *What will the weather be like?*

Estará tormentoso por todas partes.
It will be stormy everywhere.

dry — seco

Nevará en Inglaterra este invierno.
It will snow in England this winter.

It will rain — Lloverá

See p.3 for the seasons.

Hará mucho calor en el sur de Europa este verano. Sería mejor si no hiciera tanto calor porque prefiero las temperaturas más bajas.
It will be very hot in the south of Europe this summer. It would be better if it weren't so hot because I prefer lower temperatures.

It would be perfect if it were just as hot all the time. — Sería perfecto si hiciera tanto calor todo el tiempo.

Don't let revision rain on your parade...

Read this weather forecast, and then answer the questions in **English**.

Hoy en el norte de España, habrá niebla, mientras que en el sur, estará despejado. En el oeste, cerca de Portugal, hará frío, con la posibilidad de lluvia. Para el fin de semana, hará buen tiempo por toda España, pero para la semana que viene, podemos esperar que las temperaturas bajen, con un riesgo de tormentas.

e.g. What will the weather be like in the north of Spain today? **It will be foggy.**

1. Which part of Spain will have clear weather?   [1]
2. Where will it be cold?   [1]
3. What will it be like at the weekend?   [1]
4. What'll happen to the temperatures next week?   [1]
5. What else might happen next week?   [1]

Healthy Living

Time for a whole page about eating well, keeping fit and staying healthy. Pass the biscuits, then.

¿Te mantienes en forma? — *Do you keep fit?*

mantenerse en forma	*to keep fit / in shape*	entrenar(se)	*to train*	activo/a	*active*
el ejercicio (físico)	*(physical) exercise*	equilibrado/a	*balanced*	la salud	*health*
el entrenamiento	*training*	estar en forma	*to be fit*	saludable	*healthy*

Question

¿Es importante mantenerse en forma?
Is it important to keep fit?

Simple Answer

Sí, creo que es importante entrenarse y comer bien.
Yes, I think it's important to train and to eat well.

Extended Answer

Diría que es importante entrenarse, pero no tengo tiempo para hacerlo todos los días. Voy al gimnasio dos veces a la semana para mantenerme en forma. Para mí, es importante elegir comida saludable también.
I would say that it's important to train, but I don't have time to do it every day. I go to the gym twice a week to keep myself in shape. For me, it's important to choose healthy food too.

Grammar — reflexive verbs

'Mantenerse' and 'entrenarse' are reflexive verbs. Check p.84 for a reminder of how to form them.

Una vida sana — *A healthy life*

Spanish	English	Extra
Intento comer una dieta equilibrada todos los días.	*I try to eat a balanced diet every day.*	to avoid junk food — evitar la comida basura
Para mantenerme en forma, juego al tenis dos veces a la semana.	*To keep fit, I play tennis twice a week.*	I do exercise almost every day — hago ejercicio casi todos los días
Vale la pena comer menos comida rápida y más verduras.	*It's worth eating less fast food and more vegetables.*	drinking two litres of water every day — beber dos litros de agua todos los días
Para mí, es importante dormir al menos ocho horas.	*For me, it's important to sleep for at least eight hours.*	to relax a bit after school — relajarme un poco después del colegio

Time to give your Spanish a workout...

Selina has written an article about healthy living.

La salud es muy importante para mí. Voy al colegio a pie todos los días, y hago deporte tres veces a la semana. Normalmente como bien — tengo una dieta equilibrada. Recientemente he aprendido a cocinar y me encanta la comida saludable. Además es **un buen consejo**[1] beber agua en vez de **bebidas gaseosas**[2] porque contienen mucho azúcar, lo que puede llevar a problemas con los dientes. Para evitar **el estrés**[3], se debe hacer algo que te relaje todos los días. Se puede hacer ejercicio físico o escuchar música o **sencillamente**[4] hablar con tu familia. Por último, es una buena idea acostarte temprano.

Grade 8-9

[1] a good piece of advice
[2] fizzy drinks
[3] stress
[4] simply

Tick list:
✓ tenses: present, perfect, subjunctive
✓ use of impersonal verbs
✓ good topical vocab and time phrases

To improve:
+ give reasons for opinions

*Escribe aproximadamente **90** palabras en **español** para una revista. Menciona:*

- *lo que haces para mantenerte en forma;*
- *si tienes una dieta equilibrada;*
- *si tienes una vida más o menos sana que hace cinco años;*
- *dos cosas que podrías hacer para llevar una vida más sana*   [16 marks]

Unhealthy Living

You'll also need to be able to talk about drinking and smoking in your exams — what joy...

Una vida malsana — *An unhealthy life*

el cigarrillo	*cigarette*	el fumador (pasivo)	*(passive) smoker*
fumar	*to smoke*	el tabaquismo	*addiction to tobacco*
el humo	*smoke*	el síndrome de abstinencia	*withdrawal symptoms*
oler	*to smell*	la droga blanda / dura	*soft / hard drug*
los pulmones	*lungs*	el sobrepeso	*obesity*
respirar	*to breathe*	borracho/a	*drunk*
hacer daño	*to harm*	emborracharse	*to get drunk*
cansarse	*to get tired*	el botellón	*drinking party in the street*

Question

¿Qué piensas de
los cigarrillos?
*What do you think
of cigarettes?*

Simple Answer

Los cigarrillos son peligrosos
porque es difícil dejar de fumar.
*Cigarettes are dangerous because
it's difficult to stop smoking.*

Grammar — to stop ...ing

To say 'to stop ...ing', use 'dejar de'
followed by the infinitive.

Quiero dejar de fumar.
I want to stop smoking.

Extended Answer

Estoy convencido/a de que los cigarrillos perjudican la salud. Incluso cuando una persona ha dejado de
fumar, los cigarrillos causan una variedad de problemas debido al síndrome de abstinencia.
*I am convinced that cigarettes damage your health. Even when a person has stopped smoking, cigarettes
cause a variety of problems due to withdrawal symptoms.*

No quiero probar las drogas
porque son peligrosas.

*I don't want to try drugs
because they are dangerous.*

to smoke because it smells really horrible
— fumar porque huele fatal
'Oler' (to smell) is an irregular verb.

Una vez, me emborraché, pero
no me gustó.

*Once, I got drunk,
but I didn't like it.*

I went to a drinking party in the street
— fui a un botellón

No se puede fumar en espacios
públicos.

*You can't smoke in public
spaces.*

buy cigarettes if you're under 18 — comprar
cigarrillos si tienes menos de 18 años

 SPEAKING

Last night, I had four and a half pints (of tea)...

Have a look at Karima's answer to this question.

¿Piensas que el alcohol es peligroso?

Desde mi punto de vista, no hay ningún problema si
alguien quiere beber una cerveza o un poco de vino. **Grade 8-9**
A mis padres les gusta probar vinos de varios países y no
se emborrachan. Sin embargo, creo que hay problemas con
el alcohol cuando los jóvenes se emborrachan sin pensar
en las consecuencias. Es peligroso porque no saben ni
dónde están ni cuánto han bebido. Hace unos meses, mi
amigo bebió demasiado y tuvo que ir al hospital. Es muy
irresponsable beber tanto alcohol.

Tick list:
✓ tenses: present, preterite
✓ good use of quantifiers
✓ lots of opinions

To improve:
+ include another tense
  e.g. future
+ use more topical vocab

*Now answer the following questions.
Try to speak for about **2** minutes. [10 marks]*

- *¿Qué piensas de las drogas?*
- *¿Piensas que el alcohol es más peligroso
  que las drogas? ¿Por qué?*
- *¿Qué le dirías a un joven que toma drogas?*

Illnesses

Talking about feeling ill might put you off your lunch, but it'll be well worth it if it comes up in your exam.

Las enfermedades — *Illnesses*

encontrarse / sentirse mal	*to feel ill*	doler	*to hurt*	el cerebro	*brain*
encontrarse / estar enfermo/a	*to be ill*	el dolor	*pain*	el ataque cardíaco	*heart attack*
mejorarse	*to get better*	el cuerpo	*body*	el estrés	*stress*
los primeros auxilios	*first aid*	el corazón	*heart*	el sida	*AIDS*
tener dolor (de)...	*to have a pain (in)...*	el hígado	*liver*	seropositivo/a	*HIV-positive*

Question

¿Cómo te sientes?
How do you feel?

Simple Answer

Me duele la garganta.
My throat hurts.

Extended Answer

Me duelen el pie y el brazo, y tengo dolor de espalda.
My foot and arm hurt, and I have backache.

Poor Eric was feeling even greener than normal.

Grammar — 'doler' — to hurt

'Doler' works in a similar way to 'gustar' — to say what's hurting you, you need to use an indirect object pronoun (see p.69) before the verb.
You also need to add an 'n' in the plural.

Me duele la pierna.	*My leg hurts.*	← Literally, 'the leg hurts me'.
Me duelen los pies.	*My feet hurt.*	
Le duelen el brazo y la mano.	*His / her arm and hand hurt.*	

You also need to remember that 'doler' is a radical-changing verb. See p.76.

Necesito ir al médico — *I need to go to the doctor*

Hace un mes, me encontré enfermo y tuve que ir al médico.	*A month ago, I felt ill and I had to go to the doctor.* ←	the doctor gave me a prescription — el médico me dio una receta
De niño, tenía muchos problemas respiratorios.	*As a child, I had a lot of respiratory problems.*	problems with my liver — problemas con el hígado
Creo que todos deberían hacer un curso de primeros auxilios.	*I think everyone should do a first aid course.* ←	learn about what you should do if someone has a heart attack — aprender lo que se debe hacer si alguien tiene un ataque cardíaco

El sida es un problema muy grave en algunos países.	*AIDS is a very serious problem in some countries.*	The lack of doctors — La falta de médicos
Muchos jóvenes se preocupan por su peso y su apariencia.	*Many young people worry about their weight and their appearance.* ←	their exams, which causes a lot of stress — sus exámenes, lo que causa mucho estrés

A practice translation — just what the doctor ordered...

READING

Translate this text into **English**. *[9 marks]*

Me siento muy mal. La semana pasada, fui al campo, pero desafortunadamente estaba lloviendo y no había traído mi paraguas. Me duele muchísimo la garganta y apenas puedo hablar. He tenido que beber muchos líquidos durante unos días y no tengo ganas de comer. Tendré que ir al médico si no me mejoro pronto. Lo peor es que si todavía estoy enfermo el sábado, no podré ir a la fiesta de mi amigo.

Environmental Problems

Time to think green and start talking about the things that affect the environment.

El medio ambiente — *The environment*

el cambio climático	*climate change*	el combustible	*fuel*	agotar	*to use up*
el calentamiento global	*global warming*	la lluvia ácida	*acid rain*	la escasez	*shortage*
el efecto invernadero	*greenhouse effect*	nocivo	*harmful*	la inundación	*flood*
la capa de ozono	*ozone layer*	la marea negra	*oil spill*	la sequía	*drought*
los productos químicos	*chemicals*	el vertedero	*rubbish tip*	echar la culpa	*to blame*
los gases de escape	*exhaust fumes*	dañar	*to damage*	preocuparse	*to worry*

Question	**Simple Answer**	**Extended Answer**
¿El medio ambiente es importante para ti? *Is the environment important to you?*	Sí, creo que es muy importante proteger el medio ambiente. *Yes, I think it's very important to protect the environment.*	Es importantísimo proteger el medio ambiente. Si no actuamos ahora, las selvas y los bosques desaparecerán. *It's really important to protect the environment. If we don't act now, the jungles and forests will disappear.*

El cambio climático — *Climate change*

El cambio climático es un problema que me preocupa bastante. El uso de ciertos combustibles contamina el aire y causa el calentamiento global.

Climate change is a problem that worries me quite a lot. The use of certain fuels pollutes the air and causes global warming.

Exhaust fumes can be harmful and they damage the ozone layer. — Los gases de escape pueden ser nocivos y dañan la capa de ozono.

Debido al efecto invernadero, las temperaturas suben, lo que amenaza la supervivencia de unos animales, por ejemplo los pingüinos.

Due to the greenhouse effect, temperatures rise, which threatens the survival of some animals, for example penguins.

causes a shortage of water in some regions of the world — causa una escasez de agua en algunas regiones del mundo

El desperdicio de agua — *Water wastage*

El agua es necesaria para todo el mundo. Sin agua, los cultivos no pueden sobrevivir.

Water is necessary for everyone. Without water, crops can't survive.

It's an important resource that we shouldn't use up. — Es un recurso importante que no deberíamos agotar.

Debemos usar menos agua en nuestra vida diaria.

We should use less water in our daily lives.

use — utilizar
waste — malgastar

La deforestación — *Deforestation*

Los bosques son importantes porque reducen la cantidad de dióxido de carbono en la atmósfera.

Forests are important because they reduce the amount of carbon dioxide in the atmosphere.

Hoy en día cortamos muchos árboles para producir combustibles. Esto contribuye a la destrucción de los bosques, y al cambio climático.

Nowadays we cut down lots of trees to produce fuel. This contributes to the destruction of forests, and to climate change.

Environmental Problems

Raise your nature-loving credentials and impress the examiners by spicing up your opinions.

La contaminación — *Pollution*

Las mareas negras ensucian el mar y las playas. Luego, los peces y los pájaros sufren mucho y muchas veces mueren.

Oil spills make the sea and the beaches dirty. Then, the fish and birds suffer a lot and often they die.

Oil is harmful for the creatures that live in the sea. — El petróleo es nocivo para las criaturas que viven en el mar.

Aquí, tenemos un problema con la cantidad de basura. Es muy fácil olvidarse de la basura cuando está en un vertedero y no en la calle, pero sí existe.

Here, we have a problem with the amount of rubbish. It's very easy to forget about rubbish when it's in a tip and not in the street, but it does exist.

I don't understand it, because it's very easy to recycle cardboard and plastic packaging. — No lo entiendo, porque es muy fácil reciclar cartón y envases de plástico.

Algunos problemas graves — *Some serious problems*

Grammar — using the subjunctive

Use the subjunctive to give your opinion and say what you want to happen. Check how to form it on p.88-89.

You need it after 'no pienso que...' (*I don't think that...*).

No pienso que sea justo echar toda la culpa a las fábricas.
I don't think that it's fair to put all the blame on factories.

It can also be used to express an emotion about something.

Es terrible que haya tanta basura en la calle.
It's terrible that there is so much rubbish in the street.

And when you're saying what you want someone else to do, use 'quiero que' followed by the subjunctive.

Quiero que el gobierno haga más por la naturaleza.
I want the government to do more for nature.

Grammar — the future

To talk about what things might be like in the future, you can use the immediate future tense (ir + a + infinitive) or the proper future tense (iré — *I will go*, tendré — *I will have*, etc.) See p.82.

Es esencial que protejamos la naturaleza porque sin ella, no podremos vivir.

It's essential that we protect nature because we won't be able to live without it.

we combat the effects of climate change, because if not, we're going to suffer — combatamos los efectos del cambio climático porque si no, vamos a sufrir

Quiero que todos hagan más para reducir la cantidad de basura que producimos. Si no, los vertederos estarán llenos pronto.

I want everyone to do more to reduce the amount of rubbish that we produce. If not, the rubbish tips will be full soon.

think more about the environment and not waste so many things — piensen más en el medio ambiente y no gasten tantas cosas

Es terrible que no pensemos más en el futuro de la Tierra.

It's terrible that we don't think more about the Earth's future.

future generations — las generaciones del futuro

 Learn Spanish and the world's your (polluted) oyster... nice.

Translate this text into **Spanish**. [12 marks]

Climate change worries me a lot. Factories and cars contribute to the greenhouse effect. For me, the worst thing is that people in some poor countries suffer due to floods and droughts. It isn't fair. I think we should work together to reduce the effects of climate change, but it will be very difficult.

Problems in Society

Time for another cheerful topic to make your day happy and joyful — it's social problems.

Los problemas sociales — *Social problems*

el gobierno	*government*	la desigualdad	*inequality*
la libertad	*freedom*	el prejuicio	*prejudice*
el peligro	*danger*	la guerra	*war*
la pobreza	*poverty*	los "sin techo"	*homeless people*
la violencia	*violence*	el desempleo	*unemployment*
la igualdad	*equality*	estar en paro	*to be unemployed*

Although Dexter was grateful for his job, a stint as Santa wasn't quite what he'd had in mind...

Los efectos de la guerra — *The effects of war*

Grammar — 'me parece'

Use '<u>me parece</u>' to say how something '<u>seems</u>' to you. You can use it to <u>vary</u> the way you give <u>opinions</u>.

<u>Me parece</u> inquietante que...
<u>It seems</u> worrying <u>to me</u> that...

<u>Me parece</u> interesante que...
<u>It seems</u> interesting <u>to me</u> that...

Debido a la guerra, muchas personas tienen que emigrar a otro país y empezar la vida de nuevo.

Due to war, many people have to emigrate to another country and start their lives all over again.

No me parece justo que la libertad que tienes dependa tanto del país en que naciste.

It seems unfair to me that the freedom you have depends so much on the country in which you were born.

La igualdad social — *Social equality*

Sería agradable creer que todos somos iguales en nuestro país, pero no es así.

It would be nice to believe that we're all equal in our country, but that's not the case.

A veces, la desigualdad provoca violencia entre los ricos y los pobres.

Sometimes, inequality causes violence between the rich and the poor.

Me encantaría vivir en un mundo más justo.

I would love to live in a fairer world.

inequality doesn't exist — la desigualdad no existe

discrimination against immigrants — discriminación contra los inmigrantes

Here we are lucky because our country is quite fair. — Aquí tenemos suerte porque nuestro país es bastante justo.

La violencia juvenil — *Youth violence*

Question	Simple Answer	Extended Answer
¿Crees que la violencia es un problema grave hoy en día? *Do you think that violence is a serious problem nowadays?*	Sí, en mi barrio, hay un grupo de jóvenes violentos que nos dan miedo. *Yes, in my neighbourhood, there's a group of violent youths who scare us.*	Sí, hay grupos de gamberros que salen por la noche. Son muy violentos e intimidan a la gente mayor, lo que me enfada mucho. *Yes, there are groups of troublemakers who go out at night. They are very violent and they intimidate the older people, which makes me really angry.*

Problems in Society

And the social problems don't end there — you still have poverty and unemployment to get through.

La pobreza — *Poverty*

Question

¿Crees que hay mucha pobreza en este país?
Do you believe there is a lot of poverty in this country?

Simple Answer

Creo que hay más pobreza que hace diez años. El gobierno debería apoyar a los "sin techo".
I think there's more poverty than ten years ago. The government should support homeless people.

Extended Answer

Creo que hay demasiada pobreza en nuestra sociedad. Vivo en un país rico, pero todavía hay mucha gente sin comida y sin hogar. Deberíamos ayudar a los más necesitados porque es fácil acabar en la pobreza si pierdes tu trabajo. La pobreza puede afectar a cualquier persona.
I think there's too much poverty in our society. I live in a rich country, but there are still lots of people without food and without a home. We should help the most needy people because it's easy to end up in poverty if you lose your job. Poverty can affect anyone.

Grammar — 'deber'

To say what someone should do, use '<u>deber</u>' followed by the <u>infinitive</u>.

<u>Deberíamos luchar</u> **contra la pobreza.**
<u>*We should fight*</u> *against poverty.*

El desempleo — *Unemployment*

This could be the examiner's <u>favourite topic</u> in the <u>speaking</u> exam, so learn how to talk about it.

Hay mucha gente en paro en mi ciudad.

There are lots of unemployed people in my city.

Nobody has a problem finding work — Nadie tiene problemas para encontrar trabajo

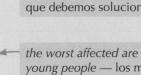

Casi todos los estudiantes por aquí se preocupan por el desempleo. Si pudiera cambiar algo, crearía más trabajos.

Nearly all the students around here worry about unemployment.
If I could change anything, I'd create more jobs.

It is a big problem that we must solve. — Es un gran problema que debemos solucionar.

El desempleo es un problema muy grave porque los que están en paro se encuentran en un círculo vicioso. Los expertos dicen que si estás en paro, es más difícil encontrar otro trabajo.

Unemployment is a very serious problem because those who are unemployed find themselves in a vicious circle. Experts say that if you're unemployed, it's harder to find another job.

the worst affected are young people — los más afectados son los jóvenes

Well, that was a bit bleak — and unfortunately, there's more...

TRACK LISTENING 09

A charity for the homeless is talking about the situation in Spain. Listen, and then fill the gaps.

e.g. __Thousands__ of people are homeless in Spain.

1. Many people have lost their jobs and homes due to .... [1]
2. Homeless people often have a .... life. [1]
3. Homeless people are often the victims of .... [1]
4. According to the report, many people think homeless people are .... [1]
5. To change the situation for homeless people, we should .... [1]

Contributing to Society

So now you've battled through all the problems, it's time to get creative and find some solutions.

¿Qué podemos hacer? — *What can we do?*

la basura	*rubbish*	renovable	*renewable*
los desechos / los residuos	*rubbish*	salvar el planeta	*to save the planet*
el reciclaje	*recycling*	la organización benéfica	*charitable organisation*
reciclar	*to recycle*	la tienda solidaria	*charity shop*

Question	**Simple Answer**	**Extended Answer**
¿Qué haces para proteger el medio ambiente? *What do you do to protect the environment?*	Apago las luces para ahorrar energía. *I turn the lights off to save energy.*	Cuando voy de compras, siempre reutilizo las bolsas en vez de comprar nuevas. *When I go shopping, I always reuse the bags instead of buying new ones.*
¿Qué haces para ayudar a otras personas? *What do you do to help other people?*	Los domingos trabajo en una tienda solidaria. *On Sundays I work in a charity shop.*	Ayudo con el club de jóvenes en mi pueblo. Es esencial que hagamos algo para los demás. *I help with the youth club in my town. It's essential that we do something for others.*

¿Cómo podemos ayudar? — *How can we help?*

Me gustaría ayudar a los refugiados que vienen a vivir en nuestro país.	*I would like to help the refugees who come to live in our country.*	the victims of natural disasters like hurricanes and fires — las víctimas de desastres naturales como huracanes e incendios
Es importante que apoyemos a las organizaciones benéficas.	*It's important that we support charitable organisations.*	'Acabar de' + infinitive means 'to have just done something'. See p.85.
Acabo de participar en una protesta en contra del uso de los combustibles fósiles.	*I have just participated in a protest against the use of fossil fuels.*	a campaign — una campaña

(SPEAKING) *I rode there and back... that's enough recycling, right?*

Look at the answers to these questions — then it's time for a photo question.

¿Recicláis mucho en casa?
¿Qué haremos en el futuro para proteger el medio ambiente?

Sí, intentamos reciclar muchas cosas. Reciclamos envases de plástico, botellas y cartón. Si no podemos reciclar algo, intentamos reutilizarlo **para que no acabe**[1] en un vertedero.

Creo que tendremos coches eléctricos. También reduciremos la cantidad de basura que producimos y reutilizaremos las cosas más antes de tirarlas.

Grade 8-9

Tick list:
✓ tenses: present, future present subjunctive
✓ topical vocab, e.g. cartón, vertedero

© iStock.com/DragonImages

To improve:
+ explain opinions more
+ more complex connectives e.g. sin embargo

Answer these questions in **Spanish**. *Talk for* **2** *minutes.*

- ¿Qué hay en la foto?
- ¿Podríamos hacer más para salvar el planeta?
- ¿Crees que es importante reciclar?   [10 marks]

[1] so that it doesn't end up

Where to Go

Grab some sun cream and pack your suitcase because you're off on holiday...

Los países y las nacionalidades — Countries and nationalities

España	*Spain*	español	*Spanish*	los Estados Unidos	*United States*
Inglaterra	*England*	inglés	*English*	Canadá	*Canada*
Escocia	*Scotland*	escocés	*Scottish*	la India	*India*
Gales	*Wales*	galés	*Welsh*	Australia	*Australia*
Irlanda	*Ireland*	irlandés	*Irish*	Rusia	*Russia*
Irlanda del Norte	*Northern Ireland*	norirlandés	*Northern Irish*	Brasil	*Brazil*
Gran Bretaña	*Great Britain*	británico	*British*	México	*Mexico*
Francia	*France*	francés	*French*	Argentina	*Argentina*
Alemania	*Germany*	alemán	*German*	Perú	*Peru*
Portugal	*Portugal*	portugués	*Portuguese*	Chile	*Chile*
Italia	*Italy*	italiano	*Italian*	Colombia	*Colombia*
Grecia	*Greece*	griego	*Greek*	Cuba	*Cuba*
Europa	*Europe*	europeo	*European*		

Mi padre es medio irlandés, así que vamos de vacaciones a Irlanda a menudo.

My father is half Irish, so we often go on holiday to Ireland.

Mi padre es griego y solía ir a Grecia para quedarme con mi familia.

My father is Greek and I used to go to Greece to stay with my family.

Luisa fue a Londres el año pasado y le gustó mucho la comida británica.

Luisa went to London last year and she really liked British food.

Grammar — nationalities

Nationalities are <u>adjectives</u> — some have an <u>accent</u> when they're used in the <u>masculine singular</u> form, but drop the accent and add '<u>a</u>' in the <u>feminine</u> form.

inglés (m., sing.) — **ingl<u>esa</u>** (f., sing.)
ingl<u>eses</u> (m., pl.) — **ingl<u>esas</u>** (f., pl.)
Las chicas <u>son inglesas</u>.
The girls <u>are English</u>.

Remember — always use the verb '<u>ser</u>' with nationalities (p.77).

Question	**Simple Answer**	**Extended Answer**
¿Adónde quisiera ir de vacaciones?	Quisiera ir al norte de España.	Me gustaría ir al norte de España porque mi tía nació en Asturias. Quisiera visitar el pueblo donde vivía.
Where would you like to go on holiday?	*I would like to go to the north of Spain.*	*I would like to go to the north of Spain because my aunt was born in Asturias. I would like to visit the town where she used to live.*

 This page about countries will have you going places...

Arturo has written a leaflet to help promote his region.

¡Ven a visitar la región bellísima de Galicia! Está situada en la costa del Océano Atlántico en el norte de España. Aquí se puede conocer las ciudades famosas de Vigo, Pontevedra, Ourense, o Santiago de Compostela, que es más conocida por su catedral y sus **peregrinaciones**[1] todos los años. ¡Hay tantas cosas que hacer! Por ejemplo, se puede **alquilar**[2] un barco en Pontevedra, explorar las calles antiguas de Vigo, o nadar en uno de los **ríos**[3] en Ourense!

[1]pilgrimages   [2]to rent, hire   [3]rivers

*Lee este texto, y luego contesta a las preguntas en **español**.*

e.g. ¿Qué región se menciona?   *Galicia.*

1. ¿Dónde está Galicia? Da dos detalles. *[2]*

2. ¿Por qué es la ciudad de Santiago de Compostela famosa? Da dos razones. *[2]*

3. ¿Qué se puede hacer en Ourense?   *[1]*

Accommodation

So you've chosen which country you're going to visit — now all you need is somewhere to stay...

Busco alojamiento... — *I'm looking for accommodation...*

alojarse / quedarse	*to stay*	las instalaciones	*facilities*
el albergue juvenil	*youth hostel*	media pensión	*half board*
la pensión	*boarding house (B&B)*	pensión completa	*full board*
el parador	*state-owned hotel*	la habitación doble	*double room*
(irse de) camping	*(to go) camping*	la habitación individual	*single room*
la tienda	*tent*	la cama de matrimonio	*double bed*
el crucero	*cruise*	el aire acondicionado	*air-conditioning*

Juliet was desperate for a room with a balcony...

Quisiera quedarme aquí cuatro noches.

I would like to stay here for four nights.

> a room with a balcony — una habitación con balcón

Siempre nos quedamos en una pensión.

We always stay in a boarding house.

> a luxury hotel — un hotel de lujo

Es esencial encontrar una habitación que tenga aire acondicionado.

It's essential to find a room that has air-conditioning.

> that has a bathroom — que tenga cuarto de baño

Question	**Simple Answer**	**Extended Answer**
¿Qué tipo de habitación quisiera usted?	Quisiera una habitación con vista al mar.	Somos una familia de tres, así que quisiéramos dos habitaciones — una individual y una doble.
What type of room would you like?	*I would like a room with a sea view.*	*We are a family of three, so we would like two rooms — a single and a double.*

Quisiera alojarme en... — *I would like to stay in...*

Mi amigo/a quisiera encontrar alojamiento de media pensión.

My friend would like to find half-board accommodation.

> full-board — pensión completa

Preferiríamos alojarnos en un parador porque tienen buenas instalaciones.

We would prefer to stay in a state-owned hotel because they have good facilities.

> on a campsite because we have a caravan and like nature — en un camping porque tenemos una caravana y nos gusta la naturaleza

Nos gustaría quedarnos en un albergue juvenil para conocer a gente nueva.

We would like to stay in a youth hostel in order to meet new people.

> to save money — ahorrar dinero

TRACK LISTENING 10

Yep, 'shop' and 'tent' are both 'la tienda' in Spanish...

Listen to this extract about hotels in Rio de Janeiro from a book by Gorgonio Petano y Mazariegos.

1. How are the hotels in general described?

   A) average   B) fantastic *[1]*

2. How many hotels are mentioned when discussing the best hotels in the city? *[1]*

3. How is the *Hotel de los Extranjeros* described? Choose the two correct adjectives from the list below.

   small   old-fashioned

   modern   strange

   elegant   ugly   *[2]*

4. What do the people of the *Cuerpo Diplomático extranjero* do at the hotel?

   A) eat dinner

   B) live

   C) have meetings   *[1]*

Getting Ready to Go

That holiday won't book itself. Thankfully, there's plenty of vocab here to help you get something sorted.

Reservando unas vacaciones — *Booking a holiday*

Spanish	English	Spanish	English
la agencia de viajes	*travel agent's*	el folleto	*leaflet*
libre / disponible	*available*	el regreso	*return*
el pasaporte	*passport*	el guía	*guide*
el carnet de conducir	*driving licence*	la guía	*guidebook*
la maleta	*suitcase*	buscar	*to look for*
el equipaje	*luggage*	informar(se)	*to find out*
la ficha / el formulario	*registration form*	el lugar / sitio	*place*

Grammar — I need...

When talking about the features of something you <u>require</u>, use the <u>subjunctive</u> (p.89).

Busco un hotel grande que <u>tenga</u> una piscina.

I'm looking for a big hotel that <u>has</u> a pool.

Question	Simple Answer	Extended Answer
¿Estás listo/a para tus vacaciones?	Sí, he hecho mi maleta.	Sí, he hecho mi maleta, pero todavía no he comprado una guía. Necesito una guía que incluya información sobre España e Italia.
Are you ready for your holidays?	*Yes, I have packed my suitcase.*	*Yes, I've packed my suitcase, but I haven't bought a guidebook yet. I need a guidebook that includes information about Spain and Italy.*

¿En qué puedo servirle? — *How can I help you?*

Por favor, ¿puedo reservar la mejor habitación disponible?

Please can I reserve the best room available?
→ a room on the ground floor — una habitación en la planta baja

Quisiera ir a un lugar donde pueda nadar.

I would like to go to a place where I can swim.
→ canoe — hacer piragüismo

¿Puede usted darnos unos folletos? Queremos informarnos sobre lo que hay en esta región.

Can you give us some leaflets? We want to find out about what there is in this region.
→ tell us if there are rooms available — decirnos si hay habitaciones libres

→ to know what time the museum opens — saber cuándo abre el museo

---

 WRITING

You shouldn't have reservations when it comes to booking...

Read the following scene from a Spanish TV show script. A travel agent is speaking to Bea.

Agente de Viajes (AV): Dígame, Señora.

Grade 6-7

Bea: Buenos días. Quisiera reservar unas vacaciones en España pero no sé el mejor lugar para quedarnos. Quiero ir con cuatro amigos.

AV: Bueno. Pues, ¿cuándo quisiera usted venir?

Bea: Preferiríamos ir durante las vacaciones de verano, desde el 3 de agosto hasta el 11 de agosto. Nos gustan las montañas.

AV: Hace buen tiempo durante agosto. Le recomendaría ir a Gijón, en el norte de España, porque se puede visitar la costa y Los Picos de Europa, que son estupendos.

Tick list:
- ✓ tenses: present, imperfect subjunctive, conditional
- ✓ superlative

To improve:
- + use subjunctive to say what you require
- + include more adjectives
- + use more conjunctions

Escribe un diálogo con un agente de viajes y menciona:
- *el tipo de lugar donde te gustaría ir;*
- *cuándo quieres ir;*
- *qué actividad quieres poder hacer;*
- *que te gustaría alquilar un coche.*

Escribe aproximadamente **90** *palabras en* **español**.   [16 marks]

How to Get There

Boats, buses, cars, coaches, trains and trams — this page will get you from A to B.

Cómo llegar a tu destino — *How to get to your destination*

el avión	*aeroplane*	el pasajero / viajero	*passenger / traveller*
el aeropuerto	*airport*	hacer transbordo	*to change, transfer*
el vuelo	*flight*	el billete (de ida / de ida y vuelta)	*(single / return) ticket*
el barco	*boat*	la estación (de autobuses / de trenes)	*(bus / train) station*
conducir	*to drive*	el andén	*platform*
la autopista	*motorway*	la red de ferrocarril	*railway network*
el tranvía	*tram*	la estación de servicio	*service station*
el viaje	*journey*	la gasolina (sin plomo)	*(unleaded) petrol*

Preferiría ir a España en avión porque me encuentro mal cuando voy en barco.

I would prefer to go to Spain by plane because I feel ill when I go by boat.

by car because it's cheaper — en coche porque es más barato

Fuimos a la playa a pie ya que está cerca de nuestro hotel.

We went to the beach on foot since it's near our hotel.

by taxi because our feet were hurting — en taxi porque nos dolían los pies

Viajaremos en autobús porque siempre nos perdemos cuando vamos en coche.

We will travel by bus because we always get lost when we go by car.

the airport workers are on strike — los empleados del aeropuerto están en huelga

Is it a boat?
Is it a car? It would appear to be both...

El tren está retrasado — *The train is delayed*

¿A qué hora sale el tranvía?

At what time does the tram leave?

does the train arrive — llega el tren

Necesito reservar un coche. ¿Tengo que rellenar una ficha?

I need to reserve a car. Do I have to fill in a registration form?

have my driving licence with me — tener mi carnet de conducir conmigo

Coge el metro porque hay un atasco en la autopista.

Take the underground because there's a traffic jam on the motorway.

the train has been cancelled — el tren ha sido cancelado

No me importa viajar en autocar, pero prefiero ir en tren porque es más cómodo.

I don't mind travelling by coach, but I prefer to go by train because it's more comfortable.

by plane because it's faster — en avión porque es más rápido

This transport stuff is driving me crazy...

Translate this text into **English**. [9 marks]

Mi ciudad tiene varios tipos de transporte. El metro, que abrió en 1924, es muy limpio y rápido. Además, existe una red de tranvías en la que se puede visitar la mayoría de los barrios de la ciudad. Desde el aeropuerto, es posible volar a todas las ciudades importantes de Europa y no está muy lejos del centro. Pronto, van a mejorar la red de autobuses, lo que será fenomenal.

What to Do

Accommodation? Check. Transport? Check. Now the fun can begin...

Hay varias actividades... — *There are various activities...*

la excursión	*trip, excursion*	caminar	*to walk*
el mar	*the sea*	esquiar	*to ski*
bañarse	*to swim*	sacar / hacer fotos	*to take photos*
tomar el sol	*to sunbathe*	el parque de atracciones	*fairground*
broncearse	*to get a tan*	el parque temático	*theme park*
los deportes acuáticos	*water sports*	el recuerdo	*souvenir*

Question	**Simple Answer**	**Extended Answer**
¿Qué actividades hiciste durante tus vacaciones? *What activities did you do during your holiday?*	Fuimos a la playa — fue muy relajante. *We went to the beach — it was very relaxing.*	Pasamos mucho tiempo en la playa porque hacía sol. Me bañé y tomé el sol con mis primos. *We spent a lot of time on the beach because it was sunny. I swam and sunbathed with my cousins.*

Grammar — la foto

<u>Watch out</u> for nouns that don't fit the masculine / feminine rule of ending with an '-o' or '-a' (p.58):

la foto	*the photo*
el agua	*the water*

('Water' is actually a feminine noun, but it takes '<u>el</u>' as its article because 'la agua' is too awkward to pronounce.)

Estamos de vacaciones — *We're on holiday*

Para mí, lo importante es encontrar un parque de atracciones.
For me, the important thing is to find a fairground. ←
- to buy souvenirs — comprar recuerdos
- to go to a museum — visitar un museo

Nos gusta nada más que dar un paseo por las calles.
We like nothing more than to go for a stroll around the streets. ←
- to try the region's typical food — probar la comida típica de la región

Cuando estoy de vacaciones, suelo sacar muchas fotos.
When I'm on holiday, I usually take lots of photos. ←
- go on various excursions — hacer varias excursiones

SPEAKING *So much to do, so little time...*

Tom and his teacher are discussing holiday activities. Look at Tom's response to this question:
¿Te gusta ir de vacaciones donde se puede hacer deportes acuáticos?

Depende del lugar. Cuando voy a un país donde hace calor, como España, tengo ganas de hacer deportes acuáticos. Voy a ir a **Noruega**[1] el año que viene. Practicaremos el piragüismo, pero pienso que el agua estará muy fría.

Grade 6-7

[1]Norway

Tick list:
✓ tenses: present, immediate future, proper future

To improve:
+ be more descriptive
+ more tenses
+ more topic vocab

Now answer these questions in **Spanish**. Try to talk for **2** minutes. *[10 marks]*

- ¿Qué hay en la foto?
- ¿Cómo fueron tus últimas vacaciones?
- ¿Cuáles serían tus vacaciones ideales?

School Subjects

School subjects — as if you don't get enough of that at school. However, it's important to learn them and to be able to say what you think about them.

Las asignaturas — *School subjects*

el español	*Spanish*	el dibujo	*art*
el alemán	*German*	el arte dramático	*drama*
el francés	*French*	la música	*music*
el inglés	*English*	las matemáticas	*maths*
las ciencias	*science*	las ciencias económicas	*economics*
la biología	*biology*	el comercio	*business studies*
la química	*chemistry*	la informática	*IT*
la física	*physics*	la cocina	*food technology*
la geografía	*geography*	los trabajos manuales	*handicrafts*
la historia	*history*	la gimnasia	*gymnastics*
la religión	*RE*	la educación física	*PE*

The thought of so many different subjects gave David a real fright.

Mi asignatura preferida es... — *My favourite subject is...*

Question	**Simple Answer**	**Extended Answer**
¿Cuál es tu asignatura preferida? *What's your favourite subject?*	Mi asignatura preferida es la música. Me encanta tocar la guitarra. *My favourite subject is music. I love to play the guitar.*	El español es mi asignatura preferida ya que es muy interesante. Es útil también porque espero ir a España el verano que viene. *Spanish is my favourite subject as it's very interesting. It's useful too because I hope to go to Spain next summer.*

Me encanta la historia. Es interesante aprender sobre el pasado.

I love history. It's interesting to learn about the past.

Nos gustan mucho las matemáticas. Es fascinante trabajar con números.

We really like maths. It's fascinating to work with numbers.

Miguel odia la química porque es tan difícil.

Miguel hates chemistry because it's so difficult.

I hate — Odio

boring — aburrido

useful — útil

José finds art awful — José encuentra el dibujo horrible

WRITING *I'm subjected to school every day...*

Gabriela has written about her school subjects in a chat room.

Generalmente, me gustan mis asignaturas. Me encantan las lenguas porque son divertidas, así que **opté por estudiar**[1] el francés y el inglés este **curso**[2]. Sin embargo, lo malo es que son difíciles. Por otro lado, me fastidia la profesora de ciencias porque es demasiado estricta. Pero a decir verdad, mi asignatura preferida es la educación física porque me gusta jugar al baloncesto.

Grade 6-7

Tick list
✓ adjectives agree
✓ range of vocabulary and conjunctions

To improve...
+ use different tenses
+ more complex adjectives
+ extend opinions

Escribe tu propio comentario. Menciona:

• *qué asignaturas (no) te gustan, y por qué;*

• *qué asignaturas quieres estudiar el curso que viene, y por qué.*

*Escribe aproximadamente **150** palabras en **español**. Responde a los dos aspectos de la pregunta.* [32 marks]

[1] I chose to study [2] school year

School Routine

Same old routine, day in, day out. At least routines are quite easy to talk about in the exam...

Mi rutina escolar — *My school routine*

el trimestre	*(school) term*
la agenda	*diary*
el horario	*timetable*
la clase	*lesson*
el recreo	*break*

Grammar — telling the time

If you're saying what time something is at, remember to put '<u>a</u>' first.
La hora de comer es <u>a la una</u>. *Lunchtime is <u>at one o'clock</u>.*
For more about time, see p.2.

Mi colegio empieza a las nueve, y a las nueve y cinco, el profesor pasa la lista.

Tengo cinco clases por día, y cada clase dura cuarenta minutos. El día escolar termina a las tres y media.

My school starts at nine o'clock, and at five past nine, the teacher calls the register.

I have five lessons a day, and each lesson lasts forty minutes. The school day finishes at half past three.

at twenty to nine — a las nueve menos veinte

we go to the assembly room — vamos al salón de actos

I return home at quarter past three. — Vuelvo a casa a las tres y cuarto.

¿Qué haces durante el recreo? — *What do you do during break?*

Durante el recreo, juego al fútbol con mis amigos, y a la hora de comer, vamos a la cantina para almorzar.

Prefiero pasar el recreo en la biblioteca porque mis amigos van al club de tenis, que a mí no me gusta.

During break, I play football with my friends, and at lunchtime, we go to the canteen to eat lunch.

I prefer to spend my break in the library because my friends go to tennis club, which I don't like.

I chat — charlo

we sit outside and eat lunch — nos sentamos afuera y almorzamos

go to gymnastics club — van al club de gimnasia

En mi mochila, pongo... — *In my school bag, I put...*

el bolígrafo	*pen*	la regla	*ruler*	el cuaderno	*exercise book*
el lápiz	*pencil*	las tijeras	*scissors*	el libro	*book*

Eduardo was ready for whatever maths could throw at him.

En mi mochila, hay un estuche.

Se me ha olvidado mi lápiz.
¿Me puedes prestar un boli por favor?

In my school bag, there's a pencil case.

I have forgotten my pencil.
Can you lend me a pen please?

In Spanish, '<u>bolígrafo</u>' (pen) is often shortened to '<u>boli</u>'.

TRACK LISTENING 11 Una clase — *let that be a lesson to you...*

*Juan y Marta hablan de su horario. Completa la tabla con las asignaturas en **español**. [3 marks]*

día / hora	08.30 — 09.20	09.20 — 10.10	10.10 — 10.30	10.30 — 11.20
lunes	las matemáticas	1)	RECREO	el inglés
martes	las ciencias	el francés	RECREO	2)
miércoles	los trabajos manuales	el español	RECREO	3)

School Life

Now's your chance to talk about what your school's like and what it has and hasn't got.

¿A qué tipo de colegio asistes? — *What type of school do you attend?*

el instituto	*secondary school*	mixto	*mixed*	privado	*private*
la escuela primaria	*primary school*	religioso	*religious*	público	*state*

Mi instituto es un colegio mixto. Está a unos cinco kilómetros de mi casa.

My school is a mixed school. It's about five kilometres from my house.

→ modern state — público y moderno

→ about 400 — unos cuatrocientos
950 — novecientos cincuenta

Hay quinientos alumnos en mi instituto y llevamos uniforme.

There are 500 students at my school and we wear a uniform.

← we don't have to wear a uniform — no tenemos que llevar uniforme

Soy alumno/a aquí desde hace tres años. Me gusta este colegio y me llevo bien con los profesores.

I've been a student here for 3 years. I like this school and I get on well with the teachers.

← the teachers are very nice — los profesores son muy simpáticos

¿Cómo es tu instituto? — *What's your school like?*

las instalaciones	*facilities*	el taller	*workshop*
el aula (f)	*classroom*	el campo de deportes	*sports field*
la pizarra interactiva	*smart board*	el gimnasio	*gymnasium*
la sala de profesores	*staffroom*	los vestuarios	*changing rooms*

Mi colegio tiene un campo de deportes grande donde podemos jugar al hockey.

My school has a big sports field where we can play hockey.

← a small gym where we can keep fit — un gimnasio pequeño donde podemos mantenernos en forma

En general, mi instituto es muy moderno. Encuentro las aulas maravillosas porque tienen pizarras interactivas.

In general, my school is very modern. I find the classrooms marvellous because they have smart boards.

← quite old — bastante antiguo

← horrible because the heating doesn't work well — horribles porque la calefacción no funciona bien

My school just had lots of fish...

Read what Sofía has written about her school below. Then in the table, indicate the three sentences that are true by ticking the correct boxes. [3 marks]

¡Hola! Soy Sofía. Te escribo para hablarte de mi colegio. Está situado en Madrid a unos siete kilómetros de mi casa y hay ochocientos alumnos. Normalmente, mi padre me lleva en coche al colegio. Tengo suerte porque puedo coger el metro también — es muy eficaz si hay atascos en las carreteras. El día empieza a las ocho menos diez. Las clases duran unos cuarenta minutos y tengo un recreo de quince minutos. El descanso para comer empieza a la una y media y dura una hora y media. Generalmente las instalaciones en mi colegio son modernas, pero lo malo es el gimnasio. Es muy sucio. ¡Qué horror! ¿Cómo es tu colegio? ¡Adiós!

1. Sofía usually takes the underground to school.	
2. Sofía is positive about the underground.	
3. Sofía is negative about the underground.	
4. The facilities are old.	
5. The facilities are modern.	
6. Sofía dislikes the gym.	

School Pressures

A chance to vent your frustrations now — should be refreshing after all this stressful revision...

Las reglas — *The rules*

(no) hay que...	*you (don't) have to...*
(no) tienes que...	*you (don't) have to...*
(no) se debe...	*you must (not)...*
(no) es obligatorio...	*it's (not) compulsory...*
(no) deberías...	*you shouldn't...*

No deberías comer chicle ni beber bebidas gaseosas.
You shouldn't eat chewing gum nor drink fizzy drinks.

Hay que levantar la mano antes de hablar.
You have to raise your hand before speaking.

Estoy muy estresado/a por... — *I'm really stressed about...*

estresante	*stressful*	el éxito	*success*	suspender	*to fail*	el apoyo	*support*
la presión	*pressure*	aprobar	*to pass*	repasar	*to revise*	apoyar	*to support*

La vida escolar es estresante. Hay mucha presión y tengo muchos deberes. Afortunadamente, los profesores apoyan a los alumnos estresados.

School life is stressful. There's a lot of pressure and I have a lot of homework. Luckily, the teachers support stressed students.

Si no saco sobresalientes, no podré ir a la universidad.

If I don't get outstanding marks, I won't be able to go to university.

I'm afraid of failing my exams — tengo miedo de suspender mis exámenes

get good marks — saco buenas notas

pass this exam — apruebo este examen

El acoso (escolar) — *(School) bullying*

El acoso es un problema muy grave en mi colegio.
Bullying is a serious problem in my school.

Bullying doesn't happen much — La intimidación no ocurre mucho

El mal comportamiento arruina las clases.
Bad behaviour ruins lessons.

is a distraction — es una distracción

SPEAKING — *It's compulsory to answer these questions carefully...*

Have a look at this photo question. Use the example to give you some inspiration.

¿Hay mucha violencia en los institutos hoy en día?

En mi instituto, la violencia no es un problema. Si la conducta de un alumno es peligrosa, el director **castigará**[1] a ese alumno. Pero a mi modo de ver, muchos institutos tienen problemas con peleas y **falta de respeto**[2]. Sería difícil estudiar en esos colegios.

Grade 6-7

© iStock.com/mactrunk

[1]will punish   [2]lack of respect

*Now answer these questions — talk for about **3** minutes.*

- *¿Qué hay en la foto?*
- *¿Cómo era la vida escolar en tu escuela primaria?*
- *¿Hay mucha violencia en los institutos hoy en día?*
  [15 marks]

After you've answered the three questions you've prepared, your teacher will ask you two more questions that you haven't seen. See p.92 for more tips for doing well in the speaking exam.

Tick list:
✓ tenses: present, future, conditional
✓ varied vocab

To improve:
+ more opinion phrases with explanations
+ use past tenses, e.g. preterite and imperfect

Education Post-16

It might not be something you've thought a lot about, but your future plans could come up in the exam. Learn this page and it might even give you some ideas...

Cuando tenga 16 años... — *When I'm 16...*

el/la aprendiz/a	*apprentice*	la academia	*academy, school post-16 (for certain careers)*
la experiencia laboral	*work experience*		
la práctica	*work placement*	las perspectivas	*employment*
hacer el bachillerato	*to do A-levels*	laborales	*prospects*

Apparently, this wasn't what Mrs Adams meant when she told me to look for work experience...

Quiero seguir mis estudios y hacer el bachillerato porque espero estudiar Derecho en la universidad.

I want to continue my studies and do my A-levels because I hope to study law at university.

to do a work placement — hacer una práctica

Para mejorar nuestras perspectivas laborales, el profesor recomienda que busquemos experiencia laboral.

In order to improve our employment prospects, the teacher recommends that we look for work experience.

to become a plumber's apprentice — hacerme aprendiz/a de fontanero

to get a degree — conseguir un título

You often need to use the subjunctive when someone wants someone else to do something. See p.89.

Después del bachillerato... — *After A-levels...*

el año libre / sabático	*gap year*	la carrera	*career, profession*
la formación (profesional)	*vocational training*	calificado	*competent, skilled*

Question

¿Qué quieres hacer después de terminar el bachillerato?
What do you want to do after you finish your A-levels?

Simple Answer

Después de terminar el bachillerato, quiero empezar a trabajar.
After finishing my A-levels, I want to start working.

Extended Answer

Voy a dedicarme a mis estudios porque quiero ser traductor/a. Si quiero ser traductor/a calificado/a, tendré que estudiar mucho.
I'm going to focus on my studies because I want to be a translator. If I want to be a competent translator, I'll have to study a lot.

Quisiera tomarme un año sabático, luego me gustaría ir a la universidad porque quiero hacer carrera en medicina.

I would like to take a gap year, then I would like to go to university because I want to have a career in medicine.

Me gustaría ser electricista, pero primero, necesito formación profesional.

I would like to be an electrician, but first, I need vocational training.

Grammar — conditional

To talk about something that could, should or would happen, use the conditional tense (p.83).

Me gustaría estudiar música.
I would like to study music.

Remember that 'quisiera' can be used to say 'I would like' too (p.83).

After school I want to have my tea and watch Hollyoaks...

Translate this text into **Spanish**. [12 marks]

When I was young, I thought I would like to be a teacher. My parents are teachers and although they find the work interesting, my father says that it is quite stressful. Now I have decided that I'm going to go to an academy to study photography. I would love to take photos of weddings!

Career Choices and Ambitions

All this revising is hard work and now you've got another job to do — learn about careers.

Los empleos — *Jobs*

albañil	*builder*	contable	*accountant*
abogado/a	*lawyer*	enfermero/a	*nurse*
bombero/a	*firefighter*	ingeniero/a	*engineer*
camionero/a	*lorry driver*	jefe/a	*boss*
carpintero/a	*carpenter*	periodista	*journalist*
cocinero/a	*chef*	policía	*police officer*
comerciante	*shop owner*	veterinario/a	*vet*

> **Grammar** — I'm a...
> When talking about jobs, <u>usually</u> you <u>don't</u> need the article '<u>un(a)</u>' (p.59).
> **Quiero ser pintor/a. *I want to be a painter*.**
> You <u>do</u> though if you use an <u>adjective</u>.
> **Soy <u>un buen</u> jardinero. *I'm <u>a good</u> gardener*.**

solicitar	*to apply*	el trabajo	*work, job*
el currículum	*CV*	estar en paro	*to be unemployed*
la entrevista	*interview*	el sueldo	*wages, salary*
empleado/a	*employee*	ganar	*to earn*

> For more jobs, have a look at the vocab list starting on p.96.

Mi empleo ideal sería periodista. Trabajaría en una oficina y escribiría artículos interesantes.

My ideal job would be a journalist. I would work in an office and I would write interesting articles.

> full time — a tiempo completo

Quisiera solicitar el puesto de contable. Adjunto mi currículum.

I would like to apply for the position of accountant. I attach my CV.

> I've got a year's experience in a bank. — Tengo un año de experiencia en un banco.

Para mí, es importante tener un empleo desafiante.

For me, it's important to have a challenging job.

> stimulating — estimulante
> rewarding — gratificante
> varied — variado

Tengo un empleo a tiempo parcial — *I have a part-time job*

Soy dependiente en una tienda de ropa. Lo mejor es charlar con los clientes.

I'm a shop assistant in a clothes shop. The best thing is chatting with customers.

> waiter/waitress in a restaurant — camarero/a en un restaurante

No tengo empleo a tiempo parcial, pero a veces cuido a mi hermana y recibo paga.

I don't have a part-time job, but sometimes I look after my sister and I receive pocket money.

> that there are discounts for employees — que hay descuentos para los empleados

Trabajo en una peluquería los sábados. Me gusta el empleo pero no gano mucho.

I work in a hairdresser's on Saturdays. I like the job, but I don't earn a lot.

> I hope to find another job and earn more money — espero conseguir otro empleo y ganar más dinero

Before you go careering into the next section...

Translate this text into **English**. [9 marks]

— Cuando yo tenía quince años, quería ser ama de casa — dijo mi madre.

— Sí, pero mucho ha cambiado en los últimos años — le respondí. — Quiero ser abogada. Ganan un buen sueldo y me gustaría ayudar a la gente. ¡El trabajo sería tan variado!

Nouns	# Words for People and Objects

Nouns are like the building blocks of a language — it's really important to know how to use them.

Every Spanish noun is masculine or feminine

1) Whether a word is masculine, feminine or plural affects lots of things.

2) All 'the' and 'a' words change depending on the word's gender, and so do any adjectives which describe the noun.

> *When you learn a new noun, learn its gender too.*

> el árbol alto (m.)   *the tall tree*
> la casa alta (f.)   *the tall house*

These rules help you guess what gender a word is

1) If you see a word with 'el' or 'un' before it, it's usually masculine.

2) 'La' or 'una' in front of a word means it's feminine.

3) If you don't have these clues, there are other tricks you can use to help you guess.

MASCULINE	Most nouns that end in: -o -l -n -r -s -ta -aje	AND	Male people, days, months, languages, seas, rivers, oceans and mountains.
FEMININE	Most nouns that end in: -a -ción -sión -tad -tud -dad -umbre	AND	Female people, letters of the alphabet.

4) You can't tell whether a noun ending in 'e' or 'ista' is masculine or feminine — you have to learn them.

el coche *the car*	la gente *the people*	el turista *the tourist (male)*	la turista *the tourist (female)*

> *These are some of the exceptions to the rules. You'll just need to learn these ones off by heart.*

el día	*day*	la foto	*photo*
el problema	*problem*	la moto	*motorbike*
el mapa	*map*	la mano	*hand*

Making nouns plural

1) Some nouns in Spanish end in a vowel. To make them plural, just add 's' — 'una cama' (*one bed*) becomes 'dos camas' (*two beds*).

2) There are some exceptions to these rules though:

Type of noun	To make it plural...	Example
ends in a consonant except 'z'	add 'es'	una flor *one flower* → dos flores *two flowers*
ends in 'z'	drop the 'z' and add 'ces'	un lápiz *one pencil* → dos lápices *two pencils*
days ending in 's'	make the article plural but keep the noun the same	el viernes *Friday* → los viernes *Fridays*
family surnames		Los Simpson *The Simpsons*

> *Sometimes you need to add or remove an accent in the plural to avoid changing the pronunciation of the word. Here are a couple of common examples.*

un inglés *one English person* → dos ingleses *two English people*
un joven *one young man* → dos jóvenes *two young men*

Ignore genders at your peril...

Write 'el' or 'la' for each of these words. Then write each one in the plural form with 'los' or 'las'.

1. sombrero	3. tradición	5. porcentaje	7. tensión	9. ciudad
2. problema	4. viernes	6. francés	8. dificultad	10. mapa

'The', 'A', 'Some' and Other Little Words

Articles + indefinite adjectives

In Spanish, 'the' and 'a' change depending on the gender of the noun and whether it's singular or plural.

El, la, los, las — *the*

'El', 'la', 'los' and 'las' are definite articles.

	Masculine	Feminine
singular	el	la
plural	los	las

1) The word for 'the' changes depending on the gender of the noun, and whether it's singular or plural.

2) Use 'el' before feminine nouns which start with a stressed 'a'.

> El agua está fría.   *The water is cold.*

3) Sometimes you need a definite article in Spanish where you wouldn't use one in English...

a) with nouns used in a general sense: No me gusta el café. *I don't like coffee.*

b) in front of the days of the week and times: los lunes a las seis *Mondays at six o'clock*

c) in front of weights and measurements: dos euros el kilo *two euros a kilo*

d) when you use a person's title: ¿Cómo está el señor Gómez? *How is Mr Gómez?*

4) There's a neuter article 'lo' for things that aren't masculine or feminine.

> *When you use 'lo' in front of an adjective, the adjective has to be in the masculine form — see p.60.*

lo mejor / peor / aburrido es que...   *the best / worst / boring thing is that...*

Un, una, unos, unas — *a and some*

'Un', 'una', 'unos' and 'unas' are indefinite articles.

1) 'Un' and 'una' mean 'a'.

2) 'Un' is used for masculine words and 'una' is used for feminine words.

> un gato   *a cat*
> una casa   *a house*

3) When you make 'un' or 'una' plural, they become 'unos' and 'unas' — they mean 'some' or 'a few'.

> unos gatos   *some cats*
> unas casas   *some houses*

4) Watch out, though — 'a' is left out...

a) ...after the verb 'ser' when talking about someone's occupation or nationality: Soy estudiante. *I'm a student.*

b) ...after a negative verb: No tengo perro. *I haven't got a dog.*

Any, another, each, all

These are known as indefinite adjectives. See p.60-61 for more adjectives.

1) There's no special word for 'any' in Spanish.   ¿Tienes manzanas?   *Have you got any apples?*

2) Use 'otro' or 'otra' for 'another'.   Lo haré otro día.   *I'll do it another day.*
> *You don't need to write 'un' or 'una' before 'otro/a'.*

3) 'Cada' means 'each'. It's the same for masculine and feminine nouns.   Cada otoño voy a Gales.   *Each autumn I go to Wales.*

4) 'Todo/a/os/as' means 'all'.   Compré todos los libros en la librería.   *I bought all the books in the bookshop.*

Articles are most definitely important...

Translate these sentences into Spanish.

1. I like chocolate.   **3.** She is a teacher.   **5.** I want to speak to Mrs López.

2. I don't have any water.   **4.** He wants some potatoes.   **6.** Each person has two dogs.

Words to Describe Things

Jazz up your work with some flashy describing words — and collect more marks while you're at it.

Adjectives describe things — *learn these common ones*

grande	*big*	guapo/a	*good-looking*		
pequeño/a	*small*	feliz	*happy*		
alto/a	*tall / high*	triste	*sad*		
bajo/a	*short / low*	fácil	*easy*		
largo/a	*long*	difícil	*difficult*		
gordo/a	*fat*	malo/a	*bad*		
delgado/a	*slim*	nuevo/a	*new*	interesante	*interesting*
viejo/a	*old*	rápido/a	*fast*	simpático	*kind*
joven	*young*	lento/a	*slow*	aburrido	*boring*

When you look up an adjective in the dictionary, it'll be in the masculine singular form.

Adjectives need to agree with the noun

1) Adjectives have to <u>agree</u> with the <u>noun</u> they refer to, <u>even if they aren't right next to it</u>.

2) This means the <u>adjective changes</u> depending on the <u>gender</u> of the <u>noun</u> and whether it's <u>singular</u> or <u>plural</u>.

3) Adjectives that end in '<u>o</u>' in the <u>masculine singular</u> form change the '<u>o</u>' to '<u>a</u>' in the <u>feminine</u> form. When <u>plural</u>, the adjective ends in '<u>os</u>' (masculine) or '<u>as</u>' (feminine).

Masculine singular	Feminine singular	Masculine plural	Feminine plural
el chico pequeño	la chica pequeña	los chicos pequeños	las chicas pequeñas
the small boy	*the small girl*	*the small boys*	*the small girls*

4) Adjectives which <u>don't</u> end in '<u>o</u>' or '<u>a</u>' <u>don't change</u> in the singular. If the noun is <u>plural</u>, add '<u>s</u>' if it ends in a vowel, or '<u>es</u>' if it ends in a consonant.

Masculine singular	Feminine singular	Masculine plural	Feminine plural
el hombre triste	la mujer triste	los hombres tristes	las mujeres tristes
the sad man	*the sad woman*	*the sad men*	*the sad women*

If the adjective ends in 'z', remove the 'z' and add 'ces'. See p.58 for nouns that work in a similar way.

Some adjectives don't change to agree

Some adjectives <u>don't change at all</u>.

Most adjectives that don't change are colours.

beis	*beige*	rosa	*pink*
lila	*lilac*	turquesa	*turquoise*
naranja	*orange*	violeta	*violet*

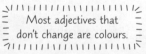

tres coches naranja   *three orange cars*
siete trenes rosa   *seven pink trains*

Adjectives agree (and I'm sure you do too) that this page is great...

Translate these phrases, making sure the adjectives agree with the nouns (where they need to).

1. the happy dog
2. seven red skirts
3. the blue cars
4. two short women
5. five small cats
6. nine violet chairs
7. four beige books
8. one sad person

Words to Describe Things

Once you know loads of adjectives, you need to know where to put them.

Most adjectives go after the word they describe

1) In Spanish, <u>most adjectives go after the noun</u> (the word they describe).

2) But that's not always the case — some adjectives always go <u>in front of the noun</u> they're describing, like these ones:

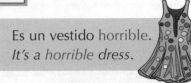

Es un vestido horrible.
It's a horrible dress.

mucho/a	*a lot of*	tanto/a	*so much*	primero/a, segundo/a...	*first, second...*
muchos/as	*lots of*	tantos/as	*so many*	próximo/a	*next*
otro/a	*another*	poco/a	*little*	último/a	*last*
otros/as	*other*	pocos/as	*few*		
alguno/a	*some*	cada	*each*		

'Otro', 'cada', and 'alguno/a' are all indefinite adjectives. For more on indefinite adjectives, see p.59.

Some adjectives change before masculine nouns...

Some adjectives <u>lose</u> the final 'o' when they go in front of a <u>masculine noun</u>.

bueno/a	*good*	tercero/a	*third*	ninguno/a	*none*
primero/a	*first*	alguno/a	*some*	malo/a	*bad*

un buen día	*a good day*	el tercer libro	*the third book*	algún día	*some day*

①	'Alguno' and 'ninguno' <u>drop</u> the final 'o' and <u>add an accent</u>.	No hay ningún taxi libre.	*There's no taxi free.*
②	'Grande' is the only adjective that <u>drops</u> 'de' in front of both <u>masculine and feminine</u> words.	una gran señora	*a great lady*

...and some change their meaning depending on their position

Paloma couldn't wait to try out the power steering in her new car.

Adjective	Before the noun...	After the noun...
grande	un gran hombre *a great man*	un hombre grande *a big man*
mismo	el mismo día *the same day*	yo mismo *I myself*
nuevo	un nuevo coche *a new (to owner) car*	un coche nuevo *a brand new car*
viejo	un viejo amigo *a long-standing friend*	un amigo viejo *an old (elderly) friend*

Don't let those adjectives trip you up — learn where they go...

Translate these phrases and sentences into Spanish, making sure the adjectives go in the right place.

1. There are lots of cats.
2. the first day
3. the same dog
4. the other pupils
5. Some people think that...
6. He's a great teacher.

Adjectives

Words to Describe Things

Adjectives are also really useful for saying what's yours and for pointing things out.

Mi, tu, nuestro — *my, your, our*

'Mi', 'tu', 'nuestro' etc. are possessive adjectives.

Words like '<u>my</u>' and '<u>your</u>' in Spanish have to <u>agree</u> with the <u>noun</u> they're describing — <u>not the owner</u>.

Possessive	Masculine singular	Feminine singular	Masculine plural	Feminine plural
my	mi (mío)	mi (mía)	mis (míos)	mis (mías)
your (inf., sing.)	tu (tuyo)	tu (tuya)	tus (tuyos)	tus (tuyas)
his/her/its/your (form., sing.)	su (suyo)	su (suya)	sus (suyos)	sus (suyas)
our	nuestro	nuestra	nuestros	nuestras
your (inf., pl.)	vuestro	vuestra	vuestros	vuestras
their/your (form., pl.)	su (suyo)	su (suya)	sus (suyos)	sus (suyas)

'Su(s)' can mean 'his', 'her', 'its', 'their' and 'your' (formal). Use the rest of the information in the sentence to work out which of these it is.

mi libro	su perro
my book	*his dog*

The forms <u>in pink</u> (in brackets) are the <u>special long forms</u> — put them <u>after the noun</u>:

las casas tuyas   *your houses*

el gato nuestro   *our cat*

The '<u>our</u>' and '<u>your (inf., pl.)</u>' forms are the <u>same</u> in the <u>short</u> and <u>long</u> forms.

Este, ese, aquel — *this, that, that over there*

'Este', 'ese' and 'aquel' are demonstrative adjectives.

1) Use '<u>este</u>' to say '<u>this</u>'. It's an adjective, so it <u>changes to agree</u> with the noun. When the noun is <u>feminine</u>, use '<u>esta</u>', and when it's <u>plural</u>, use '<u>estos</u>' (masculine) or '<u>estas</u>' (feminine).

este tigre   *this tiger*   esta leche   *this milk*   estos huevos   *these eggs*   estas caras   *these faces*

2) In Spanish, there are <u>two words</u> for '<u>that</u>', but their meanings are slightly different. '<u>Ese</u>' is used when you'd normally say '<u>that</u>' in English. Use '<u>esa</u>' for feminine nouns, and '<u>esos</u>' or '<u>esas</u>' for plural nouns.

ese tigre   *that tiger*   esa leche   *that milk*   esos huevos   *those eggs*   esas caras   *those faces*

3) '<u>Aquel</u>' is used for things that are <u>even further away</u> — in English, you might say '<u>that over there</u>'. 'Aquel' changes to '<u>aquella</u>' in the <u>feminine</u> form and '<u>aquellos</u>' and '<u>aquellas</u>' for the <u>plural</u> forms.

aquel tigre   *that tiger over there*   aquellos huevos   *those eggs over there*
aquella leche   *that milk over there*   aquellas caras   *those faces over there*

Cuyo — *whose*

'Cuyo' is a relative adjective.

To say '<u>whose</u>' in Spanish, use '<u>cuyo/a/os/as</u>'. The <u>ending</u> agrees with the <u>noun following</u>, <u>not with its owner</u>.

	Masculine singular	Feminine singular	Masculine plural	Feminine plural
whose	cuyo	cuya	cuyos	cuyas

Eva es la chica cuyo gato está allí.
Eva is the girl whose cat is there.

It's your turn now — help yourself to these quick questions...

Translate these sentences into Spanish.

1. Their books are new.
2. I want that apple.
3. That lion over there is eating.
4. These pears are good.
5. That man, whose wife is Spanish, is tall.
6. Lucas is the boy whose parents are nice.

Words to Compare Things

To make your Spanish even more brilliant, learn how to compare things.

Más, el más — *more, the most*

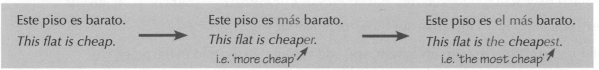
'More' is a comparative and 'the most' is a superlative.

1) In Spanish you can't say 'cheaper' or 'cheapest' — you have to say '<u>more cheap</u>' or '<u>the most cheap</u>'.

Este piso es barato.	Este piso es más barato.	Este piso es el más barato.
This flat is cheap.	*This flat is cheaper.*	*This flat is the cheapest.*
	i.e. 'more cheap' ↗	i.e. 'the most cheap' ↗

2) To say '<u>less cheap</u>' or '<u>the least cheap</u>', use '<u>menos</u>'.

Este piso es barato.	Este piso es menos barato.	Este piso es el menos barato.
This flat is cheap.	*This flat is less cheap.*	*This flat is the least cheap.*

3) To say 'the most / least' if the word you're describing is <u>feminine</u>, use 'la más / menos'. For <u>plural</u> words, use 'los/las más / menos'.

Laura es la más baja.	*Laura is the shortest.*
Jo y Ed son los menos altos.	*Jo and Ed are the least tall.*

Más / menos ... que — *more / less ... than*

1) Use '<u>más</u> ... <u>que</u>' *(more ... than)* and '<u>menos</u> ... <u>que</u>' *(less ... than)* to <u>compare</u> two things <u>directly</u>.

Catalina es más inteligente que Jorge.	*Catalina is more intelligent than Jorge.*
Jorge es menos inteligente que Catalina.	*Jorge is less intelligent than Catalina.*

2) Or to say two things are <u>as</u> young or old or brilliant <u>as</u> each other, use '<u>tan</u> ... <u>como</u>' *(as ... as)*.

Catalina es tan feliz como Jorge.	*Catalina is as happy as Jorge.*

There are some exceptions...

If the noun is feminine or plural, you'll need to change the 'el' to 'la', 'los' or 'las'.

As usual, there are a few trickier ones — learn these exceptions.

bueno	*good*	→	mejor	*better*	→	el mejor	*the best*
malo	*bad*	→	peor	*worse*	→	el peor	*the worst*
viejo	*old (for people only)*	→	mayor	*older*	→	el mayor	*the oldest*
joven	*young (for people only)*	→	menor	*younger*	→	el menor	*the youngest*

Manuela es la mayor de mis hermanas.	*Manuela is the oldest of my sisters.*

All the comparatives and superlatives stay the same for the masculine and feminine forms, but they add 'es' for the plural forms.

Blanca y Renata son las menores.	*Blanca and Renata are the youngest.*

El gorro azul es el mejor.	*The blue cap is the best.*

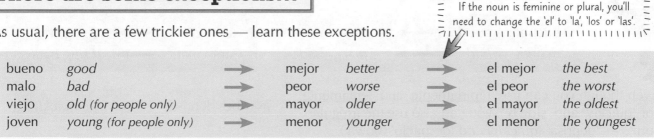

Making comparisons is the best thing ever...

Translate these sentences into Spanish — watch out for the irregular adjectives though.

1. My cat is the fattest.
2. I am as tall as my father.
3. Juan is older than Marta.
4. It was the worst day of the week.
5. The film is better than the book.
6. Our magazine is the most interesting.

Adverbs

Words to Describe Actions

Adverbs describe verbs by adding more information about how an action is done. Using them makes your Spanish much more interesting and complex, which can only be a good thing...

Adverbs help you describe how actions are done

1) If you wanted to <u>describe how you run</u>, you could say 'I run <u>slowly</u>' — 'slowly' is an <u>adverb</u>.

2) In English, you add '<u>-ly</u>' to the adjective '<u>slow</u>' to make '<u>slowly</u>'.

3) It's similar in Spanish — to form an adverb, you add '<u>-mente</u>' to the end of the <u>adjective</u>. <u>But</u>, you need to make sure the adjective is in the <u>feminine form</u> first.

> lento (*slow*) ⟶ lenta (*feminine form of 'slow'*) **+** -mente ⟶ lentamente (*slowly*)

4) With adjectives that <u>don't end</u> in '<u>o</u>', you can just add '<u>-mente</u>'.

> fácil (*easy*) **+** -mente ⟶ fácilmente (*easily*)

5) Unlike with adjectives (see p.60), adverbs don't need to <u>agree</u>. This is because they're <u>describing</u> an <u>action</u>, not the <u>person</u> doing the action.

> Hablamos sinceramente.   *We speak sincerely.*
> Habla alegremente.   *She speaks happily.*

6) Adverbs come <u>after</u> the <u>verb</u>.

> Estudio tranquilamente.   *I study quietly.*

Alexa spoke happily of the time she managed to take off her skis without falling over.

Some adverbs are formed differently

1) Just like in English, there are a couple of <u>exceptions</u>.

2) You don't say 'I sing <u>goodly</u>' in English, and you can't say '<u>buenamente</u>' in Spanish either.

> bueno/a   *good* ⟶ bien   *well*
> malo/a   *bad* ⟶ mal   *badly*

> Canto bien. ⟶ *I sing well.*
> Canto mal. ⟶ *I sing badly.*

3) Even though you can use '<u>rápidamente</u>' and '<u>lentamente</u>' for '<u>quickly</u>' and '<u>slowly</u>', you can also use the <u>irregular</u> forms — '<u>deprisa</u>' (*quickly*) and '<u>despacio</u>' (*slowly*). They <u>don't</u> add '<u>-mente</u>' or <u>change their ending</u>.

> Escribes deprisa.   *You write quickly.*

> Escribes despacio.   *You write slowly.*

Just like regular adverbs, these ones come after the verb.

Make sure you're speaking Spanish maravillosamente...

Try translating these sentences into Spanish.

1. They cry noisily.   3. She speaks clearly.   5. The baby sleeps well.   7. You dance badly.
2. He lives healthily.   4. We speak intelligently.   6. I run quickly.   8. I read slowly.

Words to Describe Actions

And here's another page on adverbs. This time, it's how to form adverbs using 'con', and some handy lists of adverbs that help you say where or when something is happening.

You can also form adverbs using 'con' + noun

1) In English, you can say someone did something 'with ease' instead of saying 'easily'.

2) You can do the same in Spanish by putting 'con' with a noun.

Lo hago con facilidad. *I do it with ease / easily.*	Hablaste con arrogancia. *You spoke with arrogance / arrogantly.*	¡Con cuidado! *With care! / Carefully!*

Adverbs can tell you where something is done...

You can put these handy words into sentences to say <u>where</u> things happen.

aquí	*here*
ahí	*(just) there*
allá / allí	*(over) there*
cerca	*near*
lejos	*far away*
en / por todas partes	*everywhere*

Mi tía trabaja aquí.　　*My aunt works here.* ← *just there — ahí*
Hay gatos por todas partes.　*There are cats everywhere.*
Está muy cerca.　　　*It's very near.* ← *far away — lejos*

To say where something is, you need the verb 'estar' (p.77).

...or when it's happening

1) Use these adverbs to help you say <u>when</u> something is being done.

ahora	*now / nowadays*	antes (de)	*before*
ya	*already*	después (de)	*after(wards)*
al mismo tiempo	*at the same time*	en seguida	*straightaway*
de momento	*at the moment*	mientras tanto	*meanwhile*
de repente	*suddenly*	pronto	*soon*
de nuevo	*again*	todavía	*still, yet*

Ya tengo un reloj.
I already have a watch.

Estaré allí pronto.
I'll be there soon.

2) These ones are really useful for saying <u>how often</u> something is done.

a diario	*daily*
a menudo	*often*
a veces	*sometimes*
de vez en cuando	*from time to time*
pocas veces	*rarely, a few times*
siempre	*always*

Siempre juego al fútbol en el parque con mis amigos.
I always play football in the park with my friends.

A veces voy a la tienda.
I sometimes go to the shop.

Use loads of adverbs and start raking in the marks with ease...

Translate these sentences into Spanish using all your adverb knowledge.

1. My shoes are here.
2. I want to do it again.
3. I did it patiently. (Use 'con'.)
4. We live far away.
5. She did it straightaway.
6. He danced enthusiastically. (Use 'con'.)

Comparatives + superlatives

Words to Compare Actions

Now you've got to grips with adverbs, you can use some of the same techniques you learned on p.63 to compare how people do things.

Using adverbs to say 'more ...ly' and 'less ...ly'

Adverbial phrases like this are called comparatives.

1) To say that something is done '<u>more ...ly</u>', use '<u>más ... que</u>'.

> Eva trabaja más alegremente que Inés.   *Eva works more happily than Inés.*

2) If you want to say that something is done '<u>less ...ly</u>', use '<u>menos ... que</u>'.

> Inés trabaja menos alegremente que Eva.   *Inés works less happily than Eva.*

3) To say that someone does something '<u>as ... as</u>' someone else, use '<u>tan ... como</u>'.

> Eva trabaja tan alegremente como Inés.   *Eva works as happily as Inés.*

Using adverbs to say the 'most ...ly'

This kind of construction is called a 'superlative'.

To say someone does something '<u>the most ...ly</u>', follow this pattern.

(Make sure you remember to change '<u>el</u>' to '<u>la</u>' if the subject is <u>feminine</u>, '<u>los</u>' if it's a <u>masculine plural</u> subject, and '<u>las</u>' for a <u>feminine plural</u> subject.)

> Daniela es la que trabaja más alegremente.   *Daniela works the most happily.*
>
> Juan es el que baila menos rápidamente.   *Juan dances the least quickly.*

Watch out for irregular comparatives and superlatives

Yes, you guessed it — there are some more <u>lovely irregular forms</u>.

bien (*well*) →	mejor (*better*) →	el que mejor ... (*the one who ... the best*)
mal (*badly*) →	peor (*worse*) →	el que peor ... (*the one who ... the worst*)

> Cocino mejor que mis amigos.   *I cook better than my friends.*
>
> Escribes peor que un niño.   *You write worse than a child.*
>
> Él es el que peor juega.   *He's the one who plays the worst.*
>
> Ellas son las que mejor bailan.   *They are the ones who dance the best.*

Use adverbs and you'll be speaking Spanish the most fluently...

Have a go at using what you know about adverbs to translate these sentences.

1. Carmen eats more quickly.
2. Luis sings as well as Adela.
3. Selina drives the best.
4. I study better than my friends.
5. We walk more slowly than Rob.
6. Ed is the one who runs the worst.

Words to Say How Much

You can use quantifiers and intensifiers with other words to give more detailed descriptions.

Use quantifiers to say how many or how much

1) Just saying 'I have apples' is boring. Use <u>quantifiers</u> to say you only have <u>a few</u> apples — or <u>loads</u>.

2) Quantifiers go <u>before the noun</u>, and most <u>change their endings</u> to agree with it, just like adjectives do.

mucho	*a lot/lots of*
poco	*only a little/only a few*
un poco de	*a bit of*
demasiado	*too much/too many*
tanto	*so much/so many*
bastante	*enough*

'Un poco de' doesn't change its ending.

Tengo muchos deberes.	*I have a lot of homework.*
Tengo pocas cartas.	*I only have a few letters.*
Haces demasiado ruido.	*You make too much noise.*
Hay tanta gente.	*There are so many people.*
Tienes bastantes zapatos.	*You have enough shoes.*
Comí un poco de chocolate.	*I ate a bit of chocolate.*

3) You don't just have to use these quantifiers with nouns — you can also use them with <u>verbs</u>. When you use them with verbs, they work like <u>adverbs</u>, so they go <u>after the verb</u> and <u>don't change their endings</u>.

Hablas demasiado.	*You talk too much.*
Come mucho.	*She eats a lot.*

Use intensifiers to strengthen what you're saying

1) You can use <u>intensifiers</u> like '<u>very</u>' and '<u>quite</u>' to <u>add detail</u> to what you're saying.

2) Intensifiers go <u>before the word they're modifying</u>, but their <u>endings don't change</u> at all.

muy	*very*
poco	*not very*
demasiado	*too*
bastante	*quite*

Simón está muy feliz.	*Simón is very happy.*
Es poco cortés.	*He's not very polite.*
Habla demasiado tranquilamente.	*She speaks too quietly.*
Comes bastante bien.	*You eat quite well*

Add '-ito' or '-ísimo' to make adjectives smaller or stronger

1) You can add '<u>ito/a/os/as</u>' to the end of most adjectives to make something seem <u>smaller or cuter</u>.

El bebé está enfermito.	*The baby is poorly.*

2) Add '<u>ísimo/a/os/as</u>' to make the meaning of what you're saying <u>stronger</u>. It's as if you're adding '<u>really</u>' to the adjective — so if '<u>bueno</u>' is '<u>good</u>', then '<u>buenísimo</u>' would mean '<u>really good</u>' or '<u>wonderful</u>'.

La película es malísima.	*The film is terrible.*

That's enough of quantifiers and intensifiers for now...

Translate these sentences into Spanish.

1. There are too many cats here.
2. It's quite interesting.
3. I have lots of friends.
4. They speak too slowly.
5. There are so many beaches in Spain.
6. The book is really good.

I, You, We

Pronouns are really handy little words that save you from needing to repeat nouns all the time.

Subject and object

Before you get started on pronouns, you need to know how to find the <u>subject</u> and the <u>object</u> of a sentence.

| The <u>subject</u> of a sentence is the noun <u>doing the action</u>. | → Pau come la pera. | *Pau eats the pear.* | ← | The <u>object</u> of a sentence is the noun <u>having the action done to it</u>. |

Yo, tú, él, ella — *I, you, he, she*

1) <u>Pronouns</u> are words that <u>replace nouns</u> — like '<u>you</u>' or '<u>them</u>'. You use them to <u>avoid repeating nouns</u>.

Jessica went to the beach and she sat on the sand. ← In English, the pronoun '<u>she</u>' replaces Jessica's name. 'She' is a '<u>subject</u> pronoun' because it <u>replaces the subject</u> of the sentence — Jessica.

2) You <u>don't normally</u> include <u>subject pronouns</u> in Spanish sentences — but you <u>still</u> need to know them.

I	yo	we	nosotros/as
you (inf., sing.)	tú	you (inf., pl.)	vosotros/as
he/it	él	they (masc.)	ellos
she/it	ella	they (fem.)	ellas
you (form., sing.)	usted	you (form., pl.)	ustedes

The masculine 'they' form is also used for <u>groups</u> made up of <u>masculine and feminine</u> nouns.

There's also 'se' which means 'one'. It's used in phrases like 'se puede' (one can / you can). It uses the third person singular form of the verb. See p.87 for more impersonal verbs.

Remember there are four ways to say 'you' in Spanish — see p.7 for more.

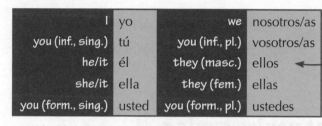

Fui a la playa y comí un helado. *I went to the beach and I ate an ice cream.*

Here, you <u>don't</u> need the pronoun '<u>yo</u>' because you can see from the first person verb forms '<u>fui</u>' and '<u>comí</u>' that the person speaking ('I') is doing the action.

You can use subject pronouns for emphasis

Although you <u>don't usually</u> need <u>subject pronouns</u> in Spanish, they help <u>emphasise</u> exactly <u>who</u> does what:

¿Qué queréis hacer el fin de semana que viene? *What would you (inf., pl.) like to do next weekend?*

Pues, yo quiero ir de compras, pero él quiere ir al cine.
Well, I want to go shopping, but he wants to go to the cinema.

You include the pronouns here to <u>emphasise</u> who wants what. They're used in Spanish in cases when <u>extra stress</u> is put on pronouns in English.

¿Quieren visitar el museo? *Do they / you (form., sing.) want to visit the museum?*

Pues, yo sí, pero ella no. *Well, I do but she doesn't.*

Remember that if you're using '<u>ustedes</u>', you need the '<u>they</u>' form of the verb.

Pronouns make your writing sound smoother — use them...

Write down the Spanish subject pronoun you'd use to replace each of these subjects.

1. Juan y Jorge
2. Anabel
3. Pedro y yo
4. Alberto y tú
5. Ramón
6. el señor Pérez y usted
7. Miranda, Alicia y Lina
8. Alberto y Tania

Me, You, Them

Now you've got to grips with subject pronouns, it's time for object pronouns — bet you didn't see that coming.

Me, te, lo — *me, you, him*

> 'Me', 'you', 'him' and 'her' are direct object pronouns. They replace the object of a sentence — the thing having an action done to it.

Use direct object pronouns when you're talking about who or what an action is done to.

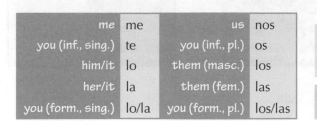

me	me	us	nos
you (inf., sing.)	te	you (inf., pl.)	os
him/it	lo	them (masc.)	los
her/it	la	them (fem.)	las
you (form., sing.)	lo/la	you (form., pl.)	los/las

The pronoun usually goes before the verb.

Ricardo lava el perro. → Ricardo lo lava.
Ricardo washes the dog. *Ricardo washes it.*

The action is done to the dog ('el perro' — masculine), so the pronoun 'it' needs to be in the masculine singular form.

Me, te, les — *to me, to you, to them*

1) If you want to talk about doing something 'to' or 'for' someone, you need an indirect object pronoun.

El perro da el cepillo a Ricardo. → El perro le da el cepillo.
The dog gives the brush to Ricardo. *The dog gives the brush to him.*

2) These pronouns are the same ones you use with the verb 'gustar' when you say you like something. This is because 'me gusta el chocolate' literally means 'chocolate is pleasing to me'.

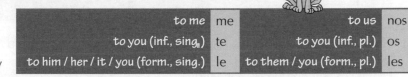

to me	me	to us	nos
to you (inf., sing.)	te	to you (inf., pl.)	os
to him / her / it / you (form., sing.)	le	to them / you (form., pl.)	les

3) If the thing you like is singular, you need 'gusta'. If it's plural, you need 'gustan'.

¿Te gusta el español? *Do you like Spanish?*
Le gustan los parques. *He likes the parks.*

Getting the order right

1) Object pronouns normally come before the verb, but they can go before or after the verb if it's an infinitive (p.75) or a present participle (p.85).

Often you need to add an accent to keep the pronunciation right.

Lo quiero ver. **OR** Quiero verlo.
I want to see it.

Le estamos hablando. **OR** Estamos hablándole.
We're talking to him.

2) With commands, the pronoun is tacked on to the end. Escríbeme, por favor. *Write to me, please.*

3) When two object pronouns come together, the indirect one comes first.

4) And if the indirect object pronoun is 'le' or 'les', it becomes 'se' when it's in front of 'lo', 'la', 'los' or 'las'.

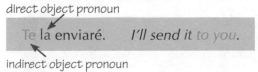

direct object pronoun
Te la enviaré. *I'll send it to you.*
indirect object pronoun

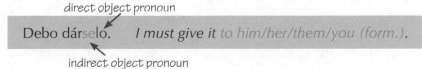

direct object pronoun
Debo dárselo. *I must give it to him/her/them/you (form.).*
indirect object pronoun

Pronouns are tricky — but if you can use them, you'll be flying...

Translate these sentences into Spanish — try to use the correct pronouns and get the order right.

1. She breaks it (the window).
2. I drink it (the milk).
3. He bought a skirt for her.
4. I send him an email.
5. I want to do it.
6. He said it to us.

More Pronouns

Pronouns can be a bit confusing — but they're really useful for adding extra detail and asking questions.

Some pronouns change after certain prepositions

Watch out — 'mí' needs an accent, but 'ti' doesn't.

1) The words for '<u>me</u>' and '<u>you</u>' (inf., sing.) become '<u>mí</u>' and '<u>ti</u>' after <u>prepositions</u> like '<u>a</u>' (*to*), '<u>para</u>' (*for*), and '<u>sobre</u>' / '<u>de</u>' (*about*).

me	mí		us	nosotros/as
you (inf., sing.)	ti		you (inf., pl.)	vosotros/as
him	él/ella		them (masc.)	ellos/as
you (form., sing.)	usted		you (form., pl.)	ustedes

No es para mí, es para él.   *It isn't for me, it's for him.*

2) '<u>With me</u>' becomes '<u>conmigo</u>' and '<u>with you</u>' becomes '<u>contigo</u>':   Está conmigo.   *He's with me.*

Que — *that, which, who*

1) '<u>Que</u>' can mean '<u>that</u>', '<u>which</u>' or '<u>who</u>' — it's a <u>relative pronoun</u>.

2) You can use it to start a <u>relative clause</u>, which is a way of <u>adding detail</u> to a sentence.

Fui a Menorca, que es una isla preciosa.   *I went to Menorca, which is a beautiful island.*
¿Dónde está el pan que compraste ayer?   *Where's the bread that you bought yesterday?*
Allí está el hombre que vive en nuestra calle.   *There's the man who lives on our road.*

3) If you're talking about an <u>idea</u> instead of an object, you need '<u>lo que</u>'.

Van a venir, lo que es maravilloso.   *They're going to come, which is wonderful.*

4) <u>After prepositions</u>, like '<u>con</u>', '<u>a</u>' and '<u>de</u>', use '<u>quien</u>' for '<u>who</u>' or '<u>el / la que</u>' or '<u>el / la cual</u>' for '<u>that / which.</u>'

el hombre con quien estoy hablando
the man with whom I'm talking

el mercado del cual compro flores
the market from which I buy flowers

If you were talking about a plural noun, you'd need to use 'con quienes' or 'de los / las cuales' instead.

Using pronouns to ask questions

Pronouns for asking questions are called 'interrogative pronouns'.

1) Normally, you can use '<u>¿Qué...</u>' to ask a question that starts with '<u>What...</u>' in English.

¿Qué te gustaría hacer?   *What would you like to do?*

If 'cuál' is being used before a noun, it needs to agree with it. Use 'cuál' for all singular nouns and 'cuáles' for all plural nouns.

2) Use '<u>¿Cuál...</u>' when you'd use '<u>Which...</u>' or '<u>Which one...</u>' in English. But remember — sometimes you need '<u>¿Cuál...</u>' when you'd actually use '<u>What...</u>' in English — see p.4.

¿Cuál es mejor?   *Which (one) is better?*

¿Cuál es tu apellido?   *What is your surname?*

3) '<u>¿Quién...</u>' means '<u>Who...</u>'. You often use '<u>¿Quién...</u>' with <u>prepositions</u>.

¿Quién es?   *Who is it?*

¿Con quién?   *With whom?*

¿De quién son?   *Whose are they?*

This page, which is very useful, will help you greatly...

Pronouns are tricky — so the best way to tackle them is by practising. Translate these sentences into Spanish.
1. My sister, who is seven, is short.
2. I went to Madrid, which is the capital of Spain.
3. What's your address?
4. Who do you live with?
5. Whose is this dog?
6. Which do you prefer?

More Pronouns

It's well worth being able to use these pronouns, so make sure you get your head around them.

El mío, el tuyo... — *mine, yours...*

'el mío', 'el tuyo', 'el nuestro' etc. are possessive pronouns.

1) Use possessive pronouns to say '<u>mine</u>' or '<u>yours</u>'.

2) Possessive pronouns <u>agree</u> in <u>gender</u> and <u>number</u> with the <u>noun</u> they're replacing.

Possessive pronoun	Masculine singular	Feminine singular	Masculine plural	Feminine plural
mine	el mío	la mía	los míos	las mías
yours (inf., sing.)	el tuyo	la tuya	los tuyos	las tuyas
his/hers/its/yours (form.)	el suyo	la suya	los suyos	las suyas
ours	el nuestro	la nuestra	los nuestros	las nuestras
yours (inf., pl.)	el vuestro	la vuestra	los vuestros	las vuestras
theirs/yours (form., pl.)	el suyo	la suya	los suyos	las suyas

¿Es tu casa?	*Is it your house?*
No, la mía es más alta.	*No, mine is taller.*

¿Es vuestro hotel?	*Is it your (inf., pl.) hotel?*
No, el nuestro está allí.	*No, ours is there.*

Algo, alguien — *something, someone*

'Algo' and 'alguien' are indefinite pronouns.

'<u>Algo</u>' means '<u>something</u>':

¿Queréis algo?	*Do you (inf., pl.) want something?*

'<u>Alguien</u>' means '<u>someone</u>':

Vi a alguien.	*I saw someone.*

When you 'see someone' in Spanish, you have to add the <u>personal 'a'</u>. See p.73.

Este, ese, aquel — *this one, that one, that one over there*

Sometimes you might see these pronouns written with an accent on the first 'e' — e.g. 'éste'.

1) <u>Demonstrative pronouns</u> are <u>the same as</u> the <u>demonstrative adjectives</u> on p.62.

2) Remember to <u>change the ending</u> to <u>agree</u> with the noun it refers back to.

Demonstrative pronoun	Masculine singular	Feminine singular	Masculine plural	Feminine plural
this/these one(s)	este	esta	estos	estas
that/those one(s)	ese	esa	esos	esas
that/those one(s) over there	aquel	aquella	aquellos	aquellas

Me gustaría este.
I'd like this one.

Prefiere esas.
She prefers those.

3) Use the <u>neuter forms</u> '<u>esto</u>', '<u>eso</u>' and '<u>aquello</u>' if you <u>don't</u> know the <u>gender</u> of the noun.

¿Qué es eso?	*What's that?*

Ahh pronouns — these will get you good marks...

Translate these sentences into Spanish, using the correct pronouns.

1. They're mine. *(cats)*
2. What's that over there?
3. This bed is bigger than that one over there.
4. This book is more interesting than that one.
5. Is it yours (inf., pl.)? *(hat)*
6. Someone's talking quietly.

Prepositions

Prepositions are sneaky little words — but you've got to learn them if you want the highest marks.

Use these words to say where something is...

> Don't forget to use 'estar' (see p.77) to say where something is.

al lado de	*next to*	bajo / debajo de	*below / under*	enfrente de	*opposite*
detrás de	*behind*	en / sobre	*on / upon*	en / dentro de	*in / into / inside*
delante de	*in front of*	encima de	*above / on top of*	al fondo de	*at the back of*
entre	*between*	contra	*against*	hacia	*towards*

A, hasta — *to*

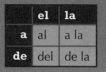

To say '<u>to</u>' in Spanish, you <u>normally</u> say '<u>a</u>'. But when '<u>to</u>' means '<u>as far as</u>', use '<u>hasta</u>'.

Va a Liverpool.	*She's going to Liverpool.*	Solo va hasta Manchester.	*He's only going to Manchester.*

En, dentro de — *in, inside*

'<u>In</u>' is just '<u>en</u>' and '<u>inside</u>' is '<u>dentro de</u>'. The verb '<u>entrar</u>' (*to go in / enter*) is normally followed by '<u>en</u>'.

En Leeds...	*In Leeds...*	dentro de la caja	*inside the box*	Entro en la tienda.	*I enter the shop.*

De — *of*

'<u>De</u>' is usually '<u>of</u>'. You can also use '<u>de</u>' to say what something's <u>made of</u>.

Es de oro.	*It's made of gold.*	al final del pasillo	*at the end of the corridor*

> You <u>can't</u> say 'de el' or 'a el' in Spanish. Instead, you <u>combine</u> '<u>a</u>' or '<u>de</u>' with the <u>definite article</u> (p.59).
>
> | | el | la |
> |---|---|---|
> | **a** | al | a la |
> | **de** | del | de la |

En, a — *at*

You can <u>normally</u> use '<u>en</u>' when you want to say '<u>at</u>'. Sometimes you need '<u>a</u>' instead...

Está en el colegio.	*He's at school.*	en casa	*at home*	a las seis	*at six o'clock*

Sobre, en — *on*

> You don't need 'on' for days of the week.

For '<u>on (top of)</u>', use '<u>sobre</u>' or '<u>en</u>'. When you mean '<u>on</u>' but not '<u>on top of</u>', use '<u>en</u>'.

Está sobre la mesa.	*It's on the table.*	Lo vi en la tele.	*I saw it on TV.*	El lunes...	*On Monday...*

De, desde, a partir de — *from*

'<u>From</u>' is normally '<u>de</u>'. Use '<u>desde</u>' when there's a <u>starting</u> and <u>ending</u> point and '<u>a partir de</u>' for dates.

Es de Kent.	*He's from Kent.*	desde Fife hasta Ayr	*from Fife to Ayr*	a partir de julio	*from July*

Learn these prepositions inside out and back to front...

Use what you know about prepositions to translate these sentences into Spanish.

1. The house is opposite the bank.
2. The train goes as far as Italy.
3. I heard it on the radio.
4. I enter the supermarket.
5. I'm from Hull, but I live in Crewe.
6. From September, I will have a job.

'Por', 'Para' and the Personal 'a'

'Por', 'para' and the personal 'a' are also prepositions, but they don't always translate easily into English.

Use 'para' to...

1) ...say <u>who</u> something is <u>for</u>.

Este dinero es para ti.   *This money is for you.*

2) ...talk about <u>destinations</u>.

el tren para Bilbao   *the train to Bilbao*

3) ...say '<u>to</u>' or '<u>in order to</u>'.

Veo la tele para descansar.   *I watch TV to relax.*

4) ...say '<u>by</u>' in <u>time phrases</u>.

para mañana   *by tomorrow*

5) ...say '<u>for</u>' in phrases like '<u>for X days</u>' when you're talking about the <u>future</u>.

Quiero el coche para un día.   *I want the car for one day.*

6) ...say '<u>in my / your opinion</u>'.

Para mí, es muy bonito.   *In my opinion, it's very pretty.*

7) ...say '<u>about to</u>'.

Según él, está para llover.   *According to him, it's about to rain.*

> '<u>Según</u>' is another <u>preposition</u>. It means '<u>according to</u>'.

Use 'por' to...

1) ...say '<u>for</u>' in phrases like '<u>for X years / months</u>' in the <u>past</u>.

Vivió allí por un año.   *He lived there for a year.*

> In certain cases, for the future you need to use 'por': Estaré en Galicia por dos años.

2) ...talk about <u>parts of the day</u> when you want to say '<u>in</u>'.

por la mañana   *in the morning*

3) ...say '<u>through</u>'.

Entré por la puerta sin hablar.   *I came through the door without speaking.*

> '<u>Sin</u>' is a <u>preposition</u> which means '<u>without</u>'.

4) ...say '<u>per</u>' or '<u>a</u>' in <u>number phrases</u>.

tres veces por día   *three times a day*

5) ...talk about <u>exchanges</u>.

Pagó dos euros por el té.   *He paid 2 euros for the tea.*

6) ...say '<u>on behalf of</u>'.

Lo hice por ti.   *I did it for you.*

7) ...say '<u>thank you</u>'.

Gracias por el pastel.   *Thanks for the cake.*

The personal 'a'

> You don't usually use the personal 'a' after 'tener' or 'ser'.

You need an <u>extra</u> '<u>a</u>' <u>before</u> the word for any <u>human being</u> or <u>pet</u> after every single <u>verb</u>.

Estoy buscando a Juan.   *I'm looking for Juan.*   **BUT**   Estoy buscando un taxi.   *I'm looking for a taxi.*

'Por' and 'para' are hard... but they're really useful to know.

Decide whether you need 'por', 'para' or 'a' in each of these sentences.

1. Esta revista es _____ ti.
2. Visito _____ mi abuelo.
3. _____ la tarde, vemos la tele.
4. Gracias _____ la carta.
5. Juego al fútbol dos veces _____ semana.
6. Lo quiero _____ el fin de semana.

Conjunctions

Conjunctions help you link your ideas together to make longer, more complex sentences.

Y — *and*

1) '<u>Y</u>' means '<u>and</u>' — you use it just like you would in English.

| Me gusta jugar al fútbol. | **AND** | Me gusta jugar al rugby. | **=** | Me gusta jugar al fútbol y al rugby. |
| *I like playing football.* | | *I like playing rugby.* | | *I like playing football and rugby.* |

2) '<u>Y</u>' changes to '<u>e</u>' <u>before</u> a word starting with '<u>i</u>' or '<u>hi</u>'.

Hablo español e inglés.   *I speak Spanish and English.*

O — *or*

1) '<u>O</u>' means '<u>or</u>'.

| Juego al fútbol los sábados. | **OR** | Juego al rugby los sábados. | **=** | Juego al fútbol o al rugby los sábados. |
| *I play football on Saturdays.* | | *I play rugby on Saturdays.* | | *I play football or rugby on Saturdays.* |

2) When '<u>o</u>' comes just <u>before</u> a word starting with '<u>o</u>' or '<u>ho</u>', it changes to '<u>u</u>'.

Cuesta siete u ocho euros.   *It costs seven or eight euros.*

Pero — *but*

1) '<u>Pero</u>' means '<u>but</u>'.

| Me gusta el fútbol. | **BUT** | No me gusta el rugby. | **=** | Me gusta el fútbol, pero no me gusta el rugby. |
| *I like football.* | | *I don't like rugby.* | | *I like football, but I don't like rugby.* |

2) When '<u>but</u>' means '<u>but rather</u>', it becomes '<u>sino</u>'.

No es español, sino francés.   *He isn't Spanish, but (rather) French.*

Porque — *because*

'<u>Porque</u>' helps you <u>give opinions</u>:   Me gusta porque es sabroso.   *I like it because it's tasty.*

> There's more about 'porque' and opinions on p.9.

Other conjunctions you need to know

cuando	*when*	así que	*so, therefore*	como	*as, since*
si	*if*	de manera que	*such that*	pues	*well, then*
sin embargo	*however*	mientras	*while*	entonces	*then*

Tiene hambre, así que va a comer.

He's hungry, so he's going to eat.

You don't want to sound like a robot, so start using conjunctions...

Translate these sentences into Spanish, deciding which conjunctions you need to use.

1. Geography is fun, but it's difficult.
2. I like history because it's easy.
3. As I'm ill, I'm staying at home.
4. I go to the park when it's hot.
5. I speak French and Italian.
6. Do you prefer blue or yellow?

Verbs in the Present Tense

There's not a lot you can do without verbs — your Spanish won't make very much sense without them.

Verbs are actions

1) A <u>verb</u> is an <u>action word</u> — for example, '<u>speak</u>', '<u>eat</u>' and '<u>live</u>'.

2) Verbs can be put into <u>different tenses</u>, such as the <u>future</u> or <u>past</u>, for example, 'Yesterday, I <u>ate</u> some cake'.

3) To use a verb, you need to know its <u>infinitive</u> — the form you find in a <u>dictionary</u>, e.g. '<u>hablar</u>' (*to speak*).

Forming the present tense

1) Most <u>regular</u> verbs in Spanish end in '<u>-ar</u>', '<u>-er</u>' or '<u>-ir</u>'. To form the <u>present tense</u> of these regular verbs, you need to find the <u>stem</u>. To do this, <u>remove</u> the <u>last two letters</u> from the <u>infinitive</u>.

Infinitive	Remove last two letters	Stem
hablar	ar	habl-

2) Then <u>add</u> the <u>endings</u> below to the <u>stem</u>.

-ar verbs

I speak	hablo	hablamos	we speak
you (inf., sing.) speak	hablas	habláis	you (inf., pl.) speak
he/she/it/you (form., sing.) speak(s)	habla	hablan	they/you (form., pl.) speak

Cantan bien. *They sing well.*

Toca el piano. *He plays the piano.*

-er verbs

I eat	como	comemos	we eat
you (inf., sing.) eat	comes	coméis	you (inf., pl.) eat
he/she/it/you (form., sing.) eat(s)	come	comen	they/you (form., pl.) eat

Bebes té. *You (inf., sing.) drink tea.*

Vendemos uvas. *We sell grapes.*

-ir verbs

I live	vivo	vivimos	we live
you (inf., sing.) live	vives	vivís	you (inf., pl.) live
he/she/it/you (form., sing.) live(s)	vive	viven	they/you (form., pl.) live

Suben la torre. *They go up the tower.*

Kevin interrumpe. *Kevin interrupts.*

When to use the present tense

For another way to say what you're doing now, see p.85.

① Use the <u>present tense</u> for actions taking place <u>now</u>.

Hablo español.   *I speak Spanish / I am speaking Spanish.*

② You also need the <u>present tense</u> for things that take place <u>regularly</u>.

Canto todos los días.   *I sing every day.*

③ Use the <u>present tense</u> with '<u>desde hace</u>' to say <u>how long</u> you've been doing something.

Toco el violín desde hace cuatro años.
I've been playing the violin for four years.

④ You can also use the <u>present tense</u> for things that are <u>about to happen</u>.

Mañana vamos al cine.   *Tomorrow we are going to the cinema.*

The present? Oh, you really shouldn't have...

Put each of the infinitives into the form given in brackets, and then translate Q8 into Spanish.

1. bailar (yo)
2. beber (nosotros)
3. nadar (vosotros)
4. correr (usted)
5. aprender (él)
6. visitar (ellos)
7. escribir (tú)
8. She has been living here for a year.

Present Tense	**Irregular Verbs in the Present Tense**

Unfortunately, not all Spanish verbs are regular — and some of the worst offenders are really common verbs...

Radical-changing verbs

These are also known as 'stem-changing verbs'.

1) A <u>radical-changing verb</u> is a verb that <u>changes its spelling</u> in the <u>present tense</u>.

2) Usually, the '<u>e</u>' in their stem changes to '<u>ie</u>', or the '<u>o</u>' or '<u>u</u>' in their stem to '<u>ue</u>'. Some <u>verbs</u> like '<u>pedir</u>' (*to order / ask for*), '<u>repetir</u>' (*to repeat*) and '<u>vestirse</u>' (*to get dressed*) change the '<u>e</u>' in their stem to '<u>i</u>'.

3) Their stem <u>changes</u> in every form apart from the '<u>we</u>' and '<u>you (inf., pl.)</u>' forms.

querer — *to want* (e to ie)

I want	quiero
you (inf., sing.) want	quieres
he/she/it/you (form., sing.) want(s)	quiere
we want	queremos
you (inf., pl.) want	queréis
they/you (form., pl.) want	quieren

These verbs also change their '<u>e</u>' to '<u>ie</u>'...

cerrar	*to close*	preferir	*to prefer*
comenzar	*to begin*	sentarse	*to sit down*
despertarse	*to wake up*	sentir(se)	*to feel*
empezar	*to begin*	tener	*to have*
pensar	*to think*	venir	*to come*

Even though their stems change, their endings are regular.

'Tener' and 'venir' have irregular first person singular forms — 'tengo' and 'vengo'.

poder — *to be able to* (o to ue)

I can	puedo
you (inf., sing.) can	puedes
he/she/it/you (form., sing.) can	puede
we can	podemos
you (inf., pl.) can	podéis
they/you (form., pl.) can	pueden

These verbs change their '<u>o</u>' or '<u>u</u>' to '<u>ue</u>'...

acostarse	*to go to bed*	encontrar	*to find*
almorzar	*to have lunch*	jugar	*to play*
costar	*to cost*	llover	*to rain*
doler	*to hurt*	morir	*to die*
dormir	*to sleep*	volver	*to return*

Kevin's perspective on life had changed — radically...

Some common irregular verbs

In Spanish, the verbs '<u>to go</u>', '<u>to give</u>', '<u>to do / make</u>' and '<u>to know</u>' are irregular.

To say you know a person, use 'conocer' instead. It also has an irregular 1st person — conozco.

ir — *to go*

<u>All</u> of the present tense forms of '<u>ir</u>' are <u>irregular</u>.

I go	voy	vamos	we go
you (inf., sing.) go	vas	vais	you (inf., pl.) go
he/she/it/you (form., sing.) go(es)	va	van	they/you (form., pl.) go

saber — *to know (something)*

I know	sé
you (inf., sing.) know	sabes
he/she/it/you (form., sing.) know(s)	sabe
we know	sabemos
you (inf., pl.) know	sabéis
they/you (form., pl.) know	saben

Only the 'I' form of 'saber' is irregular.

dar — *to give*

Only the '<u>I</u>' and '<u>you (inf., pl.)</u>' forms of '<u>dar</u>' are <u>irregular</u>.

I give	doy
you (inf., sing.) give	das
he/she/it/you (form., sing.) give(s)	da
we give	damos
you (inf., pl.) give	dais
they/you (form., pl.) give	dan

hacer — *to do*

Only the '<u>I</u>' form is <u>irregular</u>.

I do	hago	hacemos	we do
you (inf., sing.) do	haces	hacéis	you (inf., pl.) do
he/she/it/you (form., sing.) do(es)	hace	hacen	they/you (form., pl.) do

'Hacer' can also mean 'to make'.

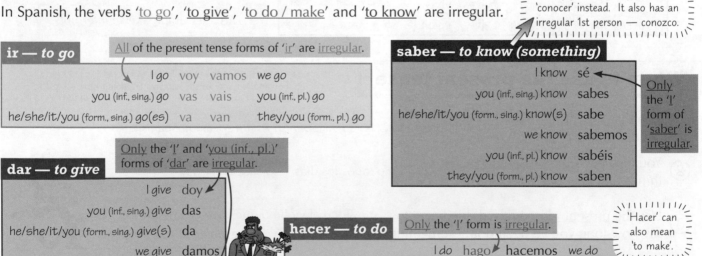

Radical verbs are just <u>so</u> out there...

Find the mistake in each of these Spanish sentences. The subject of the verb is in brackets to help you.

1. Comenza a las tres. (ella)
2. Vís a la tienda. (vosotros)
3. Quieremos leche. (nosotros)
4. Do el libro a Lola. (yo)
5. Podes conducir. (tú)
6. Sabo tu nombre. (yo)

'Ser' and 'Estar' in the Present Tense

In Spanish, there are two verbs for 'to be' — 'ser' and 'estar'. They're used differently, so it's really important to know which you need in each situation. Oh, and one more thing — they're irregular too...

Use 'ser' for permanent things

The verb 'ser' means 'to be'. It's used for permanent things. You need it to...

1) ...talk about nationalities.

> Somos galeses.   *We are Welsh.*

2) ...say someone's name or say who someone is in relation to you.

> Nerea es mi prima.   *Nerea is my cousin.*

3) ...talk about someone's job.

> Mi tío es profesor.   *My uncle is a teacher.*

4) ...describe the physical characteristics of a person or thing.

> Sois altos.   *You (inf., pl.) are tall.*

5) ...describe someone's personality.

> Son alegres.   *They are cheerful.*   Eres muy amable.   *You are very kind.*

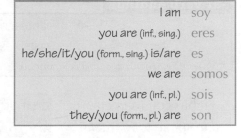

ser — to be	
I am	soy
you are (inf., sing.)	eres
he/she/it/you (form., sing.) is/are	es
we are	somos
you are (inf., pl.)	sois
they/you (form., pl.) are	son

Use 'estar' for temporary things and locations

'Estar' also means 'to be'. You use it to...

1) ...talk about things that might change in the future.

> Estoy bastante enfermo.   *I'm quite ill.*
> (But you might not be ill next week.)

> Estás muy triste hoy.   *You are very sad today.*
> (But you might not be sad tomorrow.)

Alba is positively thrilled with her parents' fashion choices.

estar — to be	
I am	estoy
you are (inf., sing.)	estás
he/she/it/you (form., sing.) is/are	está
we are	estamos
you are (inf., pl.)	estáis
they/you (form., pl.) are	están

2) ...talk about where someone or something is.

> Madrid está en España.   *Madrid is in Spain.*   Estamos en casa.   *We are at home.*

To be or to be — that's a question worth asking...

Decide whether you need 'ser' or 'estar' in each of these situations.

1. Es / Está muy hablador hoy.
2. Es / Está muy hablador en general.
3. Somos / Estamos de Escocia.
4. Soy / Estoy en Bradford.
5. Este es / está mi hermano.
6. Mi padre es / está médico.

| Preterite Tense | **Talking About the Past** |

The preterite tense ('I went' etc.) has quite a few tricky irregular forms — so pay close attention to this page.

I went — *The preterite tense*

To form the <u>preterite tense of regular verbs</u>, find the <u>stem</u> (see p.75) and then <u>add these endings</u>...

-ar verb endings

	I	-é	-amos	we
you (inf., sing.)		-aste	-asteis	you (inf., pl.)
he/she/it/you (form., sing.)		-ó	-aron	they/you (form., pl.)

-er and -ir verb endings

	I	-í	-imos	we
you (inf., sing.)		-iste	-isteis	you (inf., pl.)
he/she/it/you (form., sing.)		-ió	-ieron	they/you (form., pl.)

Habló con Marcela.
He spoke to Marcela.

<u>Don't forget the accent</u> — without it, you'd be saying 'I speak to Marcela'.

Nací en Japón.
I was born in Japan.

Bebisteis mucho.
You (inf., pl.) drank a lot.

Irregular verbs in the preterite tense

'<u>Ser</u>', '<u>ir</u>', '<u>estar</u>' and '<u>hacer</u>' are the four most important <u>irregular verbs</u> in the <u>preterite tense</u>.

ser — *to be*; ir — *to go*

I was / went	fui
you (inf., sing.) were / went	fuiste
he/she/it/you (form., sing.)	fue
was (were) / went	
we were / went	fuimos
you (inf., pl.) were / went	fuisteis
they were / went	fueron

'Ser' and 'ir' are the <u>same</u> in the <u>preterite tense</u>.

estar — *to be*

I was	estuve
you (inf., sing.) were	estuviste
he/she/it/you (form., sing.) was (were)	estuvo
we were	estuvimos
you (inf., pl.) were	estuvisteis
they/you (form., pl.) were	estuvieron

hacer — *to do / make*

I did / made	hice
you (inf., sing.) did / made	hiciste
he/she/it/you (form., sing.) did / made	hizo
we did / made	hicimos
you (inf., pl.) did / made	hicisteis
they/you (form., pl.) did / made	hicieron

Verbs ending in '<u>-car</u>' change their '<u>c</u>' to a '<u>qu</u>' in the '<u>I</u>' form of the <u>preterite tense</u> — '<u>tocar</u>' becomes '<u>toqué</u>'.
Verbs ending in '<u>-zar</u>' change their '<u>z</u>' to a '<u>c</u>' in the '<u>I</u>' form of the <u>preterite tense</u> — '<u>cruzar</u>' becomes '<u>crucé</u>'.

Even more irregular verbs

Some verbs <u>change their stem</u> in the <u>preterite tense</u>. If you know what the stem change is, you can predict what the verb is going to be in its other forms.

Infinitive	I	he/she/it
dar (*to give*)	di	dio
decir (*to say*)	dije	dijo
poder (*to be able to*)	pude	pudo
poner (*to put*)	puse	puso
querer (*to want*)	quise	quiso
tener (*to have*)	tuve	tuvo
traer (*to bring*)	traje	trajo
venir (*to come*)	vine	vino

The 'he/she/it/you (form., sing.)' form is sometimes different to what you might expect.

Le dimos un gato.   *We gave him a cat.*

Pero dijiste que te gustó.   *But you (inf., sing.) said you liked it.*

Tuvisteis una idea.   *You (inf., pl.) had an idea.*

Vinieron a mi fiesta.   *They came to my party.*

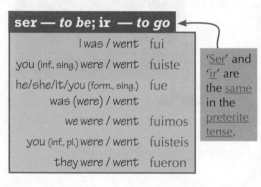
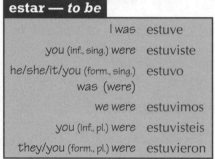
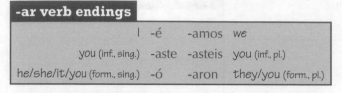

Irregular verbs are a regular pain...

Put these verbs into the preterite tense. The subject is given in brackets.

1. llorar (ellos)
2. comer (nosotros)
3. escribir (vosotros)
4. cenar (yo)
5. dar (tú)
6. poder (yo)
7. hacer (vosotros)
8. poner (usted)
9. venir (tú)
10. traer (nosotros)

Talking About the Past

The imperfect tense is used to describe things in the past. It helps you say what you 'were doing', what 'was happening' and what you 'used to do'.

I was going / I used to go — *The imperfect tense*

To form the imperfect tense, find the stem (see p.75) and then add these endings. The 'I' form and the 'he/she/it/you (form., sing.)' form look the same, so you'll have to use the context to tell which is which.

-ar verb endings

	I	-aba	-ábamos	we
you (inf., sing.)		-abas	-abais	you (inf., pl.)
he/she/it/you (form., sing.)		-aba	-aban	they/you (form., pl.)

Hablábamos por teléfono.
We were talking / used to talk on the phone.

-er and -ir verb endings

	I	-ía	-íamos	we
you (inf., sing.)		-ías	-íais	you (inf., pl.)
he/she/it/you (form., sing.)		-ía	-ían	they/you (form., pl.)

Hacía mucho deporte.
I was doing / used to do a lot of sport.

You can also say what you used to do using the imperfect tense of the verb 'soler' ('solía') and then the infinitive.

Solía viajar mucho.   *I used to travel a lot.*

Irregular verbs in the imperfect tense

1) 'Ser', 'ir' and 'ver' are the only three verbs which don't follow the pattern. 'Ser' and 'ir' are irregular...

ser — *to be*

	I was	era	éramos	we were
you (inf., sing.) were		eras	erais	you (inf., pl.) were
he/she/it/you (form., sing.) was (were)		era	eran	they/you (form., pl.) were

Mi padre era pintor.
My dad was / used to be a painter.

ir — *to go*

	I went	iba	íbamos	we went
you went (inf., sing.)		ibas	ibais	you went (inf., pl.)
he/she/it/you (form., sing.) went		iba	iban	they/you (form., pl.) went

Iba a muchos conciertos.
I went / used to go to lots of concerts.

2) ...but 'ver' is almost regular — just add the '-er' endings onto 've-', e.g. 'veía'.

Veía la tele.   *I watched / used to watch TV.*

Había — *there was / there were*

In the present tense 'hay' means 'there is' or 'there are'. The imperfect form of 'hay' is 'había', which means 'there was' or 'there were' — it stays the same, regardless of whether the noun is singular or plural.

Había un mono en el árbol.   *There was a monkey in the tree.*

Siempre había muchos niños allí.   *There were always lots of children there.*

'Hay' and 'había' come from the verb 'haber'.

Learning the imperfect — a perfect way to spend your time...

Put these verbs into the imperfect tense. The subject is given in brackets.

1. cantar (yo)
2. ser (nosotros)
3. aprender (usted)
4. decir (él)
5. volver (ustedes)
6. seguir (vosotros)
7. nadar (tú)
8. ir (ellos)

| Preterite vs. Imperfect | # Talking About the Past |

Choosing which past tense to use can be a tricky business — even for people who have been learning Spanish for ages. Here are some guidelines to get you started — read them carefully.

Use the preterite tense to...

① ...talk about a <u>single completed action</u> in the past.

> Fui al cine el jueves.   *I went to the cinema on Thursday.*

② ...talk about events that happened during a <u>set period of time</u>.

> Ayer hizo calor.   *Yesterday it was hot.*

> Remember to use '<u>hacer</u>' with nouns such as '<u>calor</u>', '<u>frío</u>', '<u>viento</u>' and '<u>sol</u>' to say '<u>it's hot</u> / <u>cold</u> / <u>windy</u> / <u>sunny</u>'. See p.38 for more <u>weather</u> vocabulary.

③ ...<u>interrupt a description of movement</u> taking place in the <u>imperfect tense</u>.

> Volvía del gimnasio cuando vi a Irene.   *I was coming back from the gym when I saw Irene.*

Use the imperfect tense to...

① ...talk about what you <u>used to do repeatedly</u> in the past.

> Iba al cine cada jueves.   *I used to go to the cinema every Thursday.*

② ...<u>describe something</u>, like the weather, in the past.

> Hacía calor, pero estaba nublado.   *It was hot, but it was cloudy.*

Camping in the rain was bad enough, but imperfect tents were unforgivable...

③ ...say <u>where you were going</u> when <u>something else happened</u>. You use the <u>imperfect</u> tense to describe the <u>background situation</u>.

> Volvía del gimnasio cuando vi a Irene.
> *I was coming back from the gym when I saw Irene.*

④ ...say <u>how long</u> something <u>had been happening for</u>. For this, you also need '<u>desde hacía</u>', which is the <u>imperfect</u> form of '<u>desde hace</u>' (see p.75).

> Leía desde hacía una hora cuando me llamó.
> *I had been reading for an hour when he called me.*

> You only need to be able to recognise this structure — you don't need to be able to use it.

Preterite or imperfect? It's a very tense business...

In each of the following sentences, choose whether you need the preterite or the imperfect tense.

1. Siempre hizo / hacía mucho viento.
2. Ayer volví / volvía de mis vacaciones.
3. ¿Fuiste / Ibas a la piscina ayer?
4. Fui / Iba al colegio cuando tuve / tenía una idea.

Talking About the Past

The perfect and pluperfect tenses allow you to say what you 'have done' or 'had done'. They're pretty easy to learn and are a useful addition to your magic bag of grammatical tricks.

Finding the past participle

1) In the sentence 'I have done', 'done' is a past participle. You need to know how to form past participles before you get started on the perfect and pluperfect tenses.

2) For '-ar' verbs, remove the 'ar' and add '-ado'.

> esperar (*to wait*) ⟶ esperado (*waited*)

3) For '-er' and '-ir' verbs, remove the 'er' or 'ir' and add '-ido'.

> comer (*to eat*) ⟶ comido (*eaten*)
> elegir (*to choose*) ⟶ elegido (*chosen*)

4) There are some irregular participles that you also need to learn...

Infinitive	Past participle	Infinitive	Past participle
abrir	abierto (*opened*)	leer	leído (*read*)
cubrir	cubierto (*covered*)	poner	puesto (*put*)
decir	dicho (*said*)	romper	roto (*broken*)
escribir	escrito (*written*)	ver	visto (*seen*)
hacer	hecho (*done / made*)	volver	vuelto (*returned*)

In these tenses, the participle stays the same — you don't need to make it feminine or plural.

He hecho — *I have done*

'I have done' is the perfect tense.

To say what you 'have done', you need the present tense of the verb 'haber' and the past participle.

haber — *to have...*

I have...	he	hemos	we have...
you (inf., sing.) have...	has	habéis	you (inf., pl.) have...
he/she/it has... you (form., sing.) have...	ha	han	they have... you (form., pl.) have...

Han jugado al tenis. *They have played tennis.*
¡Ha roto la botella! *He has broken the bottle!*

Me gustaría ir a Roma porque nunca he estado allí. *I'd like to go to Rome because I've never been there.*

Había hecho — *I had done*

'I had done' is the pluperfect tense.

To say what you 'had done', you need the imperfect tense of the verb 'haber' and the past participle.

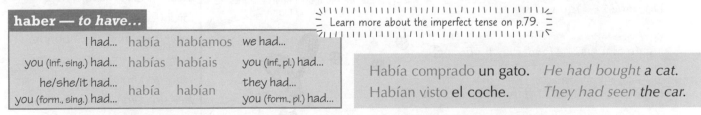

haber — *to have...*

Learn more about the imperfect tense on p.79.

I had...	había	habíamos	we had...
you (inf., sing.) had...	habías	habíais	you (inf., pl.) had...
he/she/it had... you (form., sing.) had...	había	habían	they had... you (form., pl.) had...

Había comprado un gato. *He had bought a cat.*
Habían visto el coche. *They had seen the car.*

No pude ir porque no había hecho mis deberes. *I couldn't go because I hadn't done my homework.*

If only I had learned my past participles...

Translate these sentences into Spanish using the perfect and pluperfect tenses.

1. They had sung.
2. He has travelled.
3. You have (inf., pl.) learned.
4. You have (form., sing.) seen.
5. I had drunk.
6. We had finished.
7. She has followed.
8. You have (inf., sing.) lived.

Talking About the Future

You'll need to talk about things that are going to happen at some point in the future.
There are two ways you can do it — and the first one's a piece of cake...

I'm going to... — *The immediate future*

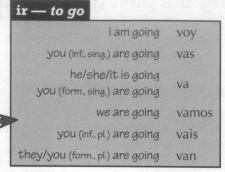

ir — *to go*

I am going	voy
you (inf. sing.) are going	vas
he/she/it is going / you (form., sing.) are going	va
we are going	vamos
you (inf., pl.) are going	vais
they/you (form., pl.) are going	van

1) The <u>immediate future</u> tense can be used to talk about something that's <u>about to happen</u>, as well as something <u>further</u> on in the future.

2) To form the immediate future, take the <u>present tense</u> of '<u>ir</u>' (*to go*) that goes with the person you're talking about.

3) Then, add '<u>a</u>' and a verb in the <u>infinitive</u>.

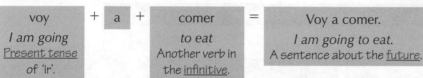

voy	+	a	+	comer	=	Voy a comer.
I am going <u>Present tense</u> of 'ir'.				*to eat* Another verb in the <u>infinitive</u>.		*I am going to eat.* A sentence about the <u>future</u>.

Susana va a leer una revista.   *Susana is going to read a magazine.*

El sábado, vamos a ir a Francia.   *On Saturday, we are going to go to France.*

Put in phrases to say when you're going to do something (p.2-3).

Just a little light reading...

I will... — *The proper future tense*

1) Use the proper <u>future tense</u> to say what will happen.

2) To form it, take the '<u>future stem</u>' of the verb —for most verbs, this is the <u>infinitive</u>.

3) Add the <u>ending</u> that matches the person you're talking about (the endings are the <u>same</u> for <u>all verbs</u>).

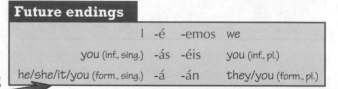

Future endings

I	-é	-emos	we
you (inf., sing.)	-ás	-éis	you (inf., pl.)
he/she/it/you (form., sing.)	-á	-án	they/you (form., pl.)

hablar	+	é	=	hablaré
infinitive		*future ending*		*I will talk.*

Dormirás.   *You will sleep.*

Jugaré al tenis.   *I will play tennis.*

Cogerá el autobús.   *He will take the bus.*

Venderemos el perro.   *We will sell the dog.*

There are a few verbs that have a special future stem, so you just have to learn them off by heart. These are the most important ones.

I will win this match...

Infinitive	'yo' form
decir (*to say*)	diré
haber (*to have...*)	habré
hacer (*to do / make*)	haré
tener (*to have*)	tendré
poner (*to put*)	pondré
querer (*to want*)	querré
saber (*to know*)	sabré
venir (*to come*)	vendré
salir (*to go out*)	saldré
poder (*to be able to*)	podré

Predicting the future might be difficult, but talking about it isn't...

Put these present tense verbs into the immediate and proper future tenses, keeping the subject the same.

1. como
2. tenemos
3. baila
4. doy
5. ponen
6. jugáis
7. puedes
8. canta
9. queremos
10. vivís

Would, Could and Should

Now it's time to talk about what could or would happen in the future.

Future stem + imperfect -er / -ir endings — *The conditional*

1) The conditional tense can be used for saying 'would'. It uses the same stems as the proper future tense (see p.82) and adds these endings:

Conditional endings

I	-ía
you (inf., sing.)	-ías
he/she/it/you (form., sing.)	-ía
we	-íamos
you (inf., pl.)	-íais
they/you (form., pl.)	-ían

comer	+	comía	=	comería
to eat		*I was eating.*		*I would eat.*
This is the infinitive. Not all verbs use the same future stem though (see p.82).		This is the -er / -ir ending of the imperfect tense.		A sentence in the conditional.

Podría ayudarme?   *Could you (form., sing) help me?*

Debería hacer mis deberes.   *I should do my homework.*

> Using 'poder' (to be able to) in the conditional lets you say 'could', and 'deber' (to have to) helps you form sentences with 'should'.

2) You can combine the conditional with other tenses to make more complicated sentences:

Bailaría, pero me duelen los pies.   *I would dance, but my feet hurt.*

Les gustaría ir a la playa, sin embargo no pueden ir porque está lloviendo.
They would like to go to the beach, however they can't go because it's raining.

> For more on conjunctions, check out p.74.

3) If you want to seriously wow the examiners, use the conditional tense of 'haber' (*to have...*) with the past participle (see p.81) to mean 'would have...'.

Habría comprado un libro, pero no tengo dinero.   *I would have bought a book, but I have no money.*

Quisiera — *I would like*

Two really common verbs sometimes get replaced in the conditional by a different form.

1) The conditional form of 'querer' (*to want*) is often replaced by 'quisiera' — it means '*I would like*'.

Quisiera un coche.   *I would like a car.*   Quisiera una manzana.   *I would like an apple.*

2) You can use 'quisiera' in polite requests.

Quisiera reservar una mesa para tres personas.   *I would like to reserve a table for three.*

3) The conditional of 'haber' (*to have...*) can also be replaced by 'hubiera'.

Hubiera venido antes.   *I would have come earlier.*

> 'Quisiera' and 'hubiera' are in the imperfect subjunctive. See p.89 for more.

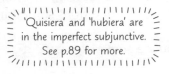

You can move on to the next topic, on one condition...

Write these verbs in the conditional. The subject has been given to you in brackets.

1. ir (tú)	3. venir (nosotros)	5. partir (yo)	7. hablar (usted)
2. cantar (él)	4. decir (vosotros)	6. salir (ellos)	8. tener (nosotros)

Reflexive Verbs

Sometimes you'll have to talk about things you do to yourself — like 'washing yourself' or 'getting yourself up' in the morning. It sounds weird in English, but in Spanish they do it all the time.

Me, te, se... — *Reflexive pronouns*

1) '<u>Se</u>' means '<u>oneself</u>'. Here are all the different ways to say 'self':

myself	me	ourselves	nos
yourself (inf., sing.)	te	yourselves (inf., pl.)	os
himself/herself/oneself		themselves, each other	
yourself (form., sing.)	se	yourselves (form., pl.)	se

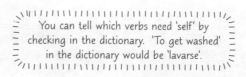
You can tell which verbs need 'self' by checking in the dictionary. 'To get washed' in the dictionary would be 'lavarse'.

2) Reflexive verbs follow a straightforward pattern, e.g. '<u>lavarse</u>' = to get washed (literally '<u>to wash oneself</u>'). The <u>reflexive pronoun</u> usually just goes in <u>front</u> of the normal <u>verb</u>.

I get washed	me lavo	we get washed	nos lavamos
you (inf., sing.) get washed	te lavas	you (inf., pl.) get washed	os laváis
he/she/it gets washed		they get washed	
you (form., sing.) get washed	se lava	you (form., pl.) get washed	se lavan

I hope that's p.m...

¿Te sientes mal?	*Do you feel ill?*

No me despierto temprano.	*I don't wake up early.*

3) There are lots of these verbs, but here are the ones you really <u>should know</u>:

'acostarse', 'sentirse', 'despertarse' and 'vestirse' are all radical-changing verbs (see p.76).

acostarse	*to go to bed*	sentirse	*to feel*	despertarse	*to wake up*	vestirse	*to get dressed*
levantarse	*to get up*	llamarse	*to be called*	irse	*to go away*	ponerse	*to put on*

Putting reflexive verbs in the perfect tense

When you want to use reflexive verbs in the <u>perfect tense</u>, put the <u>reflexive pronoun</u> (e.g. 'me', 'se') in front of the <u>verb</u> as usual:

Me		he puesto		Me he puesto **el sombrero.**
Stick the reflexive pronoun at the start.	+	Then put the whole of the perfect tense verb (see p.81).	=	*I've put on my hat.*

Use 'se' to make impersonal phrases

The reflexive pronoun '<u>se</u>' is often used in front of a verb that's not reflexive to make it <u>impersonal</u>. It's like saying '<u>one does something</u>' in English. The verb has to be in the '<u>he / she / it</u>' form.

¿Se puede comer afuera?	*Can one eat outside?*

For more about impersonal verbs, turn to p.87.

Just me, <u>myself</u> and I revising reflexive verbs...

Write these reflexive verbs in the present and perfect tenses. The subject has been given to you in brackets.

1. llamarse (yo)
2. levantarse (ellos)
3. lavarse (él)
4. acostarse (tú)
5. sentirse (nosotros)
6. irse (vosotros)
7. vestirse (usted)
8. despertarse (tú)

Verbs with '-ing' and 'Just Done'

The continuous tenses are great if you want to specify that something is ongoing at a particular moment.

Use the present continuous for something happening right now

1) <u>Most</u> of the time you'd translate phrases such as 'I am doing' and 'I was doing' with <u>normal tenses</u> — those two would be 'hago' (present tense), and 'hacía' (imperfect tense).

2) If you want <u>to stress</u> that something <u>is happening</u> at the moment, use the <u>present continuous</u>.

> Estoy almorzando.   *I'm having lunch.*

3) To form the present continuous, you need the correct part of '<u>estar</u>' (*to be*) in the <u>present</u> tense...

estar — *to be*

I am	estoy
you (inf., sing.) are	estás
he/she/it is you (form., sing.) are	está
we are	estamos
you (inf., pl.) are	estáis
they / you (form., pl.) are	están

4) ...and the '<u>-ing</u>' part — also called the <u>present participle</u> or <u>gerund</u>.

5) It's made up of the <u>stem</u> of the verb (p.75), plus the correct <u>ending</u>.

     a) if it's an -<u>ar</u> verb, add '-<u>ando</u>'.

> estoy   +   hablar   +   -ando   =   estoy hablando
> *present of 'estar'   'hablar' stem   -ar ending   I am speaking*

     b) if it's an -<u>er</u> or -<u>ir</u> verb, add '-<u>iendo</u>'.

> estás   +   comer   +   -iendo   =   estás comiendo
> *present of 'estar'   'comer' stem   -er ending   you (inf., sing.) are eating*

6) There are only a few <u>irregular</u> ones you need to <u>know</u>:

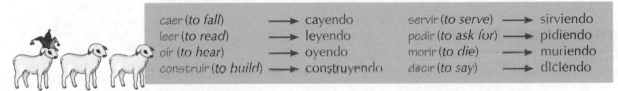

caer (*to fall*)	→	cayendo	servir (*to serve*) → sirviendo
leer (*to read*)	→	leyendo	pedir (*to ask for*) → pidiendo
oír (*to hear*)	→	oyendo	morir (*to die*) → muriendo
construir (*to build*)	→	construyendo	decir (*to say*) → diciendo

The imperfect continuous is for saying what was happening

1) If you want <u>to stress</u> that something <u>was happening</u> in the past, use the <u>imperfect continuous</u>.

2) The imperfect continuous is <u>similar</u> to the present continuous, except '<u>estar</u>' has to be in the <u>imperfect</u> tense.

> Estaba durmiendo cuando sonó el teléfono.
> *He / She was sleeping when the telephone rang.*

> The <u>preterite</u> tense is used here to show that a <u>sudden</u> action — the telephone ringing — <u>interrupted</u> an <u>ongoing</u> action in the <u>imperfect continuous</u> — i.e. the person sleeping.

'Acabar de'— *to say that something's just happened*

> 'Acabar' is a regular -ar verb.

To say what's <u>just</u> happened, use the present tense of '<u>acabar</u>', followed by '<u>de</u>' and a verb in the <u>infinitive</u>.

> Acabo de **ducharme**.   *I have just taken a shower.*   Acaba de **salir**.   *She has just left.*

Learning, learning and more learning...

Put these verbs in the present continuous, the imperfect continuous and the 'acabar de' forms.

1. caer (él)	**3.** saltar (ella)	**5.** correr (vosotros)	**7.** dar (tú)	**9.** servir (ustedes)
2. abrir (tú)	**4.** decir (ellos)	**6.** seguir (nosotros)	**8.** leer (yo)	**10.** bailar (nosotros)

Negatives	**Negative Forms**

No, I'm not going to write anything here about negatives. Nothing at all... except that they're pretty useful.

'No' in front of the verb means 'not'

1) To change a sentence to mean the <u>opposite</u> in Spanish, you have to put '<u>no</u>' in front of the <u>action word</u>:

Soy profesor.	*I'm a teacher.*	→	No soy profesor.	*I'm not a teacher.*

Hablo español.	*I speak Spanish.*	→	No hablo español.	*I don't speak Spanish.*

2) You can do the <u>same</u> with <u>all of the tenses</u> — look at these examples:

No vas a leer el libro.	*You're not going to read the book.*	No fui al parque.	*I didn't go to the park.*

Sometimes you have to say 'no' twice...

1) 'No' in Spanish means both '<u>no</u>' and '<u>not</u>'.

2) This means that if you're answering a <u>question</u>, you may need to say 'no' <u>twice</u>:

No, no quiero sopa, gracias.	*No, I don't want soup, thanks.*

No, Juan no veía la tele.	*No, Juan wasn't watching TV.*

He wasn't remotely interested in any of the programmes.

Even more negatives...

There are more negatives you need to <u>understand</u> — for top marks you should use them too.

ya no	*not any more*
no ... nadie	*not anybody (nobody)*
no ... nunca / jamás	*not ever (never)*
no ... nada	*not anything (nothing)*
no ... ni ... ni	*neither ... nor*
no ... ningún / ninguna	*none / not one / not a single (before noun)*
no .. ninguno / ninguna	*none / not one / not a single one (to replace noun)*

Ya no voy a York.	*I don't go to York any more.*

No hay nadie aquí.	*There isn't anybody here. / There's nobody here.*

Julia no va nunca al cine.	*Julia never goes to the cinema.*

No hay nada.	*There isn't anything. / There's nothing.*

Sam y Clara no van ni a Londres ni a Madrid.	*Sam and Clara go to neither London nor Madrid.*

No hay ningún plátano.	*There is not a single banana.*

No hay ninguna pera.	*There is not a single pear.*

Jo no tiene ninguno/a.	*Jo doesn't have a single one.*

p.61 has more information on 'ningún'.

On a positive note, that's the negatives finished...

Translate these sentences using negative forms.

1. I didn't go to the cinema.
2. We don't go to the gym any more.
3. You (tú) go to neither Oslo nor Faro.
4. Sally doesn't have a single apple.
5. There's nothing here.
6. There's nobody in the car.

Section 11 — Grammar

The Passive and Impersonal Verbs

Impersonal verbs and the passive come up occasionally, so it's important that you know a bit about them.

Ser + past participle — *The passive voice*

You don't need to use the passive, but you do need to be able to recognise it.

1) In an <u>active</u> sentence, the <u>subject does</u> something.   Lavé la taza.   *I washed the cup.*

2) In the <u>passive</u> voice, something is <u>done to</u> the <u>subject</u>.   La taza fue lavada.   *The cup was washed.*

3) This means you can say something is <u>happening</u> without always saying <u>who</u> is doing it.

4) The passive is formed using '<u>ser</u>' (*to be*) and the <u>past participle</u> (see p.81).

fueron	+	limpiado	=	Las mesas fueron limpiadas.
they were		*cleaned*		*The tables were cleaned.*
This is the <u>preterite tense</u> of 'ser' (see p.78). This changes depending on the tense and subject.		<u>past participle</u> of the verb '<u>limpiar</u>'		A sentence in the <u>passive</u> voice.

In the passive, the past participle must <u>always</u> match the <u>gender</u> and <u>number</u> of the <u>object</u> that you're talking about. Here 'limpiadas' is used because 'las mesas' are <u>feminine</u> and <u>plural</u>.

5) If you want to add <u>someone</u> or <u>something</u> doing the action, add '<u>por</u>' (*by*) and <u>who / what</u> did it.

El libro será leído por Jo.   *The book will be read by Jo.*   Fue escrito por Jordi.   *It was written by Jordi.*

Se + 3rd person — *Impersonal verbs*

1) You can turn <u>any</u> Spanish verb into an <u>impersonal</u> <u>verb</u> (e.g. '<u>one does</u>' rather than '*I do*') by using '<u>se</u>' and the '<u>he / she / it</u>' form of the verb:

¿Se necesita un libro?   *Does one need a book?*   ¿Se habla francés aquí?   *Does one speak French here?*

2) If there's a <u>subject</u> in the sentence, use the <u>singular</u> for a single subject, and the <u>plural</u> for plural subjects:

El arroz se cocina durante quince minutos.   *The rice is cooked for fifteen minutes.*

Las puertas se abren a las nueve.   *The doors are opened at nine.*

Some more important impersonal verbs...

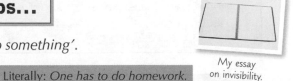

My essay on invisibility.

1) '<u>Hay que</u>' is an impersonal way of saying that '<u>one has to</u> do something'.

Hay que hacer los deberes.   *Homework has to be done.* ← Literally: *One has to do homework.*

2) '<u>Parece que</u>' means '*it seems that*':   Parece que todo ha cambiado.   *It seems that everything has changed.*

3) <u>Weather</u> verbs are <u>always impersonal</u> — they're written in the '<u>he / she / it</u>' form of the verb.

Llueve.   *It rains.*   Está nevando.   *It's snowing.*   Truena.   *It thunders.*

Tronar (to thunder) is a radical-changing verb.

One has to learn this — it's nothing personal...

A) *Decide which of these 4 sentences are in the passive voice.*
1. Comimos la sopa.   3. La mesa es puesta.
2. El poema fue escrito.   4. Cierras la puerta.

B) *Complete using the impersonal form.*
1. .... la bufanda. (comprar)
2. .... los postres. (comer)

Subjunctive

The Subjunctive

Oh yes, you're in for a treat — it's time to learn about the Spanish subjunctive...

Forming the present subjunctive

1) Sometimes, the <u>present subjunctive</u> is needed <u>instead</u> of the <u>normal present</u> tense.

2) To <u>form</u> the subjunctive, use the same <u>stem</u> as the 'I' form of the normal <u>present tense</u>.

3) For <u>-ar</u> verbs, add the -er present tense <u>endings</u>. For <u>-er</u> or <u>-ir</u> verbs, add the <u>-ar endings</u>.

infinitive	hablar	comer	vivir
'yo form'	**hablo**	**como**	**vivo**
I	hable	coma	viva
you (inf., sing.)	hables	comas	vivas
he/she/it/you (form., sing.)	hable	coma	viva
we	hablemos	comamos	vivamos
you (inf., pl.)	habléis	comáis	viváis
they/you (form., pl.)	hablen	coman	vivan

Irregular verbs in the present subjunctive

1) Some verbs are <u>irregular</u> in the 'I' form of the <u>present</u> tense, so the <u>subjunctive</u> has to <u>match</u> this.

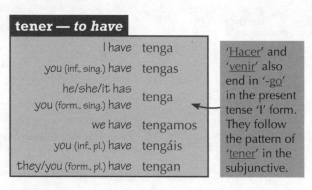

tener — *to have*	
I have	tenga
you (inf., sing.) have	tengas
he/she/it has you (form., sing.) have	tenga
we have	tengamos
you (inf., pl.) have	tengáis
they/you (form., pl.) have	tengan

'Hacer' and 'venir' also end in '-go' in the present tense 'I' form. They follow the pattern of 'tener' in the subjunctive.

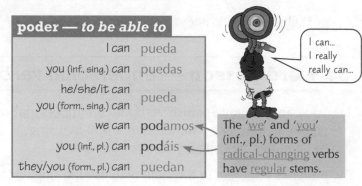

poder — *to be able to*	
I can	pueda
you (inf., sing.) can	puedas
he/she/it can you (form., sing.) can	pueda
we can	podamos
you (inf., pl.) can	podáis
they/you (form., pl.) can	puedan

I can... I really really can...

The 'we' and 'you' (inf., pl.) forms of radical-changing verbs have regular stems.

2) But <u>some verbs</u> are completely <u>irregular</u> in the <u>subjunctive</u>. Here are some of them:

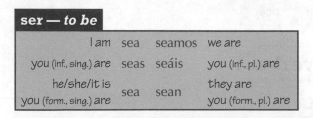

ser — *to be*			
I am	sea	seamos	we are
you (inf., sing.) are	seas	seáis	you (inf., pl.) are
he/she/it is you (form., sing.) are	sea	sean	they are you (form., pl.) are

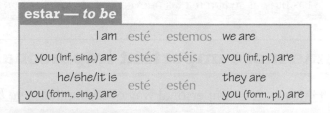

estar — *to be*			
I am	esté	estemos	we are
you (inf., sing.) are	estés	estéis	you (inf., pl.) are
he/she/it is you (form., sing.) are	esté	estén	they are you (form., pl.) are

ir — *to go*			
I go	vaya	vayamos	we go
you (inf., sing.) go	vayas	vayáis	you (inf., pl.) go
he/she/it goes you (form., sing.) go	vaya	vayan	they go you (form., pl.) go

dar — *to give*			
I give	dé	demos	we give
you (inf., sing.) give	des	deis	you (inf., pl.) give
he/she/it gives you (form., sing.) give	dé	den	they give you (form., pl.) give

I want you to revise the subjunctive...

Write these verbs in the present subjunctive. The subject has been given to you in brackets.

1. saltar (tú)　　**3.** limpiar (nosotros)　　**5.** venir (él)　　**7.** poder (ustedes)

2. escuchar (yo)　　**4.** abrir (ellos)　　**6.** hacer (nosotros)　　**8.** tener (vosotros)

The Subjunctive

Now it's time to find out when you need to use the subjunctive. It's a tricky old page so take your time.

Use the present subjunctive...

(1) ...to get <u>someone else</u> to do something:

> Ana quiere que lavemos los platos. *Ana wants us to wash the dishes.*

(2) ...to express a <u>wish</u> or <u>desire</u>:

> Espero que haya fresas en el supermercado. *I hope that there are strawberries in the supermarket.*

(3) ...after expressing an <u>emotion</u> or <u>opinion</u>:

> Es importante que estudiéis. *It's important that you (inf., pl.) study.*

(4) ...to say that something's <u>unlikely</u> to happen:

> No creo que vaya a venir. *I don't believe he's going to come.*

'sepa' is from the verb 'saber' (to know). It's also irregular in the subjunctive — its stem is 'sep'.

(5) ...when there's a <u>requirement</u>:

> Necesito a alguien que sepa cocinar. *I need someone who knows how to cook.*

Between cooking and the subjunctive, these guys had a lot on their plates.

(6) ...after '<u>cuando</u>' ('*when*'), '<u>antes de que</u>' ('*before*') and '<u>aunque</u>' ('*even if*') when talking about the future:

> Vamos al teatro cuando llegue Marta. *We're going to the theatre when Marta arrives.*

(7) ...after '<u>para que</u>' ('*so that*') to express purpose:

> Van a la tienda para que pueda comprar leche. *They're going to the shop so that he can buy milk.*

If I *were* to go to Spain...

1) The <u>imperfect subjunctive</u> is like the '<u>were</u>' in '*if I <u>were</u> to go to Spain*'. You <u>don't</u> need to use it, but you'll need to <u>recognise</u> it.

2) '<u>Quisiera</u>' ('*I would like*') is a <u>common example</u> of the imperfect subjunctive. See p.83 for more about using it in <u>polite requests</u>.

	hablar	comer	vivir
I	hablara	comiera	viviera
you (inf., sing.)	hablaras	comieras	vivieras
he/she/it/you (form., sing.)	hablara	comiera	viviera
we	habláramos	comiéramos	viviéramos
you (inf., pl.)	hablarais	comierais	vivierais
they/you (form., pl.)	hablaran	comieran	vivieran

If I were in charge, there would be no exams...

Decide which sentences use the present subjunctive and which use the imperfect subjunctive.

1. Quiere que le des el abrigo.
2. Si tuviera mucho dinero, compraría un coche.
3. Vamos a hacerlo cuando tengamos tiempo.
4. Mi madre pido que mi padre sacara la basura.

Imperative	Giving Orders

Learn what's on this page and you'll be giving out orders in no time...

Informal commands

1) To form a <u>singular informal</u> command, take the 'tú' part of the <u>present tense</u> verb and <u>take off</u> the '<u>s</u>'.

escribe<u>s</u> *you write* ➡ ¡Escribe! *Write!*   escucha<u>s</u> *you listen* ➡ ¡Escucha! *Listen!*

2) With commands, <u>pronouns</u> (e.g. *me, them, it*) are placed at the <u>end</u> of the word and you need to <u>add</u> an <u>accent</u> to show where the <u>stress</u> is.

¡Cómelo!   *Eat it!*

3) To tell <u>two or more people</u> what to do in an <u>informal</u> way, take the <u>infinitive</u> and <u>change</u> the final '<u>r</u>' to a '<u>d</u>'.

hablar (*to speak*) ➡ ¡Hablad! *Speak!*

leer (*to read*) ➡ ¡Leed! *Read!*

salir (*to go out*) ➡ ¡Salid! *Go out!*

There are a few common irregular imperatives.

Infinitive	Informal Singular
decir (*to say*)	¡Di!
hacer (*to do / make*)	¡Haz!
ir (*to go*)	¡Ve!
poner (*to put*)	¡Pon!
salir (*to go out*)	¡Sal!
ser (*to be*)	¡Sé!
tener (*to have*)	¡Ten!
venir (*to come*)	¡Ven!

Formal commands

1) To <u>politely</u> tell someone what to do, use the <u>formal 'you'</u> form of the <u>present subjunctive</u>.

¡Hable!   *Speak!*

For a reminder of the present subjunctive, head back to p.88.

Siga todo recto.   *Continue straight on.*

Infinitive	Present Subjunctive
dar (*to give*)	dé
haber (*to have...*)	haya
ir (*to go*)	vaya
saber (*to know*)	sepa
ser (*to be*)	sea

2) As always, there are some <u>irregular forms</u> that you just need to <u>learn</u>.

3) When politely telling <u>more than one</u> person what to do, use the <u>formal plural</u> of the <u>subjunctive</u>.

¡Entren!   *Enter!*

Cojan la primera calle a la derecha.   *Take the first street on the right.*

Making commands negative

1) To tell someone <u>not</u> to do something, <u>always</u> use the <u>subjunctive</u>.

¡No escuches!   *Don't listen!*

2) Watch out — any <u>pronouns</u> have to go before the verb:

¡Tócalo!   *Touch it!* ➡ ¡No lo toques!   *Don't touch it!*

Do these exercises... go on...

Write these verbs as positive and negative commands. The type of command is in brackets.

1. cantar (inf., sing.)   **3.** tener (inf., sing.)   **5.** abrir (inf., pl.)   **7.** ser (form., sing.)

2. bailar (form., pl.)   **4.** dar (form., sing.)   **6.** venir (inf., pl.)   **8.** ir (form., pl.)

The Listening Exam

Ah. Your reward for conquering all that grammar is a section about those pesky exams... Sorry about that. But there is some good news — these pages are crammed full of advice to help you tackle them head on.

There are four exams for GCSE Spanish

1) Your AQA Spanish GCSE is assessed by four separate exams — Listening, Speaking, Reading and Writing.

2) Each exam is worth 25% of your final mark. You'll get a grade between 1 and 9 (with 9 being the highest).

3) You won't sit all of the papers at the same time — you'll probably have your speaking exam a couple of weeks before the rest of your exams.

The Listening Exam has two sections

1) For the listening paper, you'll listen to various recordings of people speaking in Spanish and answer questions on what you've heard.

If you're sitting foundation tier papers, the format of your exams will be slightly different, but this advice will still be useful.

2) The paper is 45 minutes long (including 5 minutes reading time) and is split into Section A and Section B.

3) Section A is the longer section — the questions are in English, and you'll write your answers in English. Section B is shorter, but the questions are in Spanish and your answers need to be, too.

Read through the paper carefully at the start of the test

1) Before the recordings begin, you'll be given five minutes to read through the paper.

2) Use this time to read each question carefully. Some are multiple choice, and others require you to write some short answers — make sure you know what each one is asking you to do.

3) In particular, look at the questions in Section B, which are written in Spanish. Try to work out what the questions mean. There's a list of exam-style Spanish question words and phrases on the inside front cover of this book to help you prepare for this.

Miguel read 'whole model' instead of 'role-model' — it went downhill from there.

4) Reading the question titles, and the questions themselves, will give you a good idea of the topics you'll be asked about. This should help you predict what to listen out for.

5) You can write on the exam paper, so scribble down anything that might be useful.

Make notes while listening to the recordings

1) You'll hear each audio track twice, and then there'll be a pause for you to write down your answer.

2) While you're listening, it's a good idea to jot down a few details — e.g. dates, times, names or key words. But make sure you keep listening while you're writing down any notes.

Listen to the speaker's tone, too — this will hint at their mood, e.g. angry or excited.

3) Listen right to the end, even if you think you've got the answer — sometimes the person will change their mind or add an important detail at the end.

4) Don't worry if you can't understand every word that's being said — just listen carefully both times and try to pick out the vocabulary you need to answer the question.

Don't worry, I'm all ears...

If you've heard a track twice, and you're still not sure of the answer, scribble one down anyway — you never know, it might be the right one. You may as well write something sensible just in case — it's worth a shot.

The Speaking Exam

The Speaking Exam can seem daunting, but remember — no one is trying to catch you out, so try to stay calm.

There are three parts to the Speaking Exam

> During your preparation time, you can make notes to take in with you for the first two tasks. You can't keep the notes for the general conversation.

1) Your speaking exam will be conducted and recorded by your teacher.

2) The exam is in three parts. Before you start, you'll get 12 minutes to prepare for the first two sections:

① **Role-play (2 min.)**	② **Photo Card (3 min.)**	③ **Conversation (5-7 min.)**
You'll get a card with a scenario on it. It'll have five bullet points — three will be notes on what to say, in Spanish. The '!' means you'll be asked an unknown question, and '?' shows you have to ask a question about the words next to it. See p.5 for an example.	Before the exam, you'll receive a photo and three questions relating to it (look at the example on p.15). Your teacher will ask you the three questions that are on the photo card, as well as two questions you haven't seen.	You and your teacher will have a conversation. The conversation will be based on a theme that you've chosen, and the theme that hasn't been covered on the photo card. You'll have to ask your teacher at least one question.

3) The role-play card will tell you to use 'tú' or 'usted', but otherwise, use 'usted' to talk to your teacher.

Try to be imaginative with your answers

You need to find ways to show off the full extent of your Spanish knowledge. You should try to:

1) Use a range of tenses — e.g. for a question on daily routine, think of when something different happens.

Pero mañana será diferente porque jugaré al tenis después del instituto.	*But tomorrow it will be different because I will play tennis after school.*

> If you can't remember a word, just say something suitable that you do know instead, e.g. swap 'tennis' for 'hockey', or 'nephew' for 'sister'.

2) Talk about other people, not just yourself — it's fine to make people up if that helps.

Me gusta el rugby, pero mi sobrino lo odia.	*I like rugby, but my nephew hates it.*

3) Give loads of opinions and reasons for your opinions.

En mi opinión, debemos reciclar más porque producimos demasiada basura.	*In my opinion, we must recycle more because we produce too much rubbish.*

If you're really struggling, ask for help in Spanish

1) If you get really stuck trying to think of a word or phrase, you can ask for help — as long as it's in Spanish.

2) For example, if you can't remember how to say 'homework' in Spanish, ask your teacher. You won't get any marks for vocabulary your teacher's given you though.

¿Cómo se dice 'homework' en español?	*How do you say 'homework' in Spanish?*

3) If you don't hear something clearly, just ask:

¿Puede repetir, por favor?	*Can you repeat, please?*

> You could also ask this if you're desperately in need of time to think of an answer.

Don't speak too soon... wait for the teacher to tell you to start...

Given that you're only human, you're bound to have a few slip-ups in the speaking exam. Don't panic, it's completely natural. What's important is how you deal with a mistake — just correct yourself and move on.

The Reading Exam

After all that listening and speaking, the reading exam offers some nice peace and quiet. Apart from the voice inside your head that screams "WHAT ON EARTH DOES THAT WORD MEAN?!" (Or maybe that's just me...)

Read the questions and texts carefully

1) The higher tier reading paper is 1 hour long, and has three sections.

2) In Sections A and B, you'll be given a variety of Spanish texts and then asked questions about them. The texts could include blog posts, emails, newspaper reports, adverts and literary texts. Section A has questions and answers in English, and Section B has questions and answers in Spanish.

3) Section C is a translation question — you'll have to translate a short passage of text from Spanish into English. See p.95 for more tips on tackling translation questions.

4) In Sections A and B, scan through the text first to get an idea of what it's about. Then read the questions that go with it carefully, making sure you understand what information you should be looking out for.

5) Next, go back through the text. You're not expected to understand every word, so don't get distracted by trying to work out what everything means — focus on finding the information you need.

The inside front cover of this book has a list of common Spanish question words, phrases and instructions.

Don't give up if you don't understand something

1) Use the context of the text to help you understand what it might be saying. You might be able to find some clues in the title of the text or the type of text.

2) Knowing how to spot different word types (e.g. nouns, verbs) can help you work out what's happening in a sentence. See the grammar section (p.58-90) for more.

3) You can guess some Spanish words that look or sound the same as English words, e.g. el problema — *problem*, la música — *music*, el color — *colour*.

Look for words that look like ones you know, e.g. 'la comida basura'. 'La comida' means 'food', and 'basura' means 'rubbish', so you can guess it means 'junk food'.

4) Be careful though — you might come across some 'false friends'. These are Spanish words that look like an English word, but have a completely different meaning:

la nota	*mark*	la carpeta	*folder, file*	la arena	*sand*	la librería	*bookshop*	actual	*present*
el pie	*foot*	la dirección	*address*	el éxito	*success*	sensible	*sensitive*	fatal	*awful*
el campo	*countryside*	el pariente	*relative*	la ropa	*clothes*	largo	*long*	embarazada	*pregnant*

Keep an eye on the time

1) There are quite a few questions to get through in the reading exam, so you need to work at a good speed.

2) If you're having trouble with a particular question, you might want to move on and come back to it later.

Manolo and his colleagues never underestimated the importance of thyme.

3) Don't forget that the last question in the paper (Section C) is a translation — this is worth more marks than any other question, so you should leave plenty of time to tackle it.

4) Make sure you put an answer down for every question — lots of the questions are multiple choice, so even if you can't work out the answer, it's always worth putting down one of the options.

Exams are important — failing can be fatal...

Don't forget, the questions in Section B will be in Spanish. Don't panic if you don't understand them — search for any familiar vocabulary and use any answer lines or boxes to help you guess what you have to do.

The Writing Exam

The writing exam is a great way of showing off what you can do — try to use varied vocabulary, include a range of tenses, and pack in any clever expressions that you've learnt over the years.

There'll be three tasks in the Writing Exam

1) The <u>higher tier</u> writing paper is <u>1 hour and 15 minutes long</u> and has <u>three tasks</u>.

2) Each task is worth a <u>different number of marks</u>, so you should spend more time on the higher-mark tasks.

① Structured Task (16 marks)	② Open-ended Task (32 marks)	③ Translation (12 marks)
There will be <u>two tasks</u> to choose from. You'll be asked to write <u>about 90 words</u> in Spanish, based on <u>four bullet points</u>. Make sure you write about each bullet point and give some <u>opinions</u>.	There will also be <u>two tasks</u> to choose from. You'll need to write <u>about 150 words</u> in Spanish, based on <u>two bullet points</u>. This task is more creative — make sure you include some <u>opinions</u> with <u>reasons</u>.	You'll be given an <u>English passage</u> to translate <u>into Spanish</u>. The passage could be on <u>any topic</u> you've studied. There's more advice for doing translations on p.95.

Read the instructions carefully, and spend some time planning

1) Read the instructions for questions 1 and 2 carefully — you'll need to make sure you cover <u>all of the bullet points</u>. You can often use <u>words from the question</u> in your answer too.

2) Spend a few minutes for each question <u>planning out</u> your answer. Decide <u>how</u> you're going to cover everything that's required and <u>in what order</u> you're going to write things.

Try to use varied vocab and a range of tenses.

3) Write the <u>best answer</u> you can, using the Spanish <u>that you know</u> — it doesn't matter if it's not true.

Check through your work thoroughly

Checking your work is <u>really important</u> — even small mistakes can cost marks. Take a look at this checklist:

*   Are all the <u>verbs</u> in the <u>right tense</u>?
    Mañana, trabajé en el jardín. ✘   Mañana, trabajaré en el jardín. ✓

*   Are the <u>verb endings</u> correct?
    ¿No te gusta las fresas? ✘   ¿No te gustan las fresas? ✓

*   Do your <u>adjectives agree</u> with their nouns?
    La camisa es amarillo. ✘   La camisa es amarilla. ✓

    All of the points on this checklist are covered in the grammar section — see p.58-90.

*   Are your <u>adjectives</u> in the <u>right place</u>?
    Una blanca falda. ✘   Una falda blanca. ✓

*   Do your <u>reflexive verbs</u> and <u>pronouns</u> agree?
    A las siete, me levantamos. ✘   A las siete, me levanto. ✓

*   Have you <u>spelt</u> everything correctly, including using the right <u>accents</u>?
    El toca la guitar con su tio. ✘   Él toca la guitarra con su tío. ✓

And lastly, don't forget your pen...

When you're nervous and stressed, it's dead easy to miss out something the question has asked you to do. For tasks one and two, try to write about the bullet points in order, and tick them off as you go along.

The Translation Tasks

When you're studying Spanish, you do little bits of translation in your head all the time. For the translation questions, you just need to apply those skills — one sentence at a time — to a couple of short passages.

In the Reading Exam, you'll translate from Spanish to English

1) The final question of the reading paper will ask you to translate a short Spanish passage (about 50 words) into English. The passage will be on a topic you've studied, so most of the vocabulary should be familiar.

2) Here are some top tips for doing your translation:

- Read the whole text before you start. Make some notes in English to remind you of the main ideas.

- Translate the text one sentence at a time, rather than word by word — this will avoid any of the Spanish word order being carried into the English.

Ella compra la manzana roja.	*She buys the apple red.* ✘	*She buys the red apple.* ✓
Salma lo comió.	*Salma it ate.* ✘	*Salma ate it.* ✓

- Keep an eye out for different tenses — there will definitely be a variety in the passage.

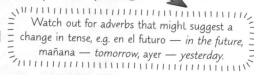

- Read through your translation to make sure it sounds natural. Some words and phrases don't translate literally, so you'll need to make sure that your sentences sound like normal English:

Watch out for adverbs that might suggest a change in tense, e.g. en el futuro — in the future, mañana — tomorrow, ayer — yesterday.

La semana pasada, Irene hizo su maleta.	*The week last, Irene made her suitcase.* ✘	*Last week, Irene packed her suitcase.* ✓

3) Make sure you've translated everything from the original text — you'll lose marks if you miss something.

In the Writing Exam, you'll translate from English to Spanish

1) In the writing paper, you will have to translate a short English passage (about 50 words) into Spanish.

2) Here are some ideas for how you could approach the translation:

- Read through the whole text before you get started so you know exactly what the text is about.

- Tackle the passage one sentence at a time — work slowly and carefully through each one.

- Don't translate things literally — think about what each English sentence means and try to write it in the most Spanish way you know. Don't worry — the translation is likely to include similar sentences to the ones you've learnt.

- Work on the word order — remember that most Spanish adjectives follow the noun. If the sentence is negative, check you've got 'no' in the right place (see p.86).

Don't try to write a perfect translation first time — do it roughly first, and then write it up properly, crossing out any old drafts. Remember to keep an eye on the time.

3) Once you've got something that you're happy with, go back through and check that you've covered everything that was in the English.

4) Now check your Spanish text thoroughly using the list from p.94.

Thankfully, none of that got lost in translation...

Elena's translations got the seal of approval.

Congratulations — you've made it to the end of the book. 95 pages is no mean feat, so give yourself a pat on the back. Make sure you still read this page properly though, and take the translation advice on board.

Vocabulary

Section One — General Stuff

Numbers (p.1)

cero	zero
uno (un) / una	one
dos	two
tres	three
cuatro	four
cinco	five
seis	six
siete	seven
ocho	eight
nueve	nine
diez	ten
once	eleven
doce	twelve
trece	thirteen
catorce	fourteen
quince	fifteen
dieciséis	sixteen
diecisiete	seventeen
dieciocho	eighteen
diecinueve	nineteen
veinte	twenty
veintiuno	twenty-one
veintidós	twenty-two
treinta	thirty
treinta y uno	thirty-one
cuarenta	forty
cincuenta	fifty
sesenta	sixty
setenta	seventy
ochenta	eighty
noventa	ninety
ciento (cien)	hundred
ciento setenta y siete	one hundred and seventy-seven
doscientos/as	two hundred
quinientos	five hundred and
veintiocho	twenty-eight
novecientos	nine hundred and
noventa y tres	ninety-three
mil	thousand
mil cuatrocientos cincuenta y tres	one thousand four hundred and fifty-three
millón	million
primero / primera	first
segundo/a	second
tercero/a	third
cuarto/a	fourth
quinto/a	fifth
sexto/a	sixth
séptimo/a	seventh
octavo/a	eighth
noveno/a	ninth
décimo/a	tenth
una docena	dozen
el número	number

un par	pair / couple
unos (diez)	about (10)

Times and Dates (p.2-3)

el lunes	Monday
el martes	Tuesday
el miércoles	Wednesday
el jueves	Thursday
el viernes	Friday
el sábado	Saturday
el domingo	Sunday
enero	January
febrero	February
marzo	March
abril	April
mayo	May
junio	June
julio	July
agosto	August
septiembre	September
octubre	October
noviembre	November
diciembre	December
la estación	season
el invierno	winter
el otoño	autumn
la primavera	spring
el verano	summer
a diario	daily / everyday
a eso de ...	at about ...
a fines de ...	at / to the end of ...
a mediados de ...	around the middle of ...
a menudo	often
a partir de	from
a veces	sometimes
ahora	now / nowadays
al mismo tiempo	at the same time
algunas veces	sometimes
anoche	last night
el año	year
anteayer	the day before yesterday
antes (de)	before
ayer	yesterday
breve	brief / short
cada (...) días / horas	every (...) days / hours
casi	nearly
de momento	at the moment / right now
de nuevo	again
de repente	suddenly
de vez en cuando	now and then / from time to time
dentro de (...) días / horas	within (...) days / hours
desde	since

desde hace	since
despacio	slowly
después (de)	after / afterwards
el día	day
durante	during / for
durar	to last
en seguida / enseguida	straightaway
esta noche	tonight
la fecha	date
el fin de semana	weekend
hace (un mes) que	it's been a month since
hace (un mes)	a month ago
hoy	today
lento	slow
los lunes etc.	(on) Mondays etc.
luego	then / afterwards
mañana	tomorrow
la mañana	morning
el mes	month
mientras tanto	meanwhile
mucho tiempo	a long time
la noche	night
otra vez	again
el pasado	past
pasado (adj)	past / last
pasado mañana	the day after tomorrow
pocas veces	seldom / a few times
por año	per year
por fin	at last
por lo general	generally
el porvenir	future
al principio	at the beginning
pronto	soon
próximo	next
que viene (el mes etc.)	next (month etc.)
quince días	fortnight
el rato	while / short time
la semana	week
siempre	always
el siglo	century
siguiente	next / following
sobre	on / around
solo (sólo)	only
tardar	to take time
tarde	late
la tarde	afternoon / evening
la temporada	period / spell / season
temprano	early
tener prisa	to be in a hurry
el tiempo	time
todas (las semanas)	every (week)
todavía	still / yet

todos (los días / meses)	every (day / month)
último	last
una vez	once
dos veces	twice

Questions (p.4-5)

¿(a)dónde?	where (to)?
¿a qué hora?	at what time?
¿cómo?	how?
¿cuál(es)?	which?
¿cuándo?	when?
¿cuánto?	how much?
¿cuánto cuesta(n)?	how much does it / do they cost?
¿cuánto es?	how much is it?
¿cuánto vale(n)?	how much does it / do they cost?
¿cuántos...?	how many?
¿cuántos años tiene(s)?	how old are you?
¿de dónde?	where from?
¿de qué color (es)?	what colour (is it)?
¿de quién?	whose?
¿es...?	is it...?
¿por cuánto tiempo?	for how long?
¿por dónde?	through where?
¿por qué?	why?
¿qué?	what?
¿qué día?	what day?
¿qué fecha?	what date?
¿qué hora es?	what time is it?
¿quién?	who?

Being Polite (p.6-7)

¡Adiós!	Goodbye!
así así	so-so
¡Basta ya!	That's enough!
¡Bienvenido/a!	Welcome!
¡Buen viaje!	Have a good trip!
¡Buena suerte!	Good luck!
¡Buenas noches!	Good night!
¡Buenas tardes!	Good afternoon! / Good evening!
¡Buenos días!	Good morning! / Good day!
¡Claro!	Of course!
¿Cómo está(s)?	How are you?
con permiso	excuse me
¡Cuidado!	Careful! Watch out!
de nada	you're welcome / don't mention it
¿De veras?	Really?
encantado/a	pleased to meet you
¡Enhorabuena!	Congratulations!
Este/a es...	This is...
fatal	terrible
¡Felices vacaciones!	Have a good holiday!
¡Felicidades!	Best wishes! Congratulations!
¡Felicitaciones!	Congratulations!
hasta el (lunes)	till / see you (Monday)
hasta luego	see you later

hasta mañana	see you tomorrow
hasta pronto	see you soon
¡Hola!	Hello!
Le presento a...	May I introduce...?
lo siento	I'm sorry
mucho gusto	pleased to meet you
(muy) bien	(very) well
no muy bien	not very well
¡Ojo!	Watch out! Careful!
perdón	sorry / excuse me
perdone	sorry / excuse me
por favor	please
¿Puedo...?	May I...?
¡Qué (+ adjective)!	How ...!
¡Qué (+ noun)!	What a ...!
¿Qué hay?	What's happening? What's the matter?
¡Que lo pase(s) bien!	Have a good time!
¿Qué pasa?	What's happening? What's the matter?
¿Qué tal?	How are you? How's ...?
¡Qué va!	Come on! Rubbish! Nonsense!
Quisiera...	I would like...
saludar	to greet / say hello
saludos	regards / greetings
¡Socorro!	Help!
vale	ok

Opinions (p.8-10)

aburrido	boring / bored
aburrirse	to get bored
adorar	to adore / to love
afortunado	lucky
agradable	pleasant
alegrar	to cheer up
alegrarse (de)	to be happy (about)
amable	nice / kind / friendly
antiguo	old
apreciar	to appreciate
apropiado	correct / appropriate
aprovechar	to make the most of
aprovecharse (de)	to take advantage (of)
barato	cheap
bonito	pretty
bueno	good
la calidad	quality
caro	expensive
creer	to believe
dar igual	to be all the same / to make no difference
decepcionado	disappointed
decepcionante	disappointing
decepcionar	to disappoint
decir	to say
desagradable	unpleasant
desear	to wish
la desventaja	disadvantage
disfrutar	to enjoy
distinto	different

divertido	amusing / entertaining / fun
divertirse	to have a good time
dudar	to doubt
duro	hard
emocionante	exciting / thrilling / moving
encantador	charming
encantar	to delight
entretenido	entertaining / amusing
esperar	to hope
espléndido	fantastic / great / terrific
estar a favor	to be in favour of
estar de acuerdo	to agree
estar en contra	to be against
estar harto de	to be fed up of
estupendo	fantastic / marvellous
fabuloso	fabulous
fácil	easy
fastidiar	to annoy / to bother
fatal	awful / fatal
fenomenal	great / fantastic
feo	ugly
genial	brilliant / great
guay	cool
hermoso	beautiful
horroroso	horrible
impresionante	impressive / striking
increíble	incredible
inseguro	unsafe / uncertain
interesante	interesting
interesar(se)	to interest / to be interested in
inútil	useless
malo	bad
maravilloso	marvellous
nuevo	new
odiar	to hate
opinar	to think / to give an opinion
parecer	to seem
pasarlo bien / mal	to have a good / bad time
pensar	to think
perfecto	perfect
ponerse de acuerdo	to agree
porque	because
precioso	precious / beautiful
preferir	to prefer
profundo	deep / profound
quedar en	to agree
querer decir	to mean
raro	strange / rare
la razón	reason
reconocer	to recognise
ridículo	ridiculous
seguro	safe / certain
sencillo	simple / plain / straightforward
sentir(se)	to feel
sorprendido	surprised

Vocabulary

tener ganas de hacer algo	to feel like doing something
tener razón	to be right
tonto	silly
tranquilo	peaceful / quiet
único	unique / only / single
útil	useful
valer la pena	to be worth the trouble
la ventaja	advantage
viejo	old

Access

abierto	open
abrir	to open
cerrado	closed
cerrar	to close
gratis	free (of charge)
gratuito	free (of charge)
libre	free / unoccupied
ocupado	engaged / occupied
permitir	to allow
prohibido	forbidden
prohibir	to forbid / ban

Colours and Shapes

amarillo	yellow
azul	blue
blanco	white
claro	light
cuadrado	square
el color	colour
la forma	shape
gris	grey
marrón	brown
morado	purple
naranja	orange
negro	black
oscuro	dark
pálido	pale
redondo	round
rojo	red
rosa / rosado	pink
verde	green
vivo	vivid / bright

Common Abbreviations

Sr (señor)	Mr
Sra (señora)	Mrs
Srta (señorita)	Miss
Sta (santa)	Saint
c/ (calle)	street
1° / primero (2°, 3° etc.)	1st (2nd, 3rd etc.)
1ª / primera (2ª, 3ª etc.)	1st (2nd, 3rd etc.)
Dr (doctor)	Dr
Dra (doctora)	Dr
el AVE	high-speed train
Renfe / RENFE	Spanish railways
IVA	VAT
Avda (avenida)	avenue
EEUU (Estados Unidos)	USA

Connectives

además	moreover / besides
aparte de	apart from
claro que	of course
dado que	given that
es decir	in other words / that is to say
por un lado / por otro lado	on the one hand / on the other hand
por una parte / por otra parte	on the one hand / on the other hand
sin duda	obviously / certainly

Correctness

cierto	certain / sure / true
equivocado	wrong
la falta	error
mal	badly
la mentira	lie / untruth
mentiroso	liar
la razón	reason
la verdad	truth
verdadero	true
corregir	to correct
estar equivocado	to be wrong
mentir	to lie
tener razón	to be right

Materials

el algodón	cotton
la cerámica	pottery
el cristal	glass / crystal
el cuero	leather
la lana	wool
la madera	wood
el oro	gold
el papel	paper
la piel	leather / skin
la plata	silver
la seda	silk
la tela	fabric / material
el vidrio	glass

Comparisons (p.63 & 66)

bastante	sufficient / enough / quite
comparar	to compare
demasiado	too, too much
igual que	same as
más (que)	more (than)
mayor	main / larger / bigger / greater / older
la mayoría	most / majority
mejor	better / best
menor	smaller / less / least / younger
menos (que)	less (than)
mismo	same
muy	very
parecido a	like / similar to
peor	worse / worst
poco (e.g. poco ruidoso)	not very
tan ... como	as ... as

tanto ... como	as much ... as

Prepositions (p.72)

a	to / at
de	from / of
en	in / at
hacia	towards
hasta	until
para	for
por	through / by / in / for / per
según	according to
sin	without

Conjunctions (p.74)

a pesar de	in spite of / despite
así que	so / therefore
aun (si)	even (if)
aunque	although / (even) though
como	as / since
cuando	when
de manera que	in such a way that
entonces	then
incluso	even
mientras (que)	while, meanwhile
o / u	or
pero	but
por eso	for that reason / therefore
por lo tanto	therefore
porque	because
pues	then / since
si	if
sin embargo	however
tal vez	maybe / perhaps
también	also
y / e	and
ya (que)	as / since

Negative Forms (p.86)

jamás	never
ni ... ni	neither ... nor
nada	nothing
nadie	nobody
ninguno	none / no-one
nunca	never
sino	but (rather) / except
tampoco	neither / not ... either ...
ya no	not any more

Important Verbs

acabar de + infinitive	to have just (done something)
comenzar	to begin
continuar	to continue
dar	to give
darse cuenta (de)	to realise
deber	must / have to
decidir	to decide
dejar de (hacer algo)	to stop (doing something)
echar	to throw

empezar	*to begin*	pasar	*to happen / to spend (time)*	tener	*to have / to own*
estar	*to be*			tener lugar	*to take place*
hace(n) falta	*to need / to be necessary*	poder	*to be able / can*	tener que	*to have to do something*
hacer	*to do / to make*	poner	*to put*	volver a hacer algo	*to do something again*
hacerse	*to become*	ponerse a (hacer algo)	*to start (doing something)*	volverse	*to become*
hay	*there is / there are*	querer	*to want / to love*		
hay que	*one must / one has to*	quisiera...	*I'd like...*		
ir	*to go*	saber	*to know (a fact / how to do something)*		
ir a (hacer algo)	*to be going to (do something)*	seguir	*to continue / to follow*		
irse	*to go away / to leave*	ser	*to be*		
necesitar	*to need*	soler	*to usually do something*		
ocurrir	*to happen*				

Section Two — Me, My Family and Friends

You and Your Family (p.11-12)

el/la abuelo/a	*grandfather / grandmother*
el apellido	*last name*
el apodo	*nickname*
el bebé	*baby*
cuidar	*to look after*
el cumpleaños	*birthday*
cumplir años	*to have a birthday*
la edad	*age*
el/la gemelo/a	*twin*
la gente	*people*
el/la hermanastro/a	*stepbrother/sister*
el/la hijo/a (único/a)	*(only) child*
los hijos	*children*
el hogar	*home*
llamarse	*to be called*
la madrastra	*stepmother*
la madre	*mother*
el miembro	*member*
nacer	*to be born*
nacido	*born*
el nacimiento	*birth*
la nacionalidad	*nationality*
el/la nieto/a	*grandchild*
el/la niño/a	*child*
el nombre	*name*
el padrastro	*stepfather*
el padre, los padres	*father, parents*
los parientes	*relatives*
el/la primo/a	*cousin*
el recuerdo	*memory*
la reunión	*get-together*
el/la sobrino/a	*nephew / niece*
tener ... años	*to be ... years old*
el/la tío/a	*uncle / aunt*
el/la vecino/a	*neighbour*

Describing People (p.13-14)

adolescente	*adolescent*
el/la adolescente	*teenager*
alegre	*happy*
alto	*tall*
(de) altura mediana	*(of) medium height*
amable	*kind*
amistoso	*friendly*
anciano	*elderly*
el/la anciano/a	*old person*
animado	*lively*
antipático	*unpleasant*
el aspecto	*appearance / looks*
atrevido	*daring / cheeky*
avaro	*mean / miserly*
bajo	*short (height)*
la barba	*beard*
el bigote	*moustache*
callado	*quiet / reserved*
calvo	*bald*
la cara	*face*
el cariño	*affection*
cariñoso	*affectionate / tender*
castaño	*chestnut / brown*
celoso	*jealous*
cobarde	*coward*
comprensivo	*understanding*
cortés	*polite*
corto	*short (length)*
cuidadoso	*careful*
débil	*weak*
delgado	*slim*
deportivo	*sporty*
educado	*polite*
egoísta	*selfish*
feliz	*happy*
fuerte	*strong*
las gafas	*glasses*
glotón	*greedy*
gordo	*fat*
gracioso	*funny*
guapo	*good-looking*
hablador	*chatty / talkative*
honrado	*honest*
joven	*young*
el/la joven	*young person*
jubilado	*retired*
el/la jubilado	*OAP / pensioner*

jubilarse	*to retire*
la juventud	*youth / young people*
largo	*long*
liso	*straight (hair)*
loco	*mad*
maduro	*mature*
maleducado	*rude*
moreno	*dark (-haired / -skinned)*
el ojo	*eye*
la oreja	*ear*
orgulloso	*proud*
parecerse a	*to look like*
las pecas	*freckles*
pelirrojo	*red-haired*
el pelo	*hair*
perezoso	*lazy / idle*
rico	*wealthy / rich*
rizado	*curly*
rubio	*blonde*
el sentido de humor	*sense of humour*
seguro de sí mismo	*self-assured*
sensible	*sensitive*
serio	*serious / responsible*
simpático	*kind / nice / pleasant*
torpe	*clumsy*
travieso	*naughty / mischievous*
triste	*sad*
valiente	*brave / bold*
viejo	*old*
el/la viudo/a	*widow(er)*

Relationships (p.15-16)

el amor	*love*
acordar	*to agree on*
aguantar	*to bear / to put up with*
el anillo	*ring*
la barrera generacional	*generation gap*
la boda	*wedding*
besar	*to kiss*

el beso	kiss
casado	married
el casamiento	wedding
casarse	to get married
el/la compañero/a	classmate / colleague
comprometerse	to get engaged
el compromiso	engagement
la confianza	trust
confiar en	to trust
conocer	to know / be familiar with / get to know
disculpar(se)	to apologise
discutir	to discuss
la disputa	argument
echar de menos	to miss (someone)
enamorado	in love
enamorarse	to fall in love
el/la esposo/a	husband / wife
el estado civil	marital status
fastidiar	to annoy / to bother
el hombre	man
juntos	together
llevarse bien / mal con	to get on well / badly with someone
el marido	husband
el matrimonio	marriage / married couple
molestar	to bother
la mujer	wife / woman
el/la novio/a	boyfriend / girlfriend
la pareja	couple / partner
la pelea	fight
pelear(se)	to fight
perdonar	to forgive
reírse	to laugh
relacionarse con	to be in contact with
romper	to break
roto	broken
salir	to go out
el sentimiento	feeling
solo	alone
soltero	single (not married)
sonreír	to smile

Section Three — Free-Time Activities

Music, Cinema and TV (p.17-19)

el/la artista	artist
el actor	actor
la actriz	actress
la actuación	performance
el anuncio (publicitario)	advert
la banda sonora	soundtrack
la batería	drums
la cadena	channel
la canción	song
el/la cantante	singer
cantar	to sing
la ciencia ficción	science fiction
el concurso	game show / contest
los dibujos animados	cartoons
la diversión	pastime / hobby / entertainment
divertir(se)	to have a good time
el documental	documentary
en directo	live
la entrada	ticket
el espectáculo	show
la estrella	star
la función	show / performance
el género	genre
la grabación	recording
el grupo	band
hacer cola	to queue
la historia	story
la letra	song lyrics
el/la músico/a	musician
la música pop	pop music
la música rap	rap music
la música rock	rock music
la música clásica	classical music
las noticias	news
el papel	role
la película	film
la película de acción	action film
la película de aventuras	adventure film
la película romántica	romantic film
la película de terror	horror film
policíaco	detective (adj.)
el programa	programme
el reality show	reality show
el reparto	cast
ser aficionado a	to be very keen on / fond of (activity)
la taquilla	box office
la telenovela	soap opera
tocar	to play (an instrument)
la trama	plot

Food and Eating Out (p.20-21)

a la plancha	grilled
el aceite	oil
el agua mineral (con / sin gas) (f)	(fizzy / still) mineral water
el ajo	garlic
la alimentación	food / nutrition
el alimento	type of food
almorzar	to have lunch
el almuerzo	lunch
apetecer	to fancy / to feel like
apto	suitable
el arroz	rice
asado	roast(ed)
el atún	tuna
el azúcar	sugar
el bacalao	cod
la barra (de pan)	loaf (of bread)
beber	to drink
la bebida	drink
el bistec	steak
el bocadillo	sandwich
los calamares	squid
el caramelo	boiled sweet
la carne	meat
de cerdo	pork
de cordero	lamb
de ternera	veal
de vaca	beef
la carta	menu
la cebolla	onion
la cena	dinner
cenar	to have the evening meal
la cerveza	beer
los champiñones	mushrooms
el chorizo	Spanish sausage
la chuleta	chop
los churros	fritters
la cocina	cuisine / cooking
cocinar	to cook
la col	cabbage
comer	to eat
la comida (basura / rápida)	junk / fast food
la comida	meal / lunch
la copa	wine glass
la cuchara	spoon
el cuchillo	knife
la cuenta	bill
desayunar	to have breakfast
el desayuno	breakfast
dulce	sweet
elegir	to choose
escoger	to choose
el filete	steak
el flan	crème caramel
la fresa	strawberry
frito	fried
la galleta	biscuit
las gambas	prawns
el gazpacho	cold soup
la grasa	fat
los guisantes	peas
la heladería	ice cream parlour
el helado	ice cream
hervido	boiled
el hielo	ice

Vocabulary

el huevo	egg	sabroso	tasty	la copa	cup / trophy
incluido	included	la sal	salt	correr	to run
el jamón (de York)	(boiled) ham	salado	salty	el deporte	sport
el jamón serrano	cured ham	la salchicha	sausage	los deportes de riesgo	adventure sports
las judías verdes	string beans	el salchichón	salami		
la leche	milk	la salsa	sauce	deportista	sporty
la lechuga	lettuce	el segundo plato	main meal / course	el / la deportista	sportsperson
las legumbres	vegetables / pulses	los servicios	toilets	el equipo	team / equipment
la mantequilla	butter	la sopa	soup	la equitación	horse riding
la manzana	apple	las tapas	nibbles / bar snacks	el estadio	stadium
los mariscos	seafood	el té	tea	ganar	to win
el melocotón	peach	el tenedor	fork	el gol	goal
merendar	to have an afternoon snack / picnic	tener hambre	to be hungry	el juego	game
		tener sed	to be thirsty	los Juegos Olímpicos	Olympic Games
la merienda	afternoon snack / picnic	tomar	to have / to take		
		la tortilla	omelette	el/la jugador/a	player
la merluza	hake	la tostada	toast	jugar	to play
la mermelada	jam	traer	to bring	marcar (un gol)	to score (a goal)
nada más	nothing else	las uvas	grapes	el monopatín	skateboard
la naranja	orange	el vaso	glass	montar	to ride
la nata	cream	las verduras	vegetables	(a caballo / en bici)	(horse / bike)
la nuez	nut / walnut	el vino (blanco / rosado / tinto)	(white / rosé / red) wine	nadar	to swim
el pastel	cake / pie			la natación	swimming
la patata	potato	la zanahoria	carrot	el partido	match
pedir	to order / ask for	el zumo (de fruta)	(fruit) juice	el patinaje	skating
la pera	pear			patinar	to skate
el perrito caliente	hot dog	**Sport (p.22-23)**		la pelota	ball
el pescado	fish	(el/la) aficionado/a	enthusiast	perder	to lose
picante	spicy	al aire libre	outdoors	la pesca	fishing
la pimienta	pepper (seasoning)	el alpinismo	mountain climbing	pescar	to fish
el pimiento	pepper (vegetable)	andar	to walk	el piragüismo	canoeing
la piña	pineapple	bailar	to dance	la pista	track / court / run / slope / rink
el plátano	banana	el baile	dancing		
el plato (combinado)	(set) dish	el baloncesto	basketball	la pista de hielo	ice rink
el pollo	chicken	la bicicleta / bici	bicycle / bike	el premio	prize
el postre	dessert	el billar	billiards	la selección	team / side
el primer plato	starter	el campeón la campeona	champion	ser aficionado a	to be very keen on / fond of (activity)
probar	to taste / to try				
la propina	tip	el campeonato	championship	el/la socio/a	member
el queso	cheese	la carrera	race	el torneo	tournament
rico	tasty	el concurso	contest / competition	la vela	sail / sailing

Section Four — Technology in Everyday Life

Technology (p.24-27)

acceder	to access	crear	to create	el mensaje (de texto)	(text) message
adjuntar	to attach	desactivar	to deactivate / block	el móvil	mobile phone
el archivo	file	descargar	to download	el muro	wall
arroba	@	el disco duro	hard drive	el navegador	browser
el blog	blog	enviar	to send	navegar	to surf
borrar	to erase / delete	funcionar	to work / function	el ordenador	computer
el buscador	search engine	grabar	to record / burn (a disk)	la pantalla	screen
el buzón	inbox / mailbox			el periódico (digital)	(digital) newspaper
cargar	load	guardar	to save	la portada	home page
charlar	to chat	el guión	hyphen	el portátil	laptop
colgar	to post (photos on social media, etc.)	el guión bajo	underscore	publicar	to publish
		hablar	to speak / talk	punto	dot / full stop
la contraseña	password	la herramienta	tool	puntocom	.com
el correo basura	spam	inalámbrico	wireless	el ratón	mouse
el correo electrónico	email	el/la internauta	Internet user	recibir	to receive
		mandar	to send	la red	network / Internet
la cuenta	account	el marcador	bookmark		

la red social	social network	la sala de chat	chat room	usar	to use
el reproductor	widget	el sitio web	website	el/la usuario/a	user
la revista digital	digital magazine / e-magazine	el servidor de seguridad	firewall	utilizar	to use
el riesgo	risk	el teclado	keyboard	el videojuego	video game

Section Five — Customs and Festivals

Customs and Festivals (p.28-30)

el Año Nuevo	New Year
la bandera	flag
la broma	joke / trick
las castañuelas	castanets
celebrar	to celebrate
la corrida	bullfight
la costumbre	custom / way
cristiano	Christian
el Día de los Inocentes	28 December (equivalent of April Fools' Day)
el Día de los Muertos	All Souls' Day
el Día de Reyes	Epiphany / 6 January
el día festivo	public holiday
el disfraz	fancy dress
disfrazarse de	to dress up as

el Eid al-Fitr	Eid al-Fitr
la fecha patria	national day to commemorate historic event
¡Feliz Año Nuevo!	Happy New Year!
¡Feliz cumpleaños!	Happy Birthday!
¡Feliz Navidad!	Merry Christmas!
la feria	fair
festejar	to celebrate
la fiesta	festival / party
el gaucho	South American cowboy
el Hannukah	Hannukah
judío	Jewish
el juguete	toy
el mariachi	Mexican musician
el/la muerto/a	dead (person)
la muñeca	doll
musulmán	Muslim
Navidad	Christmas

Nochebuena	Christmas Eve
Nochevieja	31 December
Papá Noel	Father Christmas
la Pascua	Easter
el paso	statue paraded at Easter
la plaza de toros	bullring
la procesión	procession
religioso	religious
los Reyes Magos	the Three Kings
el santo	saint's day
la Semana Santa	Easter week
la tradición	tradition
la Tomatina	tomato-throwing festival
tener suerte	to be lucky
el/la torero/a	bullfighter
el toro	bull
el turrón	Spanish nougat
el villancico	Christmas carol

Section Six — Where You Live

Where You Live (p.31-32)

las afueras	outskirts
la aldea	village
la alfombra	rug
alquilado	rented
alquilar	to rent / to hire
el alquiler	rent
el anuncio	advert / announcement
el aparcamiento	parking
el árbol	tree
el armario	wardrobe / cupboard
el ascensor	lift
el aseo	toilet
el ayuntamiento	town hall
bajar	to go down
el baño	bathroom / bath
el barrio	neighbourhood
la biblioteca	library
la bolera	bowling alley
el bosque	forest / woods
la butaca	armchair
la calefacción	heating
la calle	street
la cama	bed
el campo	countryside / grounds
la cancha (de tenis)	(tennis) court
la carnicería	butcher's

la casa (adosada)	(semi-detached) house
el centro	town centre
el centro comercial	shopping centre
el chalet / chalé	bungalow / house
el cine	cinema
la ciudad	city
el club (de jóvenes)	(youth) club
la cocina	cooker / kitchen
el comedor	dining room
la comisaría	police station
cómodo	comfortable / convenient / handy
compartir	to share
la comunidad	community
concurrido	busy / crowded
construir	to build
Correos	Post Office
la cortina	curtain
el cuarto de baño	bathroom
dar a	to look onto
de lujo	luxury
la dirección	address
el domicilio	address / home
el dormitorio	bedroom
la ducha	shower
el edificio	building
la entrada	entrance
entrar	to go in / enter

los electrodomésticos	electrical appliances
la escalera	stairs
el espacio	space
el espejo	mirror
la esquina	corner
el estanco	tobacconist's
el estante	shelf
la estantería	shelves
la fábrica	factory
el fregadero	kitchen sink
los grandes almacenes	department store
la granja	farm
la habitación	room
el/la habitante	inhabitant
el horno	oven
la iglesia	church
la joyería	jeweller's
la juguetería	toy shop
el lado	side
el lago	lake
el lavabo	washbasin
la lavadora	washing machine
el lavaplatos	dishwasher
la librería	bookcase / bookshop
la llave	key
la luz	light
la manta	blanket

la máquina	machine
el mercado	market
la mesa	table
la mezquita	mosque
el microondas	microwave oven
mudarse (de casa)	to move (house)
los muebles	furniture
el museo	museum
el negocio	business
la nevera	fridge
el paisaje	landscape / scenery
la panadería	bakery
la papelera	wastepaper basket
la papelería	stationery shop
la pared	wall
el parque	park
el parque infantil	playground
el pasillo	corridor
la pastelería	pastry shop
la peluquería	hairdresser's
las persianas	blinds, shutters
la pescadería	fishmonger's
el piso	flat / floor (of room)
la planta baja	ground floor
la planta	floor / plant
la población	population
el polideportivo	sports centre
propio	own
el pueblo	town / village / people / nation
el puente	bridge
la puerta	door
el puerto	port / harbour
el río	river
el ruido	noise
ruidoso	noisy
el salón	lounge
la segunda planta	second floor
el semáforo	traffic lights
la sierra	mountain range
la silla	chair
el sillón	armchair
el sótano	basement / cellar
subir	to go up
el suelo	floor
el teatro	theatre
la terraza	terrace
la tienda de comestibles	grocery shop
la tienda de ropa	clothes shop
la ventana	window
el vestíbulo	entrance hall / lobby / foyer
la vivienda	dwelling / housing / accommodation
la zona peatonal	pedestrian zone / area

What You Do at Home (p.33)

acostarse	to go to bed
arreglar	to tidy / to fix
ayudar	to help
cortar el césped	to mow the lawn

despertarse	to wake up
dormirse	to go to sleep
ducharse	to have a shower
hacer la cama	to make the bed
hacer las compras	to do the shopping
lavar los platos	to do the washing-up
lavarse la cara	to wash your face
levantarse	to get up
limpiar	to clean
limpio	clean
la paga	pocket money
pasar la aspiradora	to do the vacuuming
pasear al perro	to walk the dog
poner la mesa	to lay the table
quitar la mesa	to clear the table
sacar la basura	to take out the rubbish
sentarse	to sit down
la tarea doméstica	chore
vestirse	to get dressed

Shopping (p.34-36)

a mitad de precio	half price
alcanzar	to reach
alto	tall / high
la altura	height
el abrigo	coat
ahorrar	to save
ancho	wide
el ancho	width
bajo	low / short
bastar	to be enough
la blusa	blouse
el bolso	handbag
la bolsa	bag
las botas	boots
el bote	jar
la bufanda	scarf
la caja	till / box
los calcetines	socks
cambiar	to change
el cambio	change / exchange
la camisa	shirt
la camiseta	T-shirt
el camisón	nightgown
la cantidad	quantity
el cartón	carton
la cazadora (de cuero)	(leather) jacket
el céntimo	cent
el chándal	tracksuit
el cinturón	belt
el collar	necklace
comprar	to buy
las compras	shopping
contar	to count / tell / recount
la corbata	tie
la cosa	thing
el cuarto	quarter
deber	to owe
delgado	slim / thin

el/la dependiente/a	shop assistant
el descuento	discount
devolver	to return
el dinero	money
en efectivo	cash
enseñar	to show
estar de moda	to be in fashion
estrecho	narrow
la falda	skirt
la flor	flower
gastar	to spend (money) / to use (energy)
gordo	fat
la gorra	cap
grueso	thick
los guantes	gloves
hacer cola	to queue
la lata	tin
la libra (esterlina)	pound (sterling)
lleno	full
llevar (puesto)	to wear
el maquillaje	make-up
mediano	medium
las medias	stockings
medio	half
medir	to measure
la mitad	half
la moda	fashion
el monedero	purse
mostrar	to show
pagar	to pay
el pantalón corto	shorts
el panty	tights
el paraguas	umbrella
el pedazo	piece
los pendientes	earrings
pesar	to weigh
el peso	weight
un poco	a little
ponerse	to put on (clothes)
el precio	price
los probadores	changing rooms
probarse	to try on
la ración	portion
rebajar	to reduce (price / weight)
las rebajas	sales
la rebeca	cardigan
el recibo	receipt
reembolsar	to refund
el reembolso	refund
regalar	to give a present
el regalo	present / gift
el reloj	watch
repartir	to deliver
el reparto a domicilio	home delivery
la ropa (de marca)	(designer) clothes
la sudadera	sweatshirt
sugerir	to suggest
la talla	size (clothes)
el tamaño	size

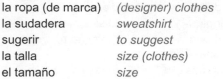

la tarjeta de crédito	credit card	a la derecha	on / to the right	caluroso	hot / warm
la tienda	shop	(todo) derecho	straight ahead	el chubasco	shower
el trozo	piece	detrás (de)	behind	el cielo	sky
vacío	empty	en / por todas partes	everywhere	el clima	climate
los vaqueros	jeans	en la esquina	on the corner	despejado	clear (skies)
el/la vendedor/a	sales assistant	en las afueras	in the outskirts	estable	stable / unchanged
vender	to sell	encima (de)	above / on top / overhead	fresco	fresh
la venta	sale	encontrarse	to be situated	el grado	degree
el vestido	dress	enfrente (de)	opposite	hacer (frío / calor etc.)	to be (cold / hot etc.)
la zapatería	shoe shop	entre	between	helar	to freeze
las zapatillas de deporte	trainers	estar situado	to be situated	el hielo	ice
los zapatos	shoes	el este	east	húmedo	humid

Directions (p.37)

		en el / al fondo	at the back / at the bottom	llover	to rain
a un paso (de)	a few steps away (from)	fuera (de)	outside	la lluvia	rain
abajo (de)	under / below	a la izquierda	on / to the left	mojar(se)	to get wet
afuera (de)	outside	al lado (de)	next to	nevar	to snow
ahí	(just) there	lejano	far away / distant / remote	la niebla	fog
aislado	isolated			la nieve	snow
al final (de)	at the end (of)	lejos (de)	far (from)	la nube	cloud
allá	(over) there	el lugar	place	nublado / nuboso	cloudy
allí	(over) there	en (el) medio (de)	in the middle of	el pronóstico	forecast
alrededor (de)	around	el norte	north	el relámpago	lightning
aquí	here	el oeste	west	seco	dry
arriba (de)	above / on top (of)	seguir	to follow / continue	el sol	sun
atrás	behind	el sitio	place	la sombra	shade / shadow
cerca (de)	near	el sur	south	templado	mild / temperate
cercano	nearby	todo recto	straight ahead	tener (frío / calor)	to feel (cold / hot)
contra	against	tomar	to take (a road)	el tiempo	weather
cruzar	to cross			la tormenta	storm
debajo (de)	under	**Weather (p.38)**		tormentoso	stormy
delante (de)	in front of	buen / mal tiempo	good / bad weather	el trueno	thunder
dentro (de)	inside	caliente	hot	el viento	wind

Section Seven — Lifestyle

Health (p.39-40)

activo	active	emborracharse	to get drunk	el propósito	aim / purpose / objective
advertir	to warn	el entrenamiento	training	provocar	to cause / provoke
el asco	disgust	entrenar(se)	to train	respirar	to breathe
asqueroso	disgusting	equilibrado	balanced	respiratorio	respiratory
el aviso	warning / notice	el esfuerzo	effort	la salud	health
el azúcar	sugar	estar en forma	to be fit	saludable	healthy
borracho	drunk	evitar	to avoid	sano	healthy / wholesome
el botellón	drinking party in the street	formar parte (de)	to be part (of)	el síndrome de abstinencia	withdrawal symptoms
caer(se)	to fall down	el/la fumador/a (pasivo/a)	(passive) smoker	el sobrepeso	overweight / obesity
cansado	tired / tiring	fumar	to smoke	el tabaquismo	addiction to tobacco
cansar(se)	to get tired	hacer daño	to injure / harm	tener sueño	to feel sleepy
el cigarrillo	cigarette	el humo	smoke	la tentación	temptation
contribuir	to contribute	malsano	unhealthy	la vida	life
el cuerpo	body	mantenerse en forma	to keep fit / in shape	vivo	alive
dedicar(se)	to do / to go in for / to devote oneself	morir	to die	**Illnesses (p.41)**	
la dieta	diet	muerto	dead	el ataque cardíaco	heart attack
dormir	to sleep	la necesidad	need	el brazo	arm
la droga (blanda / dura)	(soft / hard) drug	oler	to smell	la cabeza	head
		el olor	smell	el cerebro	brain
drogarse	to take drugs	poco sano	not healthy	el corazón	heart
el ejercicio (físico)	(physical) exercise	el porro	joint	el dedo	finger
		la posibilidad	possibility	doler	to hurt

Vocabulary

el dolor	*pain / ache*	el estrés	*stress*	los primeros auxilios	*first aid*
el dolor de oídos	*earache*	estresante	*stressful*	los pulmones	*lungs*
encontrarse bien / mal	*to feel well / ill*	la garganta	*throat*	la receta	*prescription*
la enfermedad	*illness*	el hígado	*liver*	sentirse	*to feel*
enfermo	*ill*	el/la médico/a	*doctor*	seropositivo	*HIV-positive*
la espalda	*back*	mejorar(se)	*to get better*	el sida	*AIDS*
estar bien / mal	*to be well / ill*	el pie	*foot*	tener dolor (de)...	*to have a pain (in)...*
el estómago	*stomach*	la pierna	*leg*		
		el peso	*weight*		

Section Eight — Social and Global Issues

Environmental Problems (p.42-43)

agotar	*to exhaust / use up*
el agujero	*hole*
amenazar	*to threaten*
apagar	*to turn off (lights etc.)*
arruinar	*to ruin / destroy*
el atasco	*traffic jam*
aumentar	*to increase*
el aumento	*increase*
beneficiar	*to benefit*
el beneficio	*benefit*
el calentamiento global	*global warming*
el cambio climático	*climate change*
la capa de ozono	*ozone layer*
el cartón	*cardboard*
el combustible	*fuel*
el consumo	*consumption*
contaminar	*to pollute*
el contenedor	*container*
cultivar	*to grow / cultivate*
el cultivo	*crop*
dañar	*to harm / damage*
el daño	*harm / damage*
desaparecer	*to disappear*
el desperdicio	*waste / rubbish / squandering*
ducharse	*to have a shower*
el efecto invernadero	*greenhouse effect*
encender	*to turn on (lights etc.)*
ensuciar	*to make dirty / soil / make a mess*
el envase	*wrapping / packaging / container*
la escasez	*shortage / lack*
escaso	*scarce / meagre*
estropear	*to ruin / spoil*
la falta	*lack*
faltar	*to be missing*
el fuego	*fire*
los gases de escape	*exhaust fumes*
el huracán	*hurricane*
el incendio	*fire*
la inundación	*flood*

la lluvia ácida	*acid rain*
malgastar	*to waste / misuse / squander*
la marea negra	*oil spill*
el medio ambiente	*environment*
medioambiental	*environmental*
mundial	*global / worldwide*
el mundo	*world*
la naturaleza	*nature*
nocivo	*harmful*
el pájaro	*bird*
el petróleo	*oil*
el petrolero	*oil tanker*
la pila	*battery*
la preocupación	*worry*
preocupado	*worried / anxious*
preocupante	*worrying*
los productos químicos	*chemicals*
proteger	*to protect*
químico (adj)	*chemical*
recargable	*rechargeable*
el recurso	*resource*
la selva	*jungle / tropical forest*
la sequía	*drought*
solucionar	*to solve / resolve*
sucio	*dirty*
la Tierra	*Earth*
tirar	*to throw (away)*
utilizar	*to use*
la ventaja	*advantage*
el vertedero	*rubbish dump / tip*

Problems in Society (p.44-45)

la belleza	*beauty*
combatir	*to fight / combat*
cometer	*to commit*
la culpa	*fault / blame / guilt*
el desarrollo	*development*
el desempleo	*unemployment*
los derechos	*rights*
la desigualdad	*inequality*
la discriminación	*discrimination*
echar la culpa	*to blame*
estar en paro	*to be unemployed*
el/la extranjero/a	*foreigner*
el/la gamberro/a	*hooligan / lout / troublemaker*

el gobierno	*government*
grave	*serious*
la guerra	*war*
la igualdad	*equality*
injusto	*unjust / unfair*
inquietante	*worrying / disturbing*
inquietar(se)	*to worry*
justo	*just / fair*
el ladrón / la ladrona	*thief*
la ley	*law*
la libertad	*liberty / freedom*
luchar	*to fight / struggle*
matar	*to kill*
la multa	*fine*
los necesitados	*needy people*
el peligro	*danger*
peligroso	*dangerous*
pobre	*poor*
la pobreza	*poverty*
el prejuicio	*prejudice*
el/la refugiado/a	*refugee*
robar	*to steal*
el robo	*theft / burglary*
los "sin techo"	*homeless people*
el/la testigo	*witness*
la violencia	*violence*

Contributing to Society (p.46)

la basura	*rubbish / garbage*
la campaña	*campaign*
los desechos	*rubbish / waste*
la encuesta	*poll / survey*
la obra benéfica	*charity*
la ONG	*NGO (non-governmental organisation)*
la organización benéfica	*charitable organisation*
organizar	*to organise*
la participación	*participation / taking part*
el reciclaje	*recycling*
reciclar	*to recycle*
recoger	*to collect / gather / pick up*
renovable	*renewable*
la residencia (para ancianos)	*(old people's) home*

los residuos	refuse / waste / rubbish	salvar	to save	la tienda solidaria	charity shop
reutilizar	to reuse	la tienda con fines benéficos	charity shop	voluntario	voluntary
				el/la voluntario/a	volunteer

Section Nine — Travel and Tourism

Where To Go (p.47)

alemán	German
Alemania	Germany
Argentina	Argentina
Australia	Australia
Brasil	Brazil
británico	British
las Islas Canarias	Canary Islands
Canadá	Canada
castellano	Castilian, Spanish spoken in Spain
Chile	Chile
Colombia	Colombia
Cuba	Cuba
escocés	Scottish
Escocia	Scotland
España	Spain
español	Spanish
los Estados Unidos	United States
Europa	Europe
europeo	European
en el / al extranjero	abroad
francés	French
Francia	France
Gales	Wales
galés	Welsh
Gran Bretaña	Great Britain
Grecia	Greece
griego	Greek
la India	India
Inglaterra	England
inglés	English
Irlanda	Ireland
irlandés	Irish
Irlanda del Norte	Northern Ireland
la isla	island
Italia	Italy
italiano	Italian
latinoamericano	Latin American
Londres	London
el mar	sea
el mar Mediterráneo	Mediterranean Sea
México	Mexico
la montaña	mountain
el mundo	world
norirlandés	Northern Irish
norteamericano	North American
el país	country
Perú	Peru
Portugal	Portugal
portugués	Portuguese
la playa	beach
Rusia	Russia
sudamericano	South American

Preparation (p.48-49)

la agencia (de viajes)	(travel) agent's
el aire acondicionado	air conditioning
el albergue juvenil	youth hostel
el alojamiento	accommodation
alojarse	to lodge / stay
el ambiente	atmosphere
buscar	to look for
la cama de matrimonio	double bed
cambiar	to change
el camping	campsite
la caravana	caravan
el carnet de conducir	driving licence
el carnet de identidad	identity card
el carnet	pass / card
el cheque (de viaje)	traveller's cheque
la crema solar	sun cream
decepcionar	to disappoint
la dirección	management
disponible	available
DNI	ID card
el equipaje	luggage
el formulario	registration form
la ficha	registration form
el folleto	leaflet / pamphlet
(no) fumador	(non) smoking
el/la guía	guide
la guía	guidebook
la habitación (doble / individual)	(double / single) room
informarse	to find out
irse de camping	to go camping
las instalaciones	facilities
libre	available
llevar	to take
el lugar	place
la maleta	suitcase
la máquina (de fotos)	camera
media pensión	half board
el papel higiénico	toilet paper
el parador	state-owned hotel (in Spain)
el pasaporte	passport
pensión completa	full board
la pensión	boarding house / B&B
perder	to lose

el permiso de conducir	driving licence
quedarse	to stay
la queja	complaint
quejarse	to complain
la recepción	reception
recordar	to remember
la reserva	reservation
reservar	to book / reserve
el saco de dormir	sleeping bag
la sombrilla	sunshade / parasol
el sitio	space / room / place / site
la tienda	tent
las vacaciones	holidays
la vista	view

How to Get There (p.50)

a mano derecha / izquierda	on the right- / left-hand side
a pie	on foot / walking
la aduana	customs
el aeropuerto	airport
el andén	platform
aparcar	to park
el asiento	seat
el autocar	coach
la autopista	motorway
la avería	breakdown / fault
averiado	broken down
el avión	aeroplane
el barco	boat
el billete (de ida / de ida y vuelta)	(single / return) ticket
el bonobús	bus pass
el camión	lorry
la carretera	highway
el casco	helmet
el cinturón de seguridad	seat belt
el coche	car
coger	to take / catch
conducir	to drive / lead
el/la conductor/a	driver
la consigna	left luggage office
el cruce	crossroads / intersection
el crucero	cruise
cruzar	to cross
detener(se)	to stop
doblar	to turn
esperar	to wait
la estación (de autobuses / autocares / trenes)	(bus / coach / train) station

Vocabulary

la estación de servicio	service station
el ferrocarril	railway system
la gasolina (sin plomo)	(unleaded) petrol
hacer transbordo	to change / transfer
la llegada	arrival
llegar	to arrive
el metro	underground
el motor	engine
la parada	stop
parar	to stop
el/la pasajero/a	passenger
pasar (por)	to go (through) / pass
el paso subterráneo	underpass / subway
perder (vuelo etc.)	to miss (flight etc.)
perderse	to get lost
regresar	to go back
el regreso	return
el retraso	delay
la rueda	wheel
la sala de espera	waiting room
la salida	exit

la señal	sign / signal
la taquilla	ticket office
tardar	to take (time)
torcer	to turn
el tranvía	tram
venir	to come
la vía	track / lane
viajar	to travel
el viaje	trip / journey
el/la viajero/a	traveller
volver	to return
el vuelo	flight

What To Do (p.51)

el abanico	fan
bañarse	to bathe / swim
broncearse	to get a tan
caminar	to walk
el camino	path / route / road
los deportes acuáticos	water sports
descansar	to rest
el descanso	rest / pause
el esquí	skiing

esquiar	to ski
estar de vacaciones	to be on holiday
la excursión	trip / excursion
la insolación	sunstroke
el lago	lake
la montaña	mountain
el museo	museum
la naturaleza	nature
el parque de atracciones	fairground
el parque temático	theme park
pasar (tiempo)	to spend (time)
la playa	beach
la postal	postcard
el recuerdo	souvenir
relajarse	to relax
el río	river
sacar fotos	to take photos
la tarjeta (postal)	card / (post)card
tomar el sol	to sunbathe
ver	to see

Section Ten — Current and Future Study and Employment

School Subjects (p.52)

el alemán	German
el arte dramático	drama
la asignatura	school subject
atento	attentive
la biología	biology
las ciencias económicas	economics
las ciencias	science
la cocina	food technology
el comercio	business studies
el curso	school year
el dibujo	art
la educación física	PE
enseñar	to teach
el español	Spanish
la física	physics
el francés	French
la geografía	geography
la gimnasia	gymnastics
la historia	history
el idioma	language
la informática	IT
el inglés	English
la lengua	language / tongue
las matemáticas	maths
la música	music
optar	to choose / opt for
optativo	optional
la química	chemistry
la religión	RE
riguroso	severe / harsh
sencillo	simple / easy
los trabajos manuales	handicrafts

School Life (p.53-55)

el acoso (escolar)	(school) bullying
la agenda	diary
el/la alumno/a	pupil / student
apoyar	to support / back / help
el apoyo	support / backing / help
aprender	to learn
aprobar	to approve / pass (an exam)
los apuntes	notes
el aula (f)	classroom
ausente	absent
la ayuda	help
el bolígrafo	pen
callar(se)	to shut up
el campo de deportes	sports field
la cantina	canteen
la carpeta	folder / file
castigar	to punish
el castigo	punishment
la clase	lesson
el colegio mixto	mixed school
el colegio privado	private school
el colegio público	state school
el colegio religioso	religious school
el comportamiento	behaviour
comportarse	to behave
la conducta	behaviour / conduct
contestar	to answer
charlar	to chat
el chicle	chewing gum
el cuaderno	exercise book

los deberes	homework
desobediente	disobedient
el despacho	office
dibujar	to draw
el/la director/a	head teacher / principal
diseñar	to design
educativo	educational
la enseñanza	teaching / education
entender	to understand
entregar	to hand in
escribir	to write
la escuela (primaria)	(primary) school
esforzarse	to make an effort
estresante	stressful
el estuche	pencil case
la evaluación	assessment
el examen	exam
el éxito	success
la explicación	explanation
explicar	to explain
la falta	mistake / absence
faltar	to be absent
femenino	feminine
fracasar	to fail
el fracaso	failure
el gimnasio	gymnasium
golpear	to hit
la hora de comer	lunchtime
el horario	timetable
el instituto	secondary school / institute
el intercambio	exchange
la intimidación	bullying

108

los lápices de colores	colour pencils
la lección	lesson
la lectura	reading
leer	to read
la letra	letter of the alphabet
levantar la mano	to put your hand up
el libro	book
masculino	masculine
mirar	to look
la mochila	rucksack / school bag
molestar	to annoy / bother
el nivel	level
la nota	mark
obligatorio	compulsory
oír	to listen / hear
olvidar	to forget
la página	page
la palabra	word
pasar (la) lista	to call the register
pedir prestado	to borrow
el permiso	permission
la pizarra interactiva	smart board
la pregunta	question
preguntar	to ask a question
la presión	pressure
privado	private
prometer	to promise / show promise
la prueba	test / proof
el recreo	break
la regla	rule / ruler
repartir	to hand out
repasar	to revise
la respuesta	answer
el resumen	summary
la reunión	meeting
la rutina	routine
sacar buenas / malas notas	to get good / bad marks
la sala de profesores	staffroom
el salón de actos	hall / assembly room
sobresaliente	outstanding
suspender	to fail (exam / subject)
el taller	workshop
la tarea	task / piece of homework
el tema	topic / theme
tener miedo	to be afraid
terminar	to finish
las tijeras	scissors
trabajador	hard-working
el trabajo	work
traducir	to translate
el trimestre	(school) term

el uniforme	uniform
los vestuarios	changing rooms

Education Post-16 (p.56)

a tiempo completo	full time
a tiempo parcial	part time
la academia	academy / school post-16 (for certain careers)
el aprendiz	apprentice
el aprendizaje	apprenticeship / training / learning
el bachillerato	school leaving exam (e.g. A-levels)
calificado	competent / skilled
la carrera	career / profession
el comienzo	beginning / start
los conocimientos	knowledge
conseguir	to get / achieve
dejar	to leave
Derecho	law (at university)
esperar	to hope / expect
la experiencia laboral	work experience
la formación (profesional)	vocational training
lograr	to achieve
las perspectivas laborales	employment prospects
la práctica	work placement
tomarse un año libre / sabático	to take a gap year
la universidad	university
útil	useful

Career Choices (p.57)

el/la abogado/a	lawyer / solicitor
el/la albañil	builder / brick-layer
el ama de casa (f)	housewife
el amo de casa	househusband
el/la azafato/a	flight attendant
el/la bombero/a	firefighter
el/la cajero/a	bank-teller / cashier
el/la camarero/a	waiter
el/la camionero/a	lorry driver
el/la carnicero/a	butcher
el/la carpintero/a	joiner / carpenter
la carta	letter
el/la cartero/a	postman/woman
la cita	appointment
el/la cocinero/a	cook
el/la comerciante	shop owner
el comercio	commerce / trade
el/la contable	accountant
el contrato	contract
el correo	post
el currículum	CV
el/la dependiente/a	shop assistant
desafiante	challenging
el/la ejecutivo/a	executive / officer
el ejército	army
el/la electricista	electrician
el/la empleado/a	employee / worker

el empleo	job / employment
la empresa	company
el/la encargado/a	person in charge
encargarse (de)	to be in charge of
encontrar	to find
el/la enfermero/a	nurse
la entrevista	interview
el/la escritor/a	writer
estar en huelga	to be on strike
estar en paro	to be unemployed
estimulante	stimulating
la expectativa	hope / prospect
el/la fontanero/a	plumber
ganar	to earn
el/la gerente	manager
el/la granjero/a	farmer
gratificante	rewarding
el hombre / la mujer de negocios	businessman/woman
las horas de trabajo flexibles	flexitime
el/la ingeniero/a	engineer
el/la jardinero/a	gardener
el/la jefe	boss
laboral	working
la línea	line
la llamada	call
llamar por teléfono	to telephone
llegar a ser	to become
el/la militar	serviceman/woman / soldier
el objetivo	aim / objective
el/la obrero/a	workman
obtener	to get / obtain
el/la panadero/a	baker
parado	unemployed
el paro	unemployment
el/la peluquero/a	hairdresser
el periodismo	journalism
el/la periodista	journalist
el/la pintor/a	painter / artist
el/la policía	police officer
probar	to have a go / try
pronto	ready
rellenar	to fill in
el sello	stamp
el sobre	envelope
el/la soldado	soldier
solicitar	to apply
la solicitud (de trabajo)	(job) application
el sueldo	wages / salary
el teletrabajo	work from home
el título	university degree
el/la trabajador/a	worker
trabajar	to work
el trabajo	work / job
el/la traductor/a	translator
triunfar	to triumph / succeed
variado	varied
el/la veterinario/a	veterinary surgeon

Vocabulary

Section 1 — General Stuff

Page 1: Numbers

1) Tiene diecisiete años.
2) Tiene ochenta y ocho años.
3) Vive en la segunda calle a la derecha.

Pages 2-3: Times and Dates

1) the day before yesterday   2) London   3) Friday

Page 9: Opinions

1) Luis prefers watching films at home.
2) No, he doesn't. He thinks they're boring.
3) Elena thinks sometimes they're ridiculous.

Page 10: Putting it All Together

1) F   2) T   3) F   4) T   5) F

Section 2 — Me, My Family and Friends

Page 12: My Family

I live with my mother, my older sister and my two younger sisters. They are twins. For me, it's important to have brothers and sisters because you always have someone to go out with. At the weekend, I visit my father, his wife and my stepbrother. He was born last year and he is only six months old. I would like to spend more time there with them because it's great fun / entertaining.

Page 13: Describing People

Descripción 1 = foto b   Descripción 3 = foto a
Descripción 2 = foto d   Descripción 4 = foto c

Page 16: Partnership

1a) False   1b) True   1c) False
2) Jerez

Section 3 — Free-Time Activities

Page 17: Music

1) the saxophone
2) It's very quick to get songs.
   It's cheaper than going to a shop and buying a CD.
3) Live music is always very exciting.

Page 18 — Cinema

Me encantan las películas. En mi opinión, las películas policíacas son las mejores. Son las películas más divertidas porque tienes que pensar en la trama. La semana pasada, vi una película muy divertida. Me gusta ver películas con mis amigos los fines de semana. En el futuro, me encantaría ser actriz.

Page 19: TV

1) False   2) False   3) True   4) True

Page 20: Food

The correct sentences are 2 and 3.

Section 4 — Technology in Everyday Life

Page 25: Technology

No podría vivir sin la tecnología porque es muy útil. Me gusta jugar a los videojuegos en la red con mi hermano. Hablamos con internautas en otros países. Ayer, jugué con un chico en Chile, pero para proteger mi identidad, no uso nunca mi nombre. Lo mejor de los móviles es que no tienes que estar en casa para usar la red. En el futuro, pienso que los niños tendrán móviles cuando tengan dos o tres años.

Page 26: Social Media

1) V   2) V   3) F   4) F

Section 5 — Customs and Festivals

Page 28: Customs and Festivals

1) F   2) F   3) T   4) T   5) T

Page 30: Customs and Festivals

1) A   2) C   3) C   4) B

Section 6 — Where You Live

Page 32: The Home

1) False   2) False   3) True   4) False   5) True

Page 33: What You Do at Home

I believe it's important to help at home, but I don't think it's fair if I do a lot and my younger brother does very little. I love walking the dog. My dad gives me money if I mow the lawn, so I will do it next Sunday. Last week I had to clean the bathroom. How disgusting!

Page 36: More Shopping

1) half a kilo   3) he's just sold the last bottle
2) salt   4) €6.50

Page 37: Giving and Asking for Directions

1) F   2) F   3) V   4) F

Page 38: Weather

1) the south   4) The temperatures will drop.
2) in the west (near Portugal) 5) There might be storms.
3) It'll be good weather.

Section 7 — Lifestyle

Page 41: Illnesses

I feel very ill. Last week, I went to the countryside, but unfortunately it was raining and I hadn't brought my umbrella. My throat hurts a lot and I can hardly speak. I have had to drink lots of liquids for a few days and I don't feel like eating. I will have to go to the doctor if I don't get better soon. The worst thing is that if I'm still ill on Saturday, I won't be able to go to my friend's party.

Section 8 — Social and Global Issues

Page 43: Environmental Problems

El cambio climático me preocupa mucho. Las fábricas y los coches contribuyen al efecto invernadero. Para mí, lo peor es que la gente en algunos países pobres sufre debido a las inundaciones y las sequías. No es justo. Creo que deberíamos trabajar juntos para reducir los efectos del cambio climático, pero será muy difícil.

Page 45: Problems in Society

1) economic problems   3) prejudice   5) work together
2) very difficult   4) lazy

Section 9 — Travel and Tourism

Page 47: Where to Go

1) Está en la costa del océano Atlántico en el norte de España.
2) Es famosa por su catedral y sus peregrinaciones.
3) Se puede nadar en uno de los ríos.

Page 48: Accommodation

1) A   2) 3   3) modern, elegant   4) B

Page 50: How to Get There

My city has many types of transport. The underground, which opened in 1924, is very clean and fast. Moreover, there is a tram network by which you can visit the majority of the neighbourhoods of the city. From the airport, it is possible to fly to all the important cities in Europe and it's not very far from the centre. Soon, they're going to improve the bus network, which will be great.

Section 10 — Current and Future Study and Employment

Page 53: School Routine

1) el comercio   3) la música
2) el dibujo

Page 54: School Life

Statements 2, 5 and 6 are true.

Page 56: Education Post-16

Cuando era joven, pensaba que me gustaría ser profesor/a. Mis padres son profesores y aunque encuentran el empleo interesante, mi padre dice que es bastante estresante. Ahora he decidido que voy a ir a una academia para estudiar fotografía. ¡Me encantaría sacar fotos de bodas!

Page 57: Career Choices and Ambitions

"When I was fifteen, I wanted to be a housewife," said my mother. "Yes, but a lot has changed in recent years," I replied. "I want to be a lawyer. They earn a good salary and I would like to help people. The work would be so varied!"

Section 11 — Grammar

Page 58: Words for People and Objects

1) el; los sombreros   6) el; los franceses
2) el; los problemas   7) la; las tensiones
3) la; las tradiciones   8) la; las dificultades
4) el; los viernes   9) la; las ciudades
5) el; los porcentajes   10) el; los mapas

Page 59: 'The', 'A', 'Some' and Other Little Words

1) Me gusta el chocolate.
2) No tengo agua.
3) Es profesora.
4) Quiere unas patatas.
5) Quiero hablar con la señora López.
6) Cada persona tiene dos perros.

Page 60: Words to Describe Things

1) el perro feliz   5) cinco gatos pequeños
2) siete faldas rojas   6) nueve sillas violeta
3) los coches azules   7) cuatro libros beis
4) dos mujeres bajas   8) una persona triste

Page 61: Words to Describe Things

1) Hay muchos gatos.   5) Algunas personas creen que... /
2) el primer día   Alguna gente cree que...
3) el mismo perro   6) Es un gran profesor.
4) los otros alumnos

Page 62: Words to Describe Things

1) Sus libros son nuevos. / Los libros suyos son nuevos.
2) Quiero esa manzana.
3) Aquel león está comiendo.
4) Estas peras son buenas.
5) Ese hombre, cuya mujer es española, es alto.
6) Lucas es el chico cuyos padres son simpáticos.

Page 63: Words to Compare Things

1) Mi gato es el más gordo.
2) Soy tan alto/a como mi padre.

3) Juan es mayor que Marta.

4) Fue el peor día de la semana.

5) La película es mejor que el libro.

6) Nuestra revista es la más interesante.

Page 64: Words to Describe Actions

1) Lloran ruidosamente.

2) Vive saludablemente.

3) Habla claramente.

4) Hablamos inteligentemente.

5) El bebé duerme bien.

6) Corro rápidamente / deprisa.

7) Bailas / Bailáis mal.

8) Leo lentamente / despacio.

Page 65: Words to Describe Actions

1) Mis zapatos están aquí.

2) Quiero hacerlo de nuevo. / Lo quiero hacer de nuevo.

3) Lo hice con paciencia.

4) Vivimos lejos.

5) Lo hizo en seguida.

6) Bailó con entusiasmo.

Page 66: Words to Compare Actions

1) Carmen come más rápidamente.

2) Luis canta tan bien como Adela.

3) Selina es la que mejor conduce.

4) Estudio mejor que mis amigos.

5) Andamos / caminamos más lentamente / más despacio que Rob.

6) Ed es el que peor corre.

Page 67: Words to Say How Much

1) Hay demasiados gatos aquí.

2) Es bastante interesante.

3) Tengo muchos amigos.

4) Hablan demasiado lentamente / despacio.

5) Hay tantas playas en España.

6) El libro es buenísimo.

Page 68: I, You, We

1) ellos
2) ella
3) nosotros
4) vosotros
5) él
6) ustedes
7) ellas
8) ellos

Page 69: Me, You, Them

1) La rompe.

2) La bebo.

3) Le compró una falda.

4) Le envío / mando un correo electrónico.

5) Quiero hacerlo. / Lo quiero hacer.

6) Nos lo dijo.

Page 70: More Pronouns

1) Mi hermana, que tiene siete años, es baja.

2) Fui a Madrid, que es la capital de España.

3) ¿Cuál es tu dirección?

4) ¿Con quién vives?

5) ¿De quién es este perro?

6) ¿Cuál prefieres?

Page 71: More Pronouns

1) Son los míos.

2) ¿Qué es aquello?

3) Esta cama es más grande que aquélla.

4) Este libro es más interesante que ése.

5) ¿Es el vuestro?

6) Alguien está hablando tranquilamente.

Page 72: Prepositions

1) La casa está enfrente del banco.

2) El tren va hasta Italia.

3) Lo escuché en la radio.

4) Entro en el supermercado.

5) Soy de Hull, pero vivo en Crewe.

6) A partir de septiembre, tendré un trabajo.

Page 73: 'Por', 'Para' and the Personal 'a'

1) para
2) a
3) Por
4) por
5) por
6) para

Page 74: Conjunctions

1) La geografía es divertida, pero es difícil.

2) Me gusta la historia porque es fácil.

3) Como estoy enfermo/a, me quedo en casa.

4) Voy al parque cuando hace calor.

5) Hablo francés e italiano.

6) ¿Prefieres azul o amarillo?

Page 75: Verbs in the Present Tense

1) ballo
2) bebemos
3) nadáis
4) corre
5) aprende
6) visitan
7) escribes
8) Vive aquí desde hace un año.

Page 76: Irregular Verbs in the Present Tense

1) Comienza
2) Vais
3) Queremos
4) Doy
5) Puedes
6) Sé

Page 77: 'Ser' and 'Estar' in the Present Tense

1) Está
2) Es
3) Somos
4) Estoy
5) es
6) es

Page 78: Talking About the Past

1) lloraron
2) comimos
3) escribisteis
4) cené
5) diste
6) pude
7) hicisteis
8) puso
9) viniste
10) trajimos

Page 79: Talking About the Past

1) cantaba
2) éramos
3) aprendía
4) decía
5) volvían
6) seguíais
7) nadabas
8) iban

Page 80: Talking About the Past

1) hacía
2) volví
3) Fuiste
4) Iba; tuve

112

Page 81: Talking About the Past

1) Habían cantado.
2) Ha viajado.
3) Habéis aprendido.
4) Ha visto.
5) Había bebido.
6) Habíamos terminado.
7) Ha seguido.
8) Has vivido.

Page 82: Talking About the Future

1) voy a comer; comeré
2) vamos a tener; tendremos
3) va a bailar; bailará
4) voy a dar; daré
5) van a poner; pondrán
6) vais a jugar; jugaréis
7) vas a poder; podrás
8) va a cantar; cantará
9) vamos a querer; querremos
10) vais a vivir; viviréis

Page 83: Would, Could and Should

1) irías
2) cantaría
3) vendríamos
4) diríais
5) partiría
6) saldrían
7) hablaría
8) tendríamos

Page 84: Reflexive Verbs

1) me llamo; me he llamado
2) se levantan; se han levantado
3) se lava; se ha lavado
4) te acuestas; te has acostado
5) nos sentimos; nos hemos sentido
6) os vais; os habéis ido
7) se viste; se ha vestido
8) te despiertas; te has despertado

Page 85: Verbs with '-ing' and 'Just Done'

1) está cayendo; estaba cayendo; acaba de caer
2) estás abriendo; estabas abriendo; acabas de abrir
3) está saltando; estaba saltando; acaba de saltar
4) están diciendo; estaban diciendo; acaban de decir
5) estáis corriendo; estabais corriendo; acabáis de correr
6) estamos siguiendo; estábamos siguiendo; acabamos de seguir
7) estás dando; estabas dando; acabas de dar
8) estoy leyendo; estaba leyendo; acabo de leer
9) están sirviendo; estaban sirviendo; acaban de servir
10) estamos bailando; estábamos bailando; acabamos de bailar

Page 86: Negative Forms

1) No fui al cine.
2) Ya no vamos al gimnasio.
3) No vas ni a Oslo ni a Faro.
4) Sally no tiene ninguna manzana.
5) No hay nada aquí.
6) No hay nadie en el coche.

Page 87: The Passive and Impersonal Verbs

A) Sentences 2 and 3 are written in the passive voice.
B) 1) Se compra   2) Se comen

Page 88: The Subjunctive

1) saltes
2) escuche
3) limpiemos
4) abran
5) venga
6) hagamos
7) puedan
8) tengáis

Page 89: The Subjunctive

1) present subjunctive
2) imperfect subjunctive
3) present subjunctive
4) imperfect subjunctive

Page 90: Giving Orders

1) ¡Canta!; ¡No cantes!
2) ¡Bailen!; ¡No bailen!
3) ¡Ten!; ¡No tengas!
4) ¡Dé!; ¡No dé!
5) ¡Abrid!; ¡No abráis!
6) ¡Venid!; ¡No vengáis!
7) ¡Sea!; ¡No sea!
8) ¡Vayan!; ¡No vayan!

Answers

Section 1 — General Stuff

Track 1 — p.3

E.g. **M1:** ¡Hola! Soy Carlos. Voy al gimnasio todos los días y los jueves juego al fútbol.

1) **F1:** ¡Buenos días! Me llamo Anabel. Celebré mi cumpleaños anteayer y fui a un restaurante con mi familia y mis amigos.

2) **F1:** Ayer, fuimos de compras a Londres, pero mañana por la mañana, iremos a Oxford. Me encantan las cafeterías en Oxford.

3) **F2:** ¡Hola! Me llamo Julia. Mañana voy a ir al cine con mis amigas, y el viernes vamos a ir al teatro.

Track 2 — p.10

E.g. **M1:** ¿Qué te gusta hacer los fines de semana, Carolina?
F1: Me encanta ir a la piscina.

1) **F1:** Y tú Antonio, ¿qué te gusta hacer los fines de semana?
M1: A mí me gusta ir de compras, pero no me gusta escuchar música.

2) **F1:** ¿Por qué te gusta ir de compras?
M1: Me gusta ir de compras porque es muy divertido y las tiendas en mi ciudad son estupendas. Alguna gente cree que ir de compras es para chicas, pero eso no es verdad.

3) **F1:** Ah, muy bien. Pero, ¿por qué no te gusta escuchar música?
M1: Mucha gente adora la música, pero a mí nunca me ha interesado. Prefiero leer. Acabo de terminar una novela fenomenal. Las novelas y los periódicos sí que son interesantes porque se puede aprender mucho. ¿Estás de acuerdo?

4) **F1:** Sí, estoy de acuerdo. Me encanta leer porque es relajante, pero me gusta escuchar música también.

5) **F1:** Prefiero los grupos de música pop porque la música pop me parece guay.

Section 2 — Me, My Family and Friends

Track 3 — p.13

1) **F2:** Esta persona parece bastante baja. Tiene el pelo liso y castaño, pero no lo tiene especialmente largo. Lleva unas gafas bastante grandes. Es una persona joven.

2) **M1:** Tiene el pelo negro, pero no es ni liso ni rizado. Creo que tiene los ojos marrones y que es una persona bastante alta. No lleva gafas.

3) **F2:** Esta persona no tiene ni barba ni bigote. Tiene el pelo largo y moreno, y creo que es bastante delgada. Lleva maquillaje y no tiene pecas.

4) **M1:** No es totalmente calvo, pero no tiene mucho pelo. Tiene el pelo gris, y tiene barba. No sé el color de sus ojos. No es joven — la verdad, parece bastante viejo.

Section 3 — Free-Time Activities

Track 4 — p.17

E.g. **M1:** ¡Hola Marisol! ¿Cuál es el género de música más importante para ti?
F2: Diría que mi género preferido es la música rap porque creo que es la música más original y distinta. Me encanta la música clásica también porque es relajante. Sin embargo, según mi hermana menor, la música más importante para nuestra generación sería la música pop.

1) **M1:** ¿Tocas algún instrumento?
F2: Cuando era más joven, tocaba el piano, pero en este momento, no tengo suficiente tiempo para practicar. Me encantaría aprender a tocar el saxofón porque es un instrumento fenomenal y porque el jazz es un tipo de música que siempre me ha fascinado.

2) **M1:** ¿Cómo escuchas música, Marisol?
F2: Me gusta escuchar música por Internet, porque es muy rápido descargar canciones y cuesta menos que ir a una tienda para comprar un CD.

3) **F2:** Me encanta ir a conciertos también, porque la música en directo es siempre muy emocionante.

Track 5 — p.20

E.g. **M1:** ¡Hola! Soy Joaquín. Cuando era pequeño, me gustaba comer muchos caramelos y helados y odiaba las verduras. ¡No me importaba para nada la salud!

1) **M1:** Ahora como de todo — mariscos, legumbres y carne. Odio la comida basura porque no solo engorda, sino que suele llevar cantidades enormes de sal y azúcar. ¿Qué te gusta comer, Alejandra?

2) **F1:** Creo que comes mejor que yo, Joaquín. Si pudiera comer caramelos todos los días, lo haría. Sería mejor si comiera más fruta, pero no me gusta mucho. Mis padres me dicen que bebo demasiado café, así que ahora estoy intentando beber más agua.

3) **F2:** Me llamo Raquel. No como ni pescado ni carne — soy vegetariana. Normalmente es bastante fácil evitar la carne porque me gustan las legumbres. Sin embargo, cuando voy a restaurantes con mis amigos, es más difícil porque hay pocos platos sin carne. Por otro lado, los platos vegetarianos suelen ser más baratos que los que contienen carne o pescado.

Section 5 — Customs and Festivals

Track 6 — p.30

1) **M1:** El premio es trece millones de euros y el número ganador es… ochenta mil seiscientos setenta y tres. ¡Felicitaciones a todos!

2) **F1:** ¡Hola! Soy Ana. Estoy contentísima porque gané 2.000.000 de euros en El Gordo. Voy a comprar un apartamento de lujo, y luego iré al Mediterráneo con mi novio tres semanas.

3) **F1:** Carla, ¿qué hiciste esta Navidad?
F2: En Navidad, me lo pasé fenomenal porque mis abuelos vinieron a quedarse con nosotros. Viven muy lejos de aquí, así que casi nunca los veo. En Nochebuena, mi madre preparó una cena deliciosa. Había mariscos, carne y varios postres, pero lo que más me gustó fue el turrón de chocolate.

4) **F2:** ¿Recibiste regalos, Diego?
M1: Sí, se me cayó el móvil el mes pasado, y por lo tanto, mis padres me dieron un móvil nuevo. Mi hermano había pedido unos juguetes pero le regalaron una bicicleta azul. Cuando la vio, estaba tan emocionado que ¡empezó a bailar por el salón!

Transcript

Section 6 — Where You Live

Track 7 — p.36

E.g. **F2:** ¡Hola! Quiero hacer una tortilla española para una fiesta de cumpleaños y necesito unos ingredientes. ¿Me puede ayudar?
M1: Sí, claro. ¿Qué le hace falta?

1) **F2:** Pues primero, necesito un kilo de patatas. Y póngame también medio kilo de cebollas.
M1: Claro. ¿Algo más?

2) **F2:** Sí, deme seis huevos, pero no necesito sal, porque ya la tengo en casa.
M1: Aquí tiene.

3) **F2:** ¡Ay, casi se me ha olvidado! Necesito también una botella de aceite de oliva.
M1: Desafortunadamente, no tengo aceite de oliva. Acabo de vender la última botella.

4) **F2:** ¡Qué pena! Tendré que ir a otra tienda. ¿Cuánto cuesta todo?
M1: Cuesta seis euros cincuenta.
F2: Vale, gracias. Aquí tiene. ¡Adiós!
M1: Gracias. ¡Adiós!

Track 8 — p.37

E.g. **M1:** ¡Hola! Te voy a hablar de mi barrio. Es un barrio histórico, así que hay un castillo, un ayuntamiento y un teatro.

1) **M1:** El teatro está en la parte este del barrio donde también hay muchos restaurantes. Está al lado de un museo muy impresionante.

2) **M1:** En la plaza hay un bar que es muy popular tanto con los jóvenes como con los jubilados. Había tres supermercados hace un par de años, pero ahora solo hay uno.

3) **M1:** Se puede encontrar el supermercado al fondo de la calle San Felipe, enfrente de la comisaría.

4) **M1:** Luego, si sigues esa calle y tomas la segunda calle a la derecha, encontrarás la iglesia.

Section 8 — Social and Global Issues

Track 9 — p.45

E.g. **F2:** Desafortunadamente, hay miles de personas sin techo en España.

1) **F2:** Debido a los problemas económicos que tenemos, muchas personas han perdido su trabajo y no tienen suficiente dinero para pagar el alquiler.

2) **F2:** Algunos pueden pedir ayuda a sus padres o amigos, pero otros acaban en la calle. Lo que todos tienen en común es que tienen una vida dificilísima.

3) **F2:** Sin embargo, lo peor es que frecuentemente son víctimas del prejuicio, lo que les puede dificultar la vida bastante.

4) **F2:** Este prejuicio existe porque mucha gente cree que los sin techo no pueden pagar su alquiler porque son perezosos.

5) **F2:** Si queremos cambiar la situación de estas personas, tenemos que trabajar juntos — es la única manera de hacerlo.

Section 9 — Travel and Tourism

Track 10 — p.48

1) **M1:** Los hoteles son regulares en general, contándose dos buenos.

2) **M1:** Los tres mejores que hay dentro de la ciudad son el de Pfaroux, el de las cuatro Naciones, y el de Europa. Fuera de la ciudad, y en el camino de Botafogo, hay dos ingleses y uno francés: el mejor de todos, tanto de los de la ciudad, como de los de fuera, es el Hotel de los Extranjeros en la plaza de Catette.

3) **M1:** Es una gran casa, de moderna y elegante construcción, sólida, con anchas y magníficas habitaciones: un gran jardín al pie del mar, vistas admirables, comodidades muchas.

4) **M1:** El hotel todo está alumbrado por el gas: tiene baños, billares y grande capacidad: en el Hotel de los Extranjeros, viven la mayor parte de los individuos del Cuerpo Diplomático extranjero.

Section 10 — Current and Future Study and Employment

Track 11 — p.53

1) **M1:** ¡Ay, Marta! Odio los lunes.
F1: ¿Por qué?
M1: ¿No es obvio? Tenemos matemáticas, comercio y después del recreo, inglés. Es horrible.

2) **F1:** Pero los martes son mejores, ¿no? Me gustan las ciencias y el dibujo.
M1 : ¿Y el francés?
F1: No me emociona mucho. Prefiero las asignaturas más prácticas.

3) **M1:** Estoy de acuerdo. Yo prefiero los miércoles. Es una oportunidad para ser creativo. Por ejemplo, empezamos con los trabajos manuales. Después hay el español y a las diez y media, tenemos música. Es mi día preferido.

Index

Index